REVEREND IKE

AN EXTRAORDINARY LIFE OF INFLUENCE

MARK VICTOR HANSEN
and XAVIER EIKERENKOETTER

Post Hill
PRESS

A FIDELIS BOOKS BOOK
An Imprint of Post Hill Press
ISBN: 979-8-88845-266-0
ISBN (eBook): 979-8-88845-267-7

Reverend Ike:
An Extraordinary Life of Influence
© 2023 by CNM, LLC and Rev. Ike Legacy, LLC
All Rights Reserved

Cover Design by Cody Corcoran

Post Hill Press
New York • Nashville
posthillpress.com

Published in the United States of America

To the Spirit of God in Each of You

TABLE OF CONTENTS

FOREWORD

BOB PROCTOR

If you are a student of personal development material, this biography belongs in your library. I want to recommend that as you go through this book, which contains highlights of the life of a great man, Frederick J. Eikerenkoetter II (commonly referred to as Rev. Ike), please keep your mind open, suspend all judgment, and you will find answers to many questions you frequently ask yourself.

Writing this foreword is a tremendous honor for me. I have held Reverend Ike in such high esteem for over half a century. You see, Reverend Ike and I are a year apart in age. While he was born in June of 1935, I arrived a year earlier in July of 1934. We were both born at the height of the Depression, and in 1939 the whole world was going to war. WWII was a period of great uncertainty, and almost everything—food, gasoline, you name it—was being rationed. Children were being raised solely by their mothers and grandparents as all able-bodied men were put in uniform and sent off to war.

Reverend Ike founded his ministry at an early age. His ministry was, in many respects, in total opposition to virtually everything that was being preached in the churches on almost every block.

Just think for a moment. Here is a young Black man who was raised in the Southern part of the United States in an environment that was not friendly to Blacks. Growing up in the '40s and '50s in Canada, I can remember reading about how Blacks were being treated in the south and had difficulty believing that some of the things I was told about and read about were happening. The sad truth was, they *were* happening. A young Black man was not given a fair shake to anything that would make life meaningful. So, when you think of the opposition Reverend Ike ran into merely because of the color of his skin, you could almost compound those problems when you consider he's standing tall and preaching a theology that is totally foreign to what most Southern preachers had been preaching and teaching for years. That took a tremendous amount of courage.

I became aware of Reverend Ike in the late '60s when I too had just ventured out on my own into the area of personal development. I'd been studying Napoleon Hill's *Think and Grow Rich* for several years and anything else I could get my hands on that would introduce me to more of me. I found out there are only two sources to which you can refer when you want to learn about yourself: science and theology. Science teaches that energy IS, and theology teaches that God IS. The essence is that an energy source can neither be created nor destroyed and is in every cell of our being. I had an idea that God was in every fiber of my being, but I don't know that I *really* believed it, that unshakable belief that comes from knowing.

When I was living in Chicago in '67 or '68, I would stay up until 1:00 a.m. to catch Reverend Ike's television show. I remember one evening he drove onto the stage in a Rolls Royce limousine. He got out of the car wearing a long mink overcoat, with big, bright diamonds on his fingers. This type of behavior caused many journalists and broadcasters to publicly criticize Reverend Ike.

The old paradigm that ministers should never become wealthy was showing itself in glaring form. I saw it differently.

Isn't it strange that we would believe the minister, our spiritual teacher/leader, is doing the wrong thing when he is truly demonstrating the lesson he's preaching? The abundant life is here for everyone who follows God's way. I believed that Reverend Ike was teaching and demonstrating what could be done if you worked in harmony with the God within you. When you ask, and believe you will receive, you immediately resonate with anything and everything required for the manifestation of what you have asked for. That's what the Bible teaches. God is in you and God does work by law.

I don't recall exactly what it was that caught my attention, but I can assure you, Reverend Ike had it. When I fully understood the magnitude of what he was saying, it resonated so deeply I felt I was home. It was a knowing that was innate.

"The power of the mind is not only the greatest power in the universe but the only power in the universe." He went on to explain that God was omnipresent. He continuously spoke of "GOD IN ME." The idea that God was an old White man in the sky with a long beard and arms that swept through the heavens was gone forever. What he shared was so in sync with what I was learning outside of the great minister's teachings and made so much sense that I have never stopped learning from his message.

I have been a serious student of self-development since 1961. Millions of people worldwide study personal development material every day and yet fail to produce meaningful results. Keep in mind that it is SELF we are developing, and SELF is a triune being. We live simultaneously on three planes of understanding—intellectual, spiritual, and physical—and all three must be clearly understood. It was Reverend Ike who brought it all together for me when he spoke about "GOD IN ME." That one line brought order to my mind.

At the time, it was clear that Reverend Ike was not in harmony with what all the other religious leaders were preaching and that he was in clear opposition to the piety norm of his day. He felt that the old fire and brimstone dogma of fear, doom and gloom, poverty and suffering were false teachings.

If men and women were to advance in life, they had to learn how to think and relate to God as a "vital, immediate, indwelling presence."

If you are studying your SELF and you haven't been introduced to the spiritual aspect of your personality, I strongly suggest you move on to teachings that are more in line with your being, because as Reverend Ike said, God is IN YOU!

He and I were raised through the same times, and when I found out he was cutting cardboard and putting it on the insides of his shoes so he could still wear them long after the leather had given out, I laughed because as a kid I did the same thing. This was a clear indication that neither of us were raised in abundance.

As you make your way through this wonderful book, you will discover absolute truths that Reverend Ike deals with so unabashedly. You may, as I did, begin to examine your own paradigms and free yourself from some you will soon consider absurd.

Bob Proctor
Bestselling author of *You Were Born Rich*

PREFACE

KEVIN KITRELL ROSS

Raised by a single mother in abject poverty, the religious phenomenon who became known to millions as Reverend Ike was a son of the South, a Black man who was larger than life, charismatic, fiery, brash, brilliant, and handsome.

Frederick Joseph Eikerenkoetter II dominated prime time national television and radio in the 1960s and 1970s and filled stadiums (including Madison Square Garden in New York City) without touting the traditional dogma embedded in the Christian message that the Black churches in America had become known for. In fact, while Reverend Ike did attend American Bible College, a Protestant Bible college in Chicago, he was not a favorite because he constantly challenged the dean with what he felt was a more inclusive theological perspective of God.

Despite being rejected by some of the fundamental Christian churches and highly criticized by a number of his fellow African American contemporaries, millions of mostly African Americans, but also people from all walks of life, flocked to Reverend Ike to learn what he called his "Science of Living" philosophy. And while his message ruffled the feathers of strict traditionalists, it was a breath of fresh air for freedom-seeking Black Americans who were weary of the social and economic injustices they faced.

During this time period, millions of Black people in the US lived below the poverty line, often in slums, under conditions of segregation. Some accused Reverend Ike of exploiting the condition of the poor by teaching them false doctrine and taking the little money they had. But he sincerely believed that the Christianity most African Americans were introduced to was designed to keep them shackled to an inferior position in society and in their own lives by leaving their thinking to the church, the government, and other external sources.

Rev. Ike believed that if Black people wanted to escape the hell of sickness, poverty, bad luck, unemployment, ignorance, and miseducation, they had to change their image of themselves and their relationship with God. As descendants of slaves, African Americans were systematically taught to see themselves as inferior to the dominant White society. Everything about Rev. Ike absolutely rejected this notion. He promoted a form of liberation theology that emphasized that human beings could be what they wanted to be, do what they wanted to do, and have what they wanted to have, irrespective of race. They could be, do, and have what they wanted by discovering, developing, and demonstrating the presence of God within themselves, in the here and now, not in the sweet by and by.

The fact that millions of Americans flocked to him and followed his teachings for years was proof they were ready to discard the traditional "slave theology" handed down to Black people in the United States and eager to adopt a liberation theology that reinterpreted Jesus as a revolutionary man interested in freedom, justice, and equality. Reverend Ike believed that no matter how much conditions in society had changed, if people (particularly African Americans) did not break the chains of bondage and second-class citizenship from their own minds, they would forever be relegated, by their own thinking, to being the objects of someone else's control and thinking.

If men and women were to advance in life, they had to learn how to think and relate to God as a vital, immediate, indwelling presence. Rev. Ike's entire philosophy can be summed up in three words: ***God in you***.

While some argue that his flamboyance and lavish showman-like presentation often drew focus away from the substance of his teaching, it had the exact opposite effect for millions of people. Thousands attended his services, workshops, and classes at the Science of Living Institute in New York. Millions listened to him on the radio on over 1,700 stations nationwide and viewed his nationally syndicated *Joy of Living* broadcast on network TV. Millions more corresponded with him by mail to receive his "success ideas" to support them with activating the presence of God within themselves.

Mountains of documented testimonials attested to the positive results gained through his teachings: healings, marriages, property purchases, business startups, and debts cleared. Some even became millionaires while working with Rev. Ike's philosophy. Rev. Ike always made it a point to stress that he was not the healer, but it was God moving through him that healed, in agreement with a willing soul. He placed the locus of responsibility for the various positive results of his ministry within the person who received the blessing. His role was as a conduit and demonstrator of these possibilities.

Rev. Ike often stated he was not interested in herding the masses into the folds of organized religion, nor did he seek to draw followers to himself. He wanted people to believe in themselves positively and correctly and to rely on the presence and power of God within as the source of their supply. He referred to this as positive self-image psychology. He was adept at using his gift of magnetism and media controversy to stir within people deep interest in the presence of God in themselves.

I was one of those individuals inspired by Rev. Ike at an early age. I vividly recall seeing and hearing him on television, dressed immaculately, well-spoken, and bringing a positive message. At that time, there were few positive images of African Americans on syndicated television that did not perpetuate stereotypical norms. *The Cosby Show* would not air until 1984, so Rev. Ike's prime time *Joy of Living* telecast caught my attention.

Shortly thereafter, he appeared in Chicago at my home church, Christ Universal Temple. Like Rev. Ike, my minister, Dr. Johnnie Colemon,

discarded the traditional theology of her Methodist Southern upbring-
ing, and her thriving Christ Universal Temple was a haven for thousands
of Black people looking for a message that taught them that God's will
included health, happiness, and prosperity for everyone. Her message,
her courage, her magnetism, and her massive success made her a perfect
match for Reverend Ike and his ministry. It wouldn't be long before the
pair became known as the King and Queen of Prosperity.

Their friendship grew, and the two teamed up for special services
and conferences. Rev. Ike often visited our church in Chicago. One
of the most memorable occasions occurred in October of 1985 when
Chicago Mayor Harold Washington, Rev. Jessie Jackson, Della Reese,
and Rev. Ike were present for the dedication of Dr. Johnnie's Christ
Universal Temple, the first megachurch of any denomination in the city
of Chicago.

That shining day in 1985 always stands out in my mind as the day I
adopted (in the vernacular of the Black church) my spiritual mother and
father. Shortly afterwards, when I was eleven years old, my fantasy came
true. I became the personal mentee, protégé, and spiritual son to the
King and Queen of two of the most successful African American ministries in the country, and arguably, two of the most successful African
Americans alive.

Although Reverend Ike was a highly visible television evangelist and
media mogul, he led a highly guarded, mostly quiet, private life. I felt
fortunate to have had a front row, mostly all-access pass. After all, he saw
me as his spiritual son and treated me accordingly. Among his many great
passions was that of mentoring young Black and Latino youth from the
inner cities and rural areas. It was his way of giving back to his younger
self. Through me and others like me, he wanted to correct some of the
broken theology and poverty he experienced as a boy growing up in the
Deep South. He wanted to correct some of the maltreatment he received
at the hands of his father and his own mentor.

Rev. Ike inspired me to want the best of life, to demand the best
of myself, and to demonstrate, somewhat militantly, the principles he
taught me. From the time I was a teenager until days before his death,

he was a loving, devoted, committed, and passionate spiritual father who took pleasure in knowing that he played a significant role not only in inspiring me but also in financially supporting my education and exposing me to a life beyond my wildest dreams.

As you might expect, he taught me to think, feel, look, and act prosperous. When I did not have the proper attire, he took me "shopping" in his own closet for jackets, suits, belts, and shoes that he knew would open doors for me among some of the elite circles I traveled in. While he was known as the success and prosperity preacher, he was no Pollyanna. He knew success and prosperity were produced through diligent, persistent, and excellent work. He hired me over the years to work for him and with him. Every step of the way, he intentionally opened my eyes to the degree of rigor, discipline, and pressure required to walk his talk. This gave me unique insight into his work ethic, the habits he employed, and the systems he developed that produced a ministry that touched millions of lives around the world.

While it was no secret he loved the finer things in life, Rev. Ike was actually a self-help junkie, a homebody, and at times, a recluse. He led a very public life and was often surrounded by crowds and an entourage, but he also loved time to himself. He was highly introverted, and when he was in the mood, he could withdraw from everyone and everything for hours, days, or months at a time.

Rev. Ike was always surrounded by books, recorded tapes, and papers of every kind, which filled his residences, and he always had up to four clipboards loaded with projects he was working on. With the exception of his wife, no one I knew could keep up with him, and he kept it that way. He held high standards and high expectations, and he never tolerated lateness or excuses. He could also be extremely demanding and sometimes unrealistic. Admittedly, while I did not always see the method to his madness, he would assure me that I could not lose with the stuff he used. The stuff he used was the Science of Living—the universal spiritual and mental principles that governed all of life. I am still coming to fully appreciate the impact his teachings made on my life, and I am deeply grateful that the seeds he planted more than two decades ago are beginning to take full effect.

As my mentor, Rev. Ike taught me a great deal about virtually every aspect of life. Witnessing how his amazingly busy schedule impacted the time available for him to spend with his wife and son taught me to make a concerted effort to prioritize my family and to ensure that where we lack in quantity of time, we make up in quality. Knowing how important this is, whenever I am with my children, I seek to turn minutes into moments, moments into memories, and memories into meaning.

I fully learned the mutual impact our lives had on each other when I received an invitation from Rev. Ike's wife to officiate an oceanside celebration of life ceremony and scatter Rev. Ike's ashes over the waters of Bal Harbor, Florida. I was also honored to be included as a consultant on this important book.

Rev. Ike is currently having a social media resurrection, and millions in an entirely new generation are connecting with him for the first time. His YouTube videos and recordings are going viral, his self-published study guide, *Reverend Ike's Secrets for Health, Joy, and Prosperity for You*, is selling robustly on Amazon, and this man who was once considered ahead of his time is having a "second coming" for a millennial generation whose attitude toward organized religion is very much in line with Reverend Ike's. Like him, they are not looking to be herded into the folds of organized religion but to be inspired and empowered to be a force for good in the world.

To that end, it is my pleasure to present to some and introduce to others Frederick Joseph Eikerenkoetter II, better known to millions as Reverend Ike.

INTRODUCTION

Millions of people were touched by Frederick J. Eikerenkoetter II, lovingly known by his ardent and enthusiastic followers as Reverend Ike. He was a man who presented people a new way to think about themselves, about life, and about all the riches of health, happiness, joy, love, success, prosperity, and money that could be theirs—if they only understood the principles that he had come to understand.

We, the authors of this book, are two of those people blessed to be a personal part of Reverend Ike's amazing life and journey. You'll hear Ike's story woven together through our two different perspectives. One of his only son, and another of a budding motivational speaker and author, also searching for the truth, who became a lifelong friend and protégé of Rev. Ike, and through Ike's teachings, discovered his own vast store of life's riches. Respectively, we provide an inside look at the life of this remarkable human being that most people didn't get the opportunity to see and experience.

To understand someone who has lived an extraordinary life, one must understand the road he traveled to get there. In addition to living through extreme poverty, Ike's early life was full of people who were pitted in opposition to one another behind their diametrically opposed beliefs and positions around religion, money, and morality, leaving young Frederick to either pick a side, or forge his own path forward. The emotional drama that he regularly witnessed was likely the catalyst that galvanized his desire to design a specific and clear path, which was to find and share the truth. You'll find those truths shared generously in these writings because it would be impossible to separate the man from his work and mission. You might say Rev. Ike embodied his work and his purpose to raise others up to a better life. It was who he was.

This precocious Black kid from the South who grew up in poverty in the 1930s discovered at an early age that it's not enough to live morally and ethically. He grew up in a home with a mother and a grandmother, who believed they were not worthy of the richness or the goodness of God until they died and went to Heaven. The prevailing philosophy as he was growing up was that people like him were put here on this Earth to suffer, die, and finally go to Heaven to get relief from the suffering. He came to understand you can experience Heaven on Earth when you are doing the right thinking and have the right understanding of the Bible. He developed a burning passion to share his discovery that you don't have to die to experience your heavenly treasure, that it is already inside waiting to be discovered. He understood that you must also have the proper and correct self-awareness to enjoy the riches of the Kingdom of Heaven, which Jesus wisely taught was within.

Once he accepted this remarkable truth and started to manifest abundance and opportunities that he only dreamed about as a child, Rev. Ike knew he had to share it with everyone who would listen. That's why, at the young age of seven, it seemed his calling was to become an evangelist. Unlike the concept of the faraway God in the sky that was taught to him by the fundamentalist preachers of his childhood, Ike discovered that the Presence of God is actually *inside of you*, always there, and will never let you down. That man's true identity is the Divinity within. He came to know that "the presence of God in you is the everlasting Source of all good, that no one could take away."

In stark contrast to his humble beginnings, Rev. Ike had a deep appreciation for all things elegant and beautiful, and in the height of his ministry, became known for the church's opulent church building, office and residences, cars, and tailor-made clothing. (The 2023 Tony Awards were held in this opulent building, which Rev. Ike purchased in 1969.)

As his growing ministry began to demand media attention, most media outlets of the time liked to focus on Rev. Ike's material flamboyance, like the church's Rolls Royces and his extravagant clothing, but in doing so, they often missed the transformational power in his messages that changed lives and caused people to gladly give tithes in gratitude for the value he gave to them. He was also savvy enough to know that such opulence served to attract attention and attendees to his global congregation. In truth, he was a perfect example of the power of faith in action. He overcame the odds. He came from obscurity and transformed himself to a place of great significance.

These were the very transformational principles that he taught to the hungry hearts, souls, and minds who showed up at his church meetings, workshops, and radio or TV broadcasts each week. Around the world, individuals were touched in countless ways; lifted out of poverty, anger, hopelessness, and depression, and his ministry grew, capturing the attention and devotion of millions. Ultimately, he became one of the most widely known and heard inspirational prosperity teachers of his generation, compared frequently to the impact of internationally revered Reverend Billy Graham, the soul-saving evangelist crusader known to have talked live to audiences as large as one million people at a time around the world.

By way of his endless search through God's Word in the scriptures, Rev. Ike came to know the meaning and higher purpose of a true and fulfilling spiritual life. From his deep understanding, wisdom, and biblical immersion came interpretations that were consistent and congruent with what Jesus, Moses, or Isiah said and truly meant. These interpretations were often quite different than some of the prevailing religious dogma of the time. He loved to teach what it really meant to be a child of the Most High, and how to know your true spiritual identity.

Through Rev. Ike's teachings, one would no longer think of themself in terms of race, creed, or color, but as a human creator powered by God who can create magnificently and excellently. He knew that the laws of God and life react to everyone on the same basis. This one man helped millions to access a level of possibility they hadn't previously realized was available to them. His passionate adherence to the practical implications of this came from one of his favorite passages which guided his direction from his earliest years:

> *Be ye transformed by the renewing of your mind.*
> (Romans 12:2 KJV)

He was living proof of the truth within these scriptures, and he wanted every person to know that truth. He gave all of himself to the pursuit of bringing that good news to people, particularly those downtrodden, depressed, or destitute. He knew the odds were against them, like they had been against him. Unfortunately, they had accepted the same flawed messages and failed principles that had failed him until he discovered the truth. He knew any one of them could emerge from that paradigm of accepted destitution and suffering if he could only provide that pastoral inspirational leadership and mentorship. It meant a great deal to him to help all others achieve the spiritual self-awareness and state of mindfulness that he had achieved to help lift them to their greatest levels of self-determination and self-expression.

These are the same principles and truths which took a poor Black kid from the South in the 1930s from the dreams of his most longed-for *wishes* to the manifestation of the most treasured *riches* of life.

Mark Victor Hansen and Xavier Eikerenkoetter

TWO WORLD CHANGERS MEET

Mark

I was a bankrupt twenty-six-year-old man desperate to find my way forward when Reverend Ike came into my life. Inspired by my mentor R. Buckminster Fuller, I had left graduate school and built a Geodesic Dome business in New York City, which crashed and burned when the oil embargo of the seventies hit. My primary material was large PVC (polyvinyl chloride) piping, and the sudden spike in pricing caused me to lose all of my contracts and two million dollars of business in the span of a few weeks. I had no choice but to file for bankruptcy in 1973. I was in absolute hell and felt useless and worthless. It seemed all was lost forever. I was broke, living in Hicksville, Long Island, sleeping in a sleeping bag in front of a friend's room at night. To round out my dismal days, I would tune into the negative evening news on TV each night. Ignorant of that effect on me and others, I was sharing and repeating what I heard each day and was starting to lose friendships. People clearly didn't want to be around a Danny-downer. I was eating up all the negativity and believing that was the truth. I was at the lowest point in my young life and literally considered suicide.

Struggling to pull myself out of my miserable state, searching for answers, I decided I wanted to become a speaker. I wanted to be able to talk to people about things that mattered, that would make a life-changing difference. In my attempt to rebound my life, I started as a salesman at Dale Carnegie Institute World Headquarters in Garden City, New York. One Sunday morning, two of my sales colleagues suggested that we go see Dr. Norman Vincent Peale, the author of *The Power of Positive Thinking*, who preached in his famous Marble Collegiate Church. After that we would have some lunch in the city and then go to Washington Heights to see Reverend Ike preach at his famous United Palace at three in the afternoon. I was excited and hopeful to hear these two great and inspiring preachers who preached positivity rather than negativity.

My position then was rather like that of the main character in the 1946 classic Christmas movie, *It's A Wonderful Life*. In the movie, George Bailey, a despondent man, looks at the world filled with nothing but problems and hopelessness, simultaneously wishing that he had never been born. Played by Jimmy Stewart, George has a dreamy glimpse into the question many have asked when depressed: "*What if I hadn't been born?*"

Fortunately, an angel-in-training shows him what it would have been like if he hadn't lived and helped so many people with his kind, loving, and generous spirit. When he wakes up, he decides not to end his life because he sees how important his life has been. It was meaningful, purposeful, and it truly mattered. George is able to clearly see that he served everyone in his community in quietly effective ways and was a support to the entire citizenry. George's life was important. George's life did matter—like everyone's does.

I'll never forget the day I walked into United Palace and heard Reverend Ike preach for the first time. It was there I had my George Bailey experience. Somehow this dynamic young preacher's words burned through the dark clouds that had been hanging over my soul. Something changed that day. In the space of those two hours, Rev. Ike became my angel—my model of how the future could be. A light penetrated my being during my hours there as I watched him preach from the stage:

> "*From the Mastermind, through the lips of Jesus: if you can believe, all things are possible to him who believes.*

That's from St. Mark, the 9th chapter, and the 23rd
verse. I'm going to read it again and I'm going to have
you shout it back at me as I pause. So, as a matter of
fact, I'm going to have you preach it back to me; so, all
you stand up. The words of the Mastermind, through
the lips of Jesus, from St. Mark, the 9th chapter, and
the 23rd verse; repeat it after me...

If you can believe...
If you can believe...
all things...
all things...
are possible...
are possible...
to him...
to him...
who believes.
who believes."

The negativity, struggle, and self-doubt I had felt the past few months seemed to melt away into this immersion of positivity and possibility. At the end of the service, I even bought his tapes and some books he recommended with the little money I had to my name, because I felt deeply that I needed this upliftment as much as I needed food and water. I left knowing my life was important, and that it mattered a great deal, and the idea was planted that I might actually be able to make a difference in the world. I had a hunch that what I did from then on would matter to other people. During my first immersion into the teachings of my new advocate, Reverend Ike, I realized my life was far from over. It was only just beginning.

After my first service at the United Palace, I desperately wanted to meet and personally thank Reverend Ike. I talked my two colleagues into walking up to the front of the church and waiting in line to meet Dr. Alfred Miller, who was second-in-command to Rev. Ike.

I felt Dr. Miller and I had an instant rapport and appreciation for one another. He promised me that if I kept coming, I would get backstage with Reverend Ike. He also promised to mention my name to Reverend Ike, which he memorized on the spot, chuckling about the fact that I had three names. One too many, according to him!

I kept coming faithfully not just for the opportunity to meet Rev. Ike, but to make sure I availed myself to absorbing the weekly messages that were burning into my heart, soul, and mind.

After I'd attended several more services, Rev. Ike had me believing again that the spirit of God in me could solve all my problems, end my misery, and help me become rich in every good way. He made it clear to me that being rich wasn't just about having money. It meant being healthy, happy, successful, prosperous, loving, and of course having plenty of money to be, do, and have all the good that I desired. He made me feel valuable, important, and like I could create something wonderful with my life. I had been baptized into a new awareness that would change me positively and profoundly, forever.

Later that month, Dr. Miller invited me to meet privately right after the service with Rev. Ike in his office chambers above the upper level of the United Palace. When I stepped into his office, I had an immediate appreciation for his obvious love of King Louis XIV, reflected in his regal furnishings. I loved the opulence and the luxuries.

It was there our lifelong friendship and deep conversations commenced and continued until he left us to move on to the heavenly plane. He began to ask me everything about my personal experiences.

Oh boy, was I ever learning! I'd gone from being upside down to right-side-up because of Rev. Ike. He told me to write down the most outrageous personal goal I could think of. I'd decided I was going to become a great and inspiring teacher who talked to millions of people around the world, and I planned on becoming the world's best-selling author.

I had a little diary in my hand I called my "Sunshine Diary," and when Rev. Ike asked to take a look at it, I was happy to let him.

Somehow I felt comfortable sharing my outrageous goals with Rev. Ike, goals that I wouldn't have shared with anyone else. His eyes sparkled with delight. I think he could see he'd ignited the spirit of God in me. Reverend Ike glanced through the more than 200 goals I had written, chuckling, nodding, and dignifying my dreams with affirming expressions. When he asked about my family background, I explained to him how I came from a blue-collar background, son of a Danish baker father who had a limited formal education, and how I had started being an entrepreneur at nine years old, earning enough money to buy my own bicycle. I told him that while I was in remedial reading from first to sixth grade, I was now a confirmed book addict. We talked endlessly, and he became fascinated that I went to college at Southern Illinois University, being mentored and befriended by arguably Dr. Albert Einstein's best student, Dr. R. Buckminster Fuller.

He laughed out loud when I described how I had gone to Fuller's first lecture thinking I was a hot shot with a 4.0 GPA who knew so much, and quickly realized how sophomoric I was with Fuller's first sentence. Bucky, as he was affectionately called, started the lecture listing the things we would talk about in the next hour, topics like cosmology, cosmogony, synergetic energetic mathematics, and his software project called "World Game—How to Make the World Work for One Hundred Percent of Humanity."

I explained to him Fuller's belief that God designed people. Rev. Ike kept nodding, rapt with attention. He was fascinated that Fuller's cosmological theories and research had humanity starting out on planet Earth two million years ago.

"Fuller believed humanity had commenced life here naked, helpless, and ignorant in the paradise around the Tahitian Islands that was abundantly providing for their every need with fish, fowl, fruits, and vegetables."

The reverend reveled in the imagination and probability Fuller presented that humans could just grab food off trees, easily net fish from the sea, and their first invention was a cup for carrying water.

Fuller said that "humanity went up by boat to what today we call China, migrated through India, into Africa, up to Europe, and that some of the people also went across the Bering Strait into Alaska and down through the Americas. As they evolved, their physiognomy, and especially the color of their skin, changed according to the incidence of sunshine. People nearest the equator always had the darkest skin and in the European northern climes their skins mutated into alabaster whiteness, usually with blue eyes." Over the two intensely dynamic hours we spent together, Reverend Ike pondered deeply every one of Fuller's enchanting concepts on the origins and development of the universe. I told him Fuller's original book called *Naga to Eden* got incorporated into his bestseller *Critical Path*. He agreed that whether right or wrong, true or false, it deeply stimulates one's thinking and possibilities of our original ancestry and evolution.

He was surprised to hear that Bucky wanted to kill himself after his three-year-old daughter died of spinal meningitis and he thought it was his fault. Bucky had asked himself life's two biggest questions. Question number one was, "Is there a God?" The spontaneous answer he heard inside himself was, "There is an *a priori* intelligence in the universe." Question number two was, "What is my place in the Universe?" The answer Bucky heard was, "I don't own me; the universe owns me. I am here to make humanity physically and economically one hundred percent successful." "There is enough for everyone," Bucky was known to say. "People think there isn't enough, so they take as much as they can, so many people don't have enough. Think of it… We are blessed with technology that would be indescribable to our forefathers. We have the wherewithal, the know-it-all to feed everybody, clothe everybody, and give every human on Earth a chance. We know now what we could never have known before—that we now have the option for all humanity to make it successfully on this planet in this lifetime. Whether it is to be *Utopia or Oblivion* (one of forty books Fuller wrote), it will be a touch-and-go relay race right up to the final moment." It thrilled Reverend Ike to know that Fuller believed in and often quoted what Jesus said 2,000 years ago: *I am here that you have life and have it more abundantly.*

Rev. Ike made me promise I would keep expanding my goals and serving more people. My spirit aglow, I was walking on air when I left his office. I felt I'd been anointed to do great work in the world. In that first meeting with Rev. Ike and others that would follow, I always found the reverend eager to ask endless questions, ever hungry for more knowledge from all who could teach him. His insatiable desire to learn, know, and gain more wisdom was one of the things I found so cherishable about his personality.

I became a positive spiritual addict from that point forward and attended Rev. Ike's services every Sunday, often bringing friends, colleagues, and clients during my seven years in New York City.

I was fascinated by Rev. Ike's realism and straight-up street talk. There was a brilliance to it. Even in the midst of the opulent environment he had created at the United Palace, he related to people right where they were. With the combination of visual beauty and elegance in the décor, and his immaculate attire and grooming, he stood there juxtaposed against the poverty and limitation in which he was raised, and which many of them were deeply and painfully experiencing. He awakened them to a realization that the God in them was infinite. God in them was a limitless God. God in them had extraordinary and as yet unrealized possibilities. They were filled with a God who was happy and loved His children to experience all good things.

When I was growing up, my mom was Baptist and my dad was Lutheran. I had gone to two church services most Sundays of my young life and had been bored, mostly disinterested, and only semi-listening to the pastors.

Rev. Ike was an evocator who lit my spiritual sparkplug in a way that had never happened to me before. If you had asked the starry-eyed young man I was the first time I stepped into Rev Ike's church in 1973 if I would someday be co-authoring his biographical story with his son Xavier, who was just a young boy at the time, I wouldn't have thought it possible. As a young, beginning speaker, to think I would someday be writing a book about this giant mega-church builder, media-celebrated, rock star preacher would have been totally unbelievable to me at that time in my life. I feel this book was divinely guided. Rev. Ike knew the work must go on and clearly stated just that by saying repetitively to his wife, his son, his friends, and the world in his videos, "I'm going to keep teaching, even after I go to the other side."

Well, as we write this it is twelve years after his death and his teaching and preaching are alive and thriving on YouTube. Reverend Ike was right; the work will go on, through those of us who loved him, learned from him, and gained phenomenal benefits from his wisdom and teachings. We know that it must go on. It is, was, and will continually provide tremendous value into the foreseeable future as long as individuals need and want to grow in passionate purposefulness, overcome the odds, succeed, and proceed to eradicate in their personal lives "a money rejection complex and supplant it with a money attraction complex"—that he understood, lived, and enthusiastically taught.

THE EARLY YEARS

AN UNCANNY CHILDHOOD

Xavier

People choose their parents. This is my belief. Each human soul makes these kinds of foundational decisions before incarnating into the Earthly plane. We have soul-based reasons for aligning with certain other souls who will help forge our identities and develop our strengths based on the lessons and achievements we set forth to accomplish in this lifetime. An individual's path and purpose are aided by both the encouragement and the blockages their parents present, often unwittingly, simply by being who they are. This premise holds true for me, and it holds true for my father, Frederick Joseph Eikerenkoetter II, who grew up to become the successful, wealthy, prominent, controversial, and beloved religious figure the world came to know as Rev. Ike.

My father was a brilliant man with an enigmatic nature ensconced beneath layers of a seemingly transparent public persona. In the latter years of our time together, I came to appreciate the experiences that influenced who he became as a flesh and blood person as well as an iconic celebrity. His life, a study in the sacred and worldly, bore the manifestation of human frailty and divine conviction.

My dad was born into a fertile training ground for the development of his free thinking, which was not directly supported by his parents but facilitated by their disparate views on poverty and wealth, fatalism, and self-determination. Based on his mother's rigidly religious opinions about poverty and its virtue, he figured out how a condition of destitution can be manifested. In an uncanny way, he learned how to embody prosperity principles from his father, who scoffed at ideas of piously glorified lack and, ironically, was the one who consigned little Frederick and his mother to poverty by refusing to provide funds after their marital split. He came to understand firsthand the role the mind plays in manifesting the primary beliefs it holds.

As a little boy, long before he could articulate it, my dad had a deep, innate knowing—one that transcended belief—that something bigger than him was seeking expression *through* him and that the expression of it would involve lots of money and an abundance of things he could only see in his mind. His mystical connection with something more than himself and his circumstances manifested through his imagination, and that is what he would eventually teach the world.

His parents' personal philosophies about poverty and wealth rose to the surface even more profoundly during the summer of 1940 when he was five years old. A hurricane made landfall in Beaufort, South Carolina, and poured through the nearby town of Ridgeland and the Eikerenkoetter home. The storm was so violent that it would result in the deaths of thirty-four people and cause significant property and agricultural damage in the area. This area had been the home of the Eikerenkoetter lineage at least back to my great-great grandfather Joseph Eikerenkoetter in the early 1800s, so the devastation also impacted their family and friends. My grandfather, the elder Joseph Frederick Eikerenkoetter, who went by "Fred," surveyed his yard through the window with astonishment, as a solid wall of high wind whipped across the backyard sending anything loose flying and whipping away at the pillars of his back porch.

His wife, my grandmother Rema, was startled by the roar of the hurricane-like forces, interrupted only by an occasional abrupt crash of some other piece of their homestead submitting to its forces. Another loud bang and Rema began running in circles around the living room dodging the furniture like a caged cat. Her mother, who lived with them and their young son, joined in her daughter's hysteria by screaming that the devil was riding black horses with smoldering red eyes, galloping inland from the whitecaps on the Atlantic Ocean.

"No," Rema countered. "God is pounding the sky with his raging fist because he can't tolerate the sins of the world any longer! Jesus!" she cried. "For the love of God, help us!"

The porch gave in to the storm's fury and smashed into a kitchen window, scattering fragments of glass onto the oak floor. Rema couldn't take it anymore. She bolted toward the back door with her hand stretched out in front of her, calling out to Jesus like she was ready to run straight into that storm and banish it to Hell. Or maybe she was trying to reach the storm cellar in the backyard. Regardless of what was going on in her mind, my grandfather, shaken by her loss of control, in his attempt to try to calm her down, scuffled with her in the kitchen doorway. Their fracas continued through much of the night, moving from the living room to the kitchen, outside, and back inside again. At one point he pressed his body on top of hers, pinning her to the floor for her own safety. Grandmother was drawn to the storm and my grandfather tried desperately to restrain her from racing right into it. When she resisted him with such strength she got away from his grasp, he was afraid she'd lost her mind. He chased her down, both of them collapsing in mud and water as the backyard filled up like a lake. My grandfather succeeded in keeping her from harm, and after hours of this pandemonium, she finally became motionless and trance-like on the sofa. Later, my grandmother had no memory of the raging storm, which continued to slap abruptly against the walls and roof, nor did she recall her attempt at escape from the house. Hours past her normal bedtime, she sat on the living room sofa, staring at the wall. My father witnessed it all.

"Rema, it's time to go to sleep," my grandfather repeated several times.

Four hours passed, and she did not move. Well after midnight, still silent, she finally got up, pushed away my grandfather's outstretched hand, and went upstairs to bed.

The night of the storm personified the tempest brewing in my grandparents' marriage. Eventually, their incompatibility led to a legal separation. My dad witnessed the relationship's unraveling, which included cast iron pots and pans flying over his head as he was caught between the fighting. Strangely, his parents' increasingly bitter quarrels were intensified as his mother watched his father succeed with several of his business plans.

My grandfather was a resourceful man who created multiple streams of income by becoming proficient and dependable in the work he did for mostly White folks. He had a reputation as a reliable builder who could also draw up the designs of the buildings he did. He constructed small buildings, porches, and fences on a contract basis, never working for anyone else. He was the boss. His tireless work ethic and tremendous pride in what he produced allowed him to quickly establish a reputation for excellence and timeliness. Naturally frugal, he saved much of his considerable earnings, creating an increasingly comfortable lifestyle for his wife and young son.

He was determined to make something of himself, never shirking from opportunities that arose to work a little harder or expand his offerings, hiring himself out to keep his nest egg growing. He wasn't afraid to dream, and his dreams had big plans. He saw the way it worked in the White man's world. A man could incorporate his services and become a real businessman. Why not him? The differences aggravated him. He did some of the best work around, and time after time other men, especially White folks, told him as much. He would put up some nice advertisement signs like the rest of them, *Frederick Eikerenkoetter, Architect. Builder. Real Estate Developer. Finest Quality Work Around.*

Deep inside he knew he was more than a hired hand and had plans in his future to sit at a desk in a real office and conduct his business dealings. He was tired of bumping around in beat-up old trucks that kept falling apart on him and wasting his time trying to fix them. The indignity of the disparities of the time irked him and must have been painful because he was a man whose talent and drive eclipsed many of those who called him "boy" or looked down on him but benefitted from his gifts.

My grandmother would get nervous when he started having all of these "highfalutin notions" and reminded him she was the granddaughter of a house slave, and to be grateful to the Lord for how far they'd come. Rema's mother, Annie Mae Thomas Matthews, was the daughter of an African house slave, Nancy Masters, and her White slave master, Thomas Thomas, who owned the sprawling Thomasville, Georgia slave plantation starting in the early 1800s. All four of Annie Mae's children, one son and three daughters, were at some time educators. In the 1930s in Georgia, when they finished eighth grade, they were able to get jobs teaching for a sum of sixty-five dollars a month.

Grandmother Rema warned her husband to be content with what he had, and to stop pushing so much. Being so brazenly ambitious would surely end up offending some of the White folks who had been good to him. She couldn't get through to him. "Pride goeth before a fall!" she would cry. He just wouldn't listen, and when he came home one day talking about the new car he was going to buy, that was it for her. She decided he was more wedded to his flamboyant dreams than he was to her, and she wasn't willing to subject herself to a man who was a renegade in the eyes of the Lord. He could go ahead and make absurd plans but now she would make her own plans to leave and save herself and her son from the sins of greed and gluttony. Her roots led through a maze of stories where Black men had been lynched in the South for getting too full of themselves and she concluded that the Eikerenkoetter men had dangerously large heads filled with too many fancy ideas. Ideas that could lead to big trouble.

Their marriage did not turn out the way either of them had imagined. When they met, my grandfather was reaping the benefits of having grown up with a demanding, impatient father who implemented a literal translation of Proverbs 27:17 (NIV): "*As iron sharpens iron, so one man sharpens another.*"

My great-grandfather accepted no excuses in demanding discipline from his son, which included having my grandfather read and memorize long Biblical passages. He said he knew of no better way to make sure his son was literate in his knowledge of the Word and sharpen his faculties in reading and speaking. In the early 1930s, Grandfather made Ridgeland his permanent home. Right away he decided to utilize his knowledge of the Bible and began to preach to eager, enthusiastic crowds. People liked his style and thought he delivered a captivating message.

One clear, bright morning, my grandfather had just finished baptizing a young man down at the lake when he glanced up and locked eyes with an attractive young woman named Rema Matthews. A few minutes later when they were introduced by a mutual friend, Rema couldn't help but notice that Frederick Eikerenkoetter, in addition to his curly hair and his handsome countenance, was extremely well mannered. Rema was articulate and conversant, and he admired her education in literature, music, and science that was atypical of most of the residents of Ridgeland.

At his request, she gave him permission to visit her later that week, and their courtship began. She liked the way he took charge and made their time together interesting and fun. It was a beautiful, sunny afternoon when he took her for a lovely picnic he had planned. After they arranged themselves in the shade of a big tree, he admitted, "I thought you were something special the first time I met you down by the lake."

"Why?" she asked.

"Because you were one of the few girls who could say my name without giggling or stumbling over every letter," he replied.

"Well, tell me about the origins of your name. I am curious," Rema asked directly, looking right into his eyes.

He was several years older than her and found her confidence amusing. He answered with a big grin, "My people are descended from Dutch East Indians who settled around Savannah. The name means 'little acorn carrier' in Dutch."

It mattered that there was warmth and understanding when she laughed at his response, not the sarcasm he experienced in the laughter of so many other women. My grandfather looked at her intently for several minutes before kissing the woman he decided was going to be his wife. He had found the woman who had the intellectual sophistication to get behind him and his plans. She had found a hard worker and a preacher who would love the scripture as she did.

The romance of the honeymoon period did not last long. My grandmother had listened to him share his plans for operating his own contracting business, which would allow him to make a name for himself and become wealthy. During their courtship, it all sounded so dreamy. Once they were married, however, she expected him to stop the nonsensical talk and begin to behave more practically by getting a regular job.

Years later, as she packed her clothes to leave the small but comfortable house he had built for her and their son, she said, "You Eikerenkoetters have big minds—too big for anybody's good, especially your own."

"You go right ahead, you stubborn woman," he replied. "You're so damned high and mighty with all your education, see if you can make it alone out here!" He didn't think she'd ever go through with it.

Grandmother was determined to stick to her principles. If she did, God would see they would endure. She knew she could. Her education and her faith in Jesus would be enough to persist and subsist. She would have to withstand some hardship, but nothing she couldn't bear. She was a survivor who was willing to withstand more than necessary to stand up for what she thought was right. She had planned her exit, secured a house to rent, and hired a local moving company to take her belongings to her new residence, all while my grandfather was out working.

It had been a long, grueling day in the country helping to raise a barn for a wealthy White farmer and all Grandfather could think about was a hot meal and a soak in the tub. Instead, he walked into an empty house that had just been abandoned hours before by his wife and son. The kitchen table, the dishes, the sofa, and all their clothes were gone. The big trunk and two suitcases were also gone. He was furious and heartbroken at the same time. How could she do this? His family was gone in an instant, without notice. In his rage over her departure, he swore he would never give her one red cent—not for her support and not even for his son.

Never one to show weakness, Rema told church members and friends that it was necessary for her to leave her husband, that he didn't understand the true nature of religious conviction, which should be guided by a willingness to reject worldly things like fancy motor cars, fine furniture, and clothing. A man of Jesus would pursue meekness rather than wealth. In addition to his lack of interest in true spiritual piety, her former husband refused to discipline his mind with reading and fine music. She was not willing to allow her son to grow up around a man who was so fixated on material wealth that he paid too little attention to spiritual provisions and the salvation of the soul.

The years following his parents' divorce became difficult for my dad. Keeping his vow, his father gave them nothing. Sneers from other children were painful to him as they learned his parents had split. Being a child of divorced parents and a single mother made life for a young Black boy more difficult than it already was. The only saving grace was that my grandmother kept the Eikerenkoetter name, so people understood he wasn't fatherless.

As the married Mrs. Eikerenkoetter, my grandfather's success made it possible for her salary as a schoolteacher to go into the bank under her name. Her meager salary was now needed for daily life. Since she and her son shared a home with her aging mother, there were three of them to house, feed, and clothe, not to mention all the other necessities of living to pay for, including a tithe paid at church every week without fail.

From the first day of her marriage, Rema had taken a backseat role in anything financial. Like the other women at the time who were housewives and mothers, she wasn't demanding of any luxuries, but expected that her husband would provide money for all of the things a working-class household needed, including food, clothing, and personal products. The man of the household was supposed to be in charge of the money. This was the structure of a normal, stable family in the thirties.

From her lonely spot under the dim, solitary lightbulb hanging from the kitchen ceiling, Grandma now realized she hadn't before experienced this combined pressure of being provider, single mother, and teacher. A proud woman, she wouldn't admit how overwhelmed she felt with bills that devoured every penny of her sixty-five-dollars-a-month salary. Each weekday she still faced fifty students from seven different grades whom she taught in one room, managing the ever-fluctuating scale of compliance or defiance a teacher faces. Whenever she reached out to my grandfather for money, he made sure she understood the question was open and shut. He would give her absolutely nothing. He would not forgive her for leaving him.

When Dad would ask why he couldn't have a little more supper because he was still hungry or why he had to wear newspapers in his shoes, she shuddered, struggling to offer her little son a good explanation for this meager life through which they were trying to navigate.

While their circumstances had tremendous impact on him, Dad's mind periodically poked through into a different reality, prompted by an inner soulful longing that included a form of hope, a kind of divine reach that allowed him to visualize a life exceedingly more prosperous than what his eyes saw. It was a possible future that became more and more probable as he matured in his gift.

> *"As a kid, I would lie in bed at night and project my own mental movies up onto the ceiling of my room. I could see the beautiful cars I wanted. That's why I was different than my friends. They didn't know how to do what I did. I knew how to make beautiful and exciting pictures with me sitting inside. I could tell by the things they said the other kids couldn't do it. In their pictures, they were always outside, always looking in. But I made my own dreams. I wasn't watching that beautiful car drive by, I was riding in it. My mind had the best pictures of me throwing the best parties in the huge houses where rich White folks lived. But instead I lived there. I was not a servant; I was a host. I imagined myself as the owner of that fine house. I had a different vision of myself. At one point, I decided in my dreams I didn't want to see fine clothes sitting in a store window. Instead I dreamed I was wearing those beautiful things. I dreamt of having things and being somebody.*

Somehow the parties in my mind were always silent, and a lot of nights the sound of my mother's voice singing filled my dreams. The words about clinging to the old rugged cross would travel down the hallway uninvited, right into my party, her sad old song interrupting all that fun I had going on. And she'd sing such a long time. Way too long. Far into the night. Long after my dream was over."

As angry as Fred Eikerenkoetter was to have been forced to live apart from his wife and small son, his refusal to support them financially allowed my grandfather to save his earnings to invest in various properties. He developed a good nose for knowing how much to pay for a piece of farmland or an empty lot in town he felt was a good potential site for a building. I still have a parcel of Grandfather's property with remnants of a house he built by hand. He saw the value in collecting rents and now owned a building in Ridgeland that housed a beauty parlor the ladies frequented and a barbershop that was a favorite for Blacks. A friend convinced him that joining a couple of other local men to buy part of a restaurant would be lucrative. He did, and that too started to spin off a little extra cash each month.

He started to shift his focus away from weekend revivals and visiting minister assignments around the state. The success of his business interests allowed him to limit his preaching to a handful of local services, baptisms, and funerals. He was still a favorite and continued to make money and raise spirits with his arousing delivery as Reverend Freddie.

His distraction from the unhappiness he felt being away from his son caused him to immerse himself in his accomplishments. He already had a respectable level of success in finding opportunities and making money, but being away from his wife and mother-in-law with their poverty mentality allowed him to flourish even more as a businessman and become more commanding in the pulpit. He had to keep moving forward because he could never live with a wife who rigidly ennobled lack. He often found himself drifting back to the same questions. Why had he chosen to marry a woman who was willing to settle for a deficient, substandard life? She was the mother of his child. Why couldn't she have appreciated a man who had dreams and desires for something better for his family?

Regardless of how she behaved during their courtship, the truth was, she had never believed in him and didn't want him to succeed as a dignified businessman. To her, a Negro was a sufferer, a person to whom God's promises didn't apply, and pain and sacrifice were the trade-off for the hope and possibility of some future glory in the afterlife. In Rema's world, this was what the Lord expected and decent people accepted. Only the lowest Hell-bound sinners would dare question this truth.

For Fred Eikerenkoetter, the true transgression was that she had left him. He could have pardoned her constant pestering. If it had just been little irritations like bad housekeeping or plain-tasting cooking, no problem. Even though she was good at pushing him from exasperation to anger, he still would have hung in there and worked to make their home and life ever better. But leaving him and rejecting him as a man? She could never atone for that. He would not forgive her.

There were not a lot of secrets in the Ridgeland Negro community, and he was well aware of her struggle to get by financially. He'd never hear it from her lips, but he knew her desperation. With her education and proper speech, my grandmother was a target for verbal jabs of gossip from other Blacks less accomplished than her. During back-fence talk, they took some delight in sharing the buzz about Rema Eikerenkoetter who "didn't have a pot to pee in nor a window to throw it out of."

Whether she realized it or not, she had hurt my grandfather irreversibly. The bitterness never seemed to subside, and he would forever offer reminders of her great loss. My dad's fifth birthday in June 1940 was a perfect opportunity for such. Grandfather paid a surprise visit, driving up to the modest little row house where his former wife was living with her mother and their son to deliver a vivid symbol of what she had left behind.

His son was getting ready for school as Grandfather knew he would be at this time of the morning. Grandfather strode confidently to the front door, which young Frederick opened with excitement, inviting his dad into the living room. As soon as both the ladies entered the living room to see what the fuss was, Frederick's father presented him with a finely crafted fishing rod. The device was far too intricate for a five-year-old, but that wasn't the point. Neither woman could afford anything like it, and it made their gifts to young Frederick—new pencils for school, a white Sunday shirt, or new black socks—pale considerably by comparison.

His point made, my grandfather gave his son a hug and a pat on the head, and after a minute or two of polite banter with his ex-wife and ex-mother-in-law, he bid them all a pleasant day and departed. Trying to maintain their dignity, they watched through the living room window as he walked to the street and glided into a gleaming new Chevrolet coupe, the first of its kind ever owned by a Black man in Ridgeland. He drove away without looking back. Even at five, the extravagance of the fishing rod was not lost on my dad. It reminded him just how rich his father was and how selective he was with his wealth.

Just a few years later, when he was eight, Dad had an experience that forged his sense of self-reliance and fierce independence. Because his shoes were worn through and his feet hurt from walking to and from school, he asked his mother for a new pair of shoes. She did not have the money for them, so she appealed to his father to buy them. "You took that boy away from me. You can buy him new shoes," Frederick Sr. replied. When my father heard this, something ripped inside of him. Extremely hurt, he vowed to do it all for himself from then on and never ask for anything again, especially from his father.

This hardheartedness towards his former wife that collaterally punished his son was probably his biggest character flaw, and it impacted my father profoundly. I believe that, in turn, impacted his relationship with me. I sensed that, in many ways, Dad's eventual accumulation of material assets was an attempt to make up for this deeply hurtful slight from his father and the sense of worthlessness that resulted from being abandoned in penury.

Psychologically, a state of pennilessness can equate to a lack of personal value. It is not true that those who have less are worth less, but the sting of poverty lived as a state of being over time can have that effect.

It makes sense that my father's central message became that as a child of the king I/we deserve it all. Identifying as God's true child—taking this as the literal a priori status for himself and human beings as a species—instead of seeing it as a platitude took care of the self-worth question.

My father challenged the old religion with its tired thinking and banal assumptions by saying, "You call yourself a child of God, child of the King, and you are struggling, nay suffering through life impoverished and self-deprecating? That makes absolutely no sense. I'm going up to live in the palace. Join me if you will! You say the Lord is your shepherd. Why are you wanting? I'm going to dine upon those green pastures and drink of the sweet, still waters. Join me if you dare."

The basis of my father's philosophy was the divinity of the human being. Part of it was sparked by the necessity of believing that God was better than his Earthly father and could never abandon him. The divinity factor put an unbreakable lock on value, both personal/human and material.

That fall, my father began to go with his mother to the segregated grammar school for Negro children in Ridgeland. There was no transportation available to them, so they walked the four miles to school. She spent each weekday in this tiny wooden building, lecturing, encouraging, and often berating her pupils. Even with these challenges, she was a teacher first, and her students were all better for it. Then, when the day was done, she walked the four miles back home, her young son trudging along at her side.

Although Rema was frequently sick, her pride and work ethic wouldn't allow her to miss workdays because of any illness and she demanded the same of my dad. If she went to school, he did too. You wouldn't ever find him at home under warm covers if he had sniffles. It didn't matter that other kids stayed home with coughs, colds, or sore throats; those were excuses, according to my grandmother. She insisted that church and school were two places you unfailingly attended if you could stand and walk. That suited my dad just fine because he excelled in both. Rema's mother had also taught school, so Dad was constantly immersed in the intellectual conversations between his mother and grandmother, supplemented by a wide variety of books in their home. School was a happy place for him, and he was always eager to learn.

My grandmother organized her household with a meticulous set of routines that made certain the shopping, cooking, laundry, and house cleaning were executed with competence. She demanded maximum productivity from her son and her mother. Troubled emotions lurking beneath the surface were veiled by the overtone of constant perfection and order. Despite their calm public appearances and immaculate home, the family's scarce resources kept them desperately impoverished. They never had quite enough food, and what they did have was basic and often of poor quality. Dad didn't dare ask for a second helping, and desserts were so rare that even getting a small piece of cake felt like a holiday to him.

Neat, organized, and educated, but still poor, the family resided in a neighborhood of small row houses in the Negro section of town. Every home was made of wood, and each looked the same as the next. The residents were largely unskilled workers. As the only educated professional, my grandmother felt isolated into a life that was mostly limited to church, school, and home. She resented having to live this way. It was beneath her, and she was unable to hide her consuming rage for her ex-husband who allowed it. Disguised by a cool demeanor, her anger was constantly brewing just below the surface and the most innocent misbehavior from my dad could set her off, resulting in severe punishment that often left him confused. He came home one day after playing with a couple of friends on the street, and enthusiastically showed his grandmother a pair of dice the kids had been tossing around for fun. When his mother found out, she thrashed his hands so hard with a wooden stick that for the rest of his life, just the sight of a set of dice caused him pain.

Her threats about the dice and any other "sinful" activities were filled with a fury that left deep impressions on him. When she felt she wasn't satisfactorily getting his attention with her fiery admonishments, the Word of God became her weapon. Fear and silence dominated their home. With the exception of his mother's voice demanding his attention and his grandmother's hands emphatically pounding a table in her outrage, noise of any kind was not permitted in the household.

In this environment, my dad learned to speak softly and politely, no matter what situation arose or how he felt about it. This was the only behavior allowed by his mother. There was no space in his home life to express his emotions, regardless of what they might be. He escaped by spending much of his time alone in his room, imagining something different. His fantasies and visions were the only access he had to a world beyond the one he lived in, and he created pictures in his mind of travels to rich, exciting cities and daring, exotic places.

It was a secret world that only he could enter. The few close friends he had wouldn't understand if he tried to share them, and he had learned the hard and painful way to not ever discuss "other worlds" with his mother or grandmother. Other worlds were dangerous and full of sin. They were filled with wild temptations like liquor, loud music, gambling, and heathens who sought things of the flesh. Godly people did not even think about entering these places or participating in these aspects of human experience. Tools of the devil like cards, radio music, and dancing were not allowed in their home. Except for a few gospel spirituals that facilitated her deepest lamentations, Rema didn't even allow singing. "The Old Rugged Cross" was one of her favorites, and it was a perfect outlet for venting nearly all her complaints.

As a kid, my dad got to briefly see a lighthearted side of his mother that had remained completely hidden from him, until one night when she called him into her room and had him help her pull out a large trunk from under the bed. She opened the trunk and took out a gold linen tablecloth with beautifully patterned edges and an extravagantly woven silk shawl. After placing them across the bed like she was setting a fancy tabletop, she took China, silver, crystal glasses, and starched napkins and placed them in neat rows. She pulled out necklaces, along with shining bracelets and beautiful rings for her fingers. Her son didn't know she owned anything this nice. He'd never seen her wear anything that pretty. She even set out two silver hand mirrors with an elaborate initial "R" hammered onto them. For the young, well-disciplined child that my father was, it was like watching a magic show, with everything in the room shining and glowing. He watched her go back in time and become someone he'd never seen before. As she pulled out various lovely music boxes and wound up each one, there was an odd but lovely symphony of different tunes playing all at the same time.

She brought out perfumes and sachet powders, laughing as she told the stories about boyfriends who had given her these gifts back in Savannah before she got married. There were fancy hats relatives had given her that she paraded around in, pretending she was back on the Fourth of July boat rides having ice cream with her friends, taking pictures with them and their dates from the state college. My dad watched in wonder as Rema reminisced about her life before her marriage.

With quiet, breathless excitement, he asked his mother when they would use all the fancy silverware, dishes, and linen. When would they put up mantle clocks and all the other beautiful items she kept packed away?

"Why son, we'll wait for company," she replied with a big smile.

In all those years of living with his mother and grandmother, there were seldom any visitors. Rema's sister came to visit once and stayed a while. Cousins visited. But that special "company" for whom she was saving all of her finery never came.

The hidden treasures my dad witnessed that day were part of her private stash of "riches." Rema was not free to bring them out and enjoy them, because in her belief system, rich people could not get into Heaven. If God didn't punish the rich here and now, they would certainly receive the ultimate exclusion after death. They wouldn't fit through the "eye of the needle." The apprehension she carried about being worthy of Heaven was likely compounded by the nervousness she had concerning her husband and son. It was a time when mistreatment and lynchings still happened to Black men in South Carolina when they "stepped out of place." That constant fear concerning her ambitious husband caused her enough angst to leave him and the good life he was providing. Whatever mistreatment at the hands of racist White people she may have witnessed in her life likely created trauma that she would have personally felt and that the Black community generally lived with. The pressure from her beliefs and the conditions of the times kept her in a state of constant anxiety that often resulted in her punishing herself and her family.

Not long after my dad's thirteenth birthday, the family made a change that would result in a universal conspiracy of strange but wonderful events for him. My grandmother decided the three of them would move into a house directly across the street from a popular local nightclub. Ironically, this "juke joint," as people in the South called it, would end up having a life-changing impact on the youngster who would grow up to become Reverend Ike.

Southern jukes were notoriously questionable places. In small towns, they often served as the social and recreational hub for adults, particularly those who didn't "belong" to any other institution, especially a church community. In the segregated South, these places were the social epicenter for Black people who were constantly floundering between coarse poverty and spiritual guilt and confusion fueled by religious fervor. A juke joint was a beacon for drinkers, gamblers, and sometimes troublemakers looking to express unbridled pleasures and passions.

My father knew that Sadie's Place represented the incarnate evil he'd been warned about. Yet as a young boy reaching adolescence, he secretly couldn't help feeling intrigued by this forbidden den of iniquity. Forbidden to play cards, dance, or even think carnal thoughts for as long as he could remember, he was now within sight of what his mother quickly described as the hell that surrounded him on Earth, hell that would rise to devour him if he was not strong and ever vigilant.

It was disquieting to him to think that inside that menacing structure was more sin in one hour than might exist among decent people in a lifetime. It mercilessly teased his thoughts as he imagined that amongst the smoke and the shadows was a world of wild, lost souls whom his mother assured him were irredeemably damned.

Settled into their new house that first night, the family of three got on their knees and prayed for themselves in this neighborhood of living purgatory and especially for the survival of my dad's youthful, innocent soul. Clashing against the soul-saving petitions the family offered up to God was raucous screamin' and hollerin' from the uninhibited crowd across the street at Sadie's Place. Young Freddie tried to concentrate as he felt squeezed between his hallowed prayers and the Earthly noises drifting toward him. Try as he might, he couldn't shut off the fascination.

As if reading his mind, a jukebox sprang into a jazzy blues number, the kind he'd heard schoolmates whisper about as "devil's music." Pretending to be deaf to the noise his mother began to sing "Amazing Grace." He tried to focus on her words, but the music blared across the street, and he felt too warm to concentrate as he thought of his friend telling him this was the kind of music that made folks act crazy, screaming and shaking like wild animals.

"Amazing Grace, how sweet the sound…"

Moving right through the walls of their home came the wicked opposition to his mother's singing. A fiery electric guitar coaxing out sensual love calls. Struggling against the forbidden, beckoning to him, he breathed deeply.

"I once was lost, but now I'm found…"

These wildly divergent strains of song crashed against each other like booming retorts in a battlefield of the divine and the profane, and the adolescent who would someday become my father found himself simultaneously thrilled by a deeply emotional mixture of terror and burgeoning desire.

Tucked away in his upstairs bedroom later that night, he tiptoed to the window to gaze across Koming Street, nearly abandoned at this late hour. He couldn't help but fixate on the doors and windows at Sadie's, searching for the faces and the bodies that laughed and moved to all that music. He felt a little jolt each time the door opened to release or admit new customers, the sound of the jukebox erupting inside his belly like rolling thunder.

Exhausted from all the emotional excitement, he drifted off to the hushed tones of his mother's voice down the hall.

"I once was blind but now I see..."

Returning home from a revival meeting in Beaufort with his mother one day, they saw some kind of bedlam going on in the street. It had only been six days since they had moved in and a neighbor had reported someone had just been killed at Sadie's Place while they were gone. A man walked away from his fish sandwich for a moment, and another man had taken a bite without permission. An argument ensued, knives were drawn, and the fight began—ending when one of them fell over dead from stab wounds.

My dad was more astounded by people's casual reaction to the loss of life than he was by the shocking news of the killing. He listened as several men began arguing about exactly how long it had been since the last murder in Sadie's while they watched the police remove the body.

"Look at that! Do you see that?" Rema insisted, grabbing her son's face and turning it around fiercely toward Sadie's as the limp body was dumped into the trunk of a police car. "You see! This is where sin will take you. All that liquor and wickedness going on! This is exactly what happens in the presence of evil."

Afraid to close his eyes, Dad stared at the ceiling all that night. He wanted to shut away the memory of that lifeless body as he tried desperately to fall asleep. His body was tense with fear as if a brawl from Sadie's Place might suddenly break into his house, bringing random, careless death along with it. Instead, the sound of loud, booming laughter brought him to his window.

Only hours after the fatal showdown between two of her customers, it was business as usual at Sadie's. With contempt, his mother described Sadie and her regulars, claiming that the demise of those who chose to live among the riffraff was the price they paid for their madness. People were filling up the place again like nothing had happened. The normal crowd had the place hopping. The liquor was flowing and the music blasting to the sound of a young blues singer named Dinah Washington. In spite of the trauma he'd felt, Dinah's confident young voice made my dad feel a little more confident, and with a big sigh he floated off to sleep. He slept through the early morning revenge killings of two people on the sidewalk outside the nightclub—retaliation murders committed by the deceased stabbing victim's relatives.

A strange twist of fate precipitated by an unexpected rainstorm pulled together sacred and the secular one night at Sadie's. The uncooperative weather had interfered with the tent meeting of a group of traveling Pentecostal revivalists. They were forced to pack up all their equipment and gear into a station wagon and drive to the nearest town, which happened to be Ridgeland. They needed to find a place to stay for the night. Elder Davis, an aging but energetic preacher, was the troupe's leader. Three musicians and two female vocalists rounded out the traveling gospel caravan. Davis preached wildly animated Pentecostal sermons that left a lasting impression. Some of the locals who had attended a Davis and Company revival around South Carolina said, "Those people don't hold back nothin'!"

In the prominent church organizations around the town, there were subtle but well-known distinctions. The Black Methodists considered themselves more important than the larger but less organized Baptist sects in Ridgeland. But you'd never catch either of those denominations publicly endorsing the unfiltered, party-like atmosphere the Pentecostal folks were known for at their loud, steamy revival meetings, although they would sometimes curiously participate in the revivals.

Elder Davis' entourage included a guitarist, drummer, and a keyboardist with a portable electric organ. His band would often invite some local musicians to create a large, soul-rocking orchestra. Somehow, these Pentecostal travelers decided to stop at Sadie's that rainy night. The storm deluge had served to keep most of the regulars at home, so the place was unusually empty. The few people there were mostly enjoying a meal of fried chicken or spareribs accompanied by some kind of soda pop. Deflated from the lack of business, Sadie suddenly perked up when they entered the "joint" and she asked the musicians if they would play there that night. Elder Davis thought it was a wonderful idea so until the wee hours of the morning, an improvised Pentecostal revival blared like a stranger from a foreign land out of the juke joint.

Rema was seething. She was being robbed of her sleep by the sinful sounds from across the street, which she despised with every fiber of her being. The music kept growing louder and more insistent. How dare that lewd woman disrupt the sleep of hard-working true believers and righteous Christians? Especially troubling was the realization that even with a cotton pillow pressing into her ears, she couldn't avoid the mocking tunes that were deceptively splashing in spiritual words. How dare that sinful woman have the nerve to insult the Lord by playing jukebox tunes that sounded like church music!

Dad lay there awake hearing the whole thing too. It was hopping over at Sadie's, and he was surprised that the heavy rain wasn't keeping everyone home. He also noticed the sound radiating into his bedroom didn't sound like the normal musical offering that he had fallen asleep to so many nights. There was a peculiarly "churchy" feel mixed with a Blue Grass sound, a blend he didn't quite recognize, though he could swear he was hearing the words "Heaven" and "Jesus" floating out. His wonder and curiosity had him standing at the window of his room staring across the street, straining to see what was happening inside the dimly lit room beyond the windows.

Sadie had instant affection for the revival group. They were talented players and singers, all of them strongly rooted in a familiar spiritual culture that even made outcasts and sinners who frequented her bar feel comfortable. Their music created an atmosphere which made the community feel at home regardless of how spiritually lost they were.

Sadie was a clever one and was able to keep them on by convincing Elder Davis to stay around town to support her in her sudden self-proclaimed conversion to the Pentecostal faith. Davis, who couldn't resist her welcoming attitude, eagerly accepted a room above the juke joint, at no charge to him as long as he was willing to conduct three gospel meetings a week. Sadie claimed the early evening sessions were for those in town with no place to worship. Truthfully, any church in Ridgeland would welcome a willing attendee, but there was nowhere else one might experience the living gospel accompanied by a band that played all night with such intensity that Sadie swore they "put flames on her ice cubes from fifteen feet away."

Sadie was baptized by Elder Davis in the glow of the early morning dawn in a ritual that lured both her most devoted customers, some curious onlookers, and quite a few of the most well-known religious radicals in Ridgeland. From that day forward, Sadie's place served a dual purpose as a part-time gospel sanctuary, part-time nightclub on other evenings. Oftentimes the worshippers and the bar patrons were one and the same, praying there one day and "shakin 'em down" on another.

On those increasingly frequent occasions when Elder Davis was absent from his makeshift pulpit, the evening services continued with chants, songs, and readings from the Bible, inspiring those who attended to embrace a renewed zeal for the gospel. Rema had made it clear to my father that regardless of Sadie's newly proclaimed conversion, he was forbidden to even walk on the side of the street where her establishment was located. Perhaps it was the lure of forbidden fruit or maybe just plain destiny in motion, but by the age of fourteen, Dad had started slipping over to the juke joint and peeping through a rear window to watch the nightly ceremonies going on inside. He gradually got the courage to walk inside on one of the three gospel nights and sit at one of the back tables. He discovered that the music and the penetrating emotional drama was even more exciting close up.

Rema had made sure he was at church every Sunday morning and present at some of the Baptist Wednesday night activities since he was an infant. But the insatiable fervor that happened at these meetings was something he had never seen. The sort of music they played had certainly never been a part of any church service he had attended. These new gospel meetings mesmerized him and he became completely enthralled when he was able to attend, usually by convincing his mother he was going to a friend's home to study and do homework.

He noticed that when Elder Davis wasn't in attendance because he was evangelizing elsewhere, the female vocalists started an exciting new activity in which they would lay down their tambourines and begin to shout passages from the Bible. This was a signal to start passing the Bible around to the attendees who were dubbed "saint" by Elder Davis who blessed them for their unwavering support of his traveling gospel troupe.

On what would turn out to be an experience of divine destiny, Dad sneaked over to Sadie's on an evening when Elder Davis was away.

"They were passing the Bible in that typical old way Southern folks will do when there's no official preacher around. They fill in with scripture just reading one passage after another and passing it along to the next person. Well, this was something you had to be kind of special to do. People needed to know you and like you for you to be able to jump and take that Bible and go to reading. I was just a kid, so I didn't even worry about having to take a turn. Surely no one would pick me. The thought of getting up and saying a word, even opening my mouth in front of all those grown people scared me half-silly.

"They were just about to pass the Bible to a woman who was already worked up emotionally with religious fervor when the band began playing a song that apparently struck a deep mournful nerve in that woman with the line, 'When my mother was livin', I could take this old world with ease.'

"Now maybe this woman thought about her departed mother at that moment because all of a sudden, she threw her head back, called Jesus, and fell flat on the floor in a dead faint. Well, her friends started jumping around and fanning her with handkerchiefs, and while all that was happening, somebody just thrust this great big Bible into my hands. It was filled with these pretty red satin markers, and I just pulled it open to

this one section and started reading. Well, I don't know exactly what happened, but the screaming went higher, and the praying and the music all got louder, by the time I got to the sixth chapter of the Book of Romans I had to scream out the entire thing, just to be heard over this din. But boy, oh boy, could I read. Growing up in that house full of schoolteachers, I'll tell you, I could read the Word like nobody ever heard. And by the time I reached the final verse, everything was blazing up like some spiritual forest fire and I was right in the middle of it. So, I sent them all into the stratosphere with a big, booming finale: And the wages of sin is death, but the gift of God is eternal life through Jesus Christ our Lord.

"Pandemonium broke out! I mean, people were rushing to the windows for air. Fans going everywhere. People almost passed out on the floor. Folks gasping for breath. Lord have mercy, it was really something."

Thankfully for my dad, his father got wind of his nightclub-preaching debut before his mother did. People at the senior pastor's revival told him about his son's sermonizing abilities, prompting him to visit his son at school. He made a point some time before to never visit the house because the arguments with his ex-wife and ex-mother-in-law were vicious. He found my dad on the school grounds and pulled him aside away from any curious eyes.

"Fred," he said, "I hear you think you're a preacher."

"Naw," Freddie replied, "I just got up and read the Bible. That's all there is to that."

A FOURTEEN-YEAR-OLD
MINISTER AND A PROSTITUTE

Xavier

My father turned fourteen in 1949. In that same year, he was ordained as a Baptist minister. He had been working hard that entire year to prepare to meet with an ordination board which was composed of some respected country preachers. My grandfather had taken on Dad's tutoring himself. He knew this group prided themselves on their biblical knowledge and he wanted to make sure Dad was prepared and unintimidated.

Even at his young age, he impressed them. His ability to cite entire passages from both the Old and New Testament and weave it into an exhilarating sermon based on the premise that God is alive, well, and ready to reveal himself left all the elders pleasantly surprised.

The fact that my grandfather was still in the circuit preaching by appointment helped significantly when it came time for them to pay attention to my dad and his skills. Grandpa was still expanding his small business empire, but it mattered a lot to him to help his young son achieve his spiritual calling. He was able to help secure some solid assignments to get my dad started.

He performed well with those and attracted more and more duties as a young preacher. By the time he was fifteen, he officially had a career and was invited to accept the position of assistant pastor at Bible Way Baptist. At sixteen, he was the church's sole minister for a while. He was pleased with, but not the least bit surprised by, his growing popularity as a religious figure. It was what he expected.

Nevertheless, amidst his budding career, one thing meant more to him than anything else: his father's approval. He had a complicated relationship with his father, but he held him in high esteem.

> *"My father, through all the bitter years, was my hero. I don't know how many Black men have ever said that in this country, but a hell of a lot more should, and I'm glad I can. Oh, my father had been cruel to me, I could remember. Yet he stood for something I couldn't help admiring—excellence."*

One of the complicating factors in the relationship was the fact that my grandfather spoke highly of my father to everyone but him. Instead of telling my father directly that he was pleased with him, during my dad's haircut, he would tell the barbers and their customers how proud he was of his son who was going far as a preacher. But there were no firsthand compliments to fill the void in his heart where his father's love belonged, so my dad tried to fill it himself by recalling good times with his father.

He thought about the days he went down to the dump with him to collect cans, discarded bottles, metal, and even old picture frames that would end up looking pretty in somebody's house. He visualized the times he'd heard his father preach, and recalled his father's tips about timing and developing his premise, his themes, and his stories in a way that would resonate deeply with people, subconsciously binding them to him and his message. Importantly, although it left a lasting scar that even abundant success in adulthood would not completely heal, he saw clearly the blessing from his father's refusal to buy him those shoes when he needed them so badly.

Nevertheless, my father understood that the science of the mind is impersonal and manifests experiences, without fail, based on our thoughts. Practicing what he preached about the magnificent power of forgiveness, even as he repressed some of the pain, he pardoned his dad, choosing instead to focus on precious memories, as evidenced by a portion of this beautiful poem he wrote as an adult celebrating their relationship:

My Father Always Kissed Me

He did not give to me or do for me,
What I thought he should, or could;
But one little thing I always cherish;
As I look back in my mind, I see
My Father always kissed me.
He brought me the sweetest, finest fruits,
Figs, bananas, oranges, apples, grapes
And persimmons from his own tree,
Which now belongs to me.
But nothing is as sweet as the memory,
My Father always kissed me.
He held me in his arms,
He rode me on his shoulders
Through his fields of golden corn,
To Grandpa's house in the meadow.
And when he put me down, you guessed it,
My Father always kissed me.
He sat me in his lap
And let me "drive" his brand-new car
Before my feet could touch the floor—
Before my little eyes over the hood could see,
But more precious than that I remember
My Father always kissed me.

Much later, when he was a father himself, Dad made up for his father's lack of providing for his son by giving me almost anything money could buy, which was how he expressed his love for me and assuaged some of the pain from his early years. Yet just as his own father had not provided deep emotional connection and support for him, he was unable to provide me with those things. Just as he had needed those things to affirm his selfhood as a child, so did I. The errors and missteps of one generation are repeated in subsequent generations until they are healed. This is something I worked on later in my life to finally come to a level of peace and understanding.

From fifteen to seventeen years of age, Dad deeply studied Southern religious tradition. He compartmentalized its punitive ideology while simultaneously allowing his innate notion of a far more enjoyable God to flourish. Shortly after his seventeenth birthday, he acted on an innocent desire to elevate a stodgy religious ceremony into a more festive affair at Bible Way Baptist.

His pastor got a chance to go to Georgia and preach a big visitation service. Dad was left in charge of conducting a small, quiet Sunday service, beginning with a baptism at dawn and going all day with sermons, folks coming forth to testify, and some visiting choirs from Beaufort stopping in to join them. He had a thought to make the day something special. He was already noted around the area as a fine young speaking preacher, so when folks arrived at the creek that Sunday morning, he wanted them to know they were in for something special. He'd convinced Mr. Willis, the principal of the high school, to sing. Mr. Willis prided himself on having a fine baritone voice and was always looking for a chance to solo before a crowd. He sang at baptismal services that Sunday, even though Bible Way Baptist wasn't his church.

Picking up on the principal's enthusiasm, Dad suggested that the school band accompanied him.

That Sunday morning, twenty marching musicians who were usually forced to work their way through Semper Fidelis and all those other boring marches accompanied their principal on behalf of Bible Way Baptist. Willis was so worked up that by the time they got to the water that morning, he told them to "go for broke, just like the gamblers do!" A swinging version of "Just a Closer Walk with Thee" came to life as they marched up to the creek.

The older church folks, the ones who made every baptism, wedding, funeral, christening—people who just loved any old kind of church you could put together for them—well, they just about passed out. They'd never seen anything like it. Principal Willis got to soloing on his favorite hymn and a couple of other numbers, and some young folks caught the spirit and started dancing out into the shallow water, white dresses and dark neckties just swirling all over the place, people laughing with joy, clapping and screaming.

Dad was there to preach! And he went all out. The word must have gotten out because people who hadn't had baptism on their minds ever in life showed up at that creek and said, "Reverend, I'm ready." Soon enough, he was doing immersions every minute. Willis did his part keeping his little school orchestra music bouncing. They were having more fun with his service than they ever had at some football game, and no one wanted it to end.

About ten thirty in the morning, Dad told everybody they were going to march on back to the church, and the band was going right along with them. Willis was just beside himself with glee, he was having such a good time. With Willis and my dad up front, they marched on back, the band playing, people singing and clapping, and Dad preaching, leading the parade all the way.

My dad figured if the band could make music for the football team, then it could certainly make some music for the Holy Spirit. If you could have a party for the neighborhood hoodlums and nightlife crowd, then you could jitterbug for Jesus too.

They just carried on. Even some of the older folks got with it, brought their tambourines out of their handbags and went to town. They conducted a truly great celebration unto the Lord, was how Dad looked at it, but little did he know it wasn't to be quite that simple. Before the day was over, his career at Bible Way Baptist would take a unexpected turn that would change everything.

While many viewed the dawn baptism as a creative church service with grand style and energy, some elderly church members described it

37

as a devil ceremony conducted by that young boy who had such big ideas about himself.

Dad pleaded his case, but he was ordered out of the church. He was stunned. His intention had been to honor and serve God, to make a joyful noise unto the Lord. The church pastor had not seen things quite that way, and neither had the church deacons, a group of aging townsmen who had no sense of humor. I guess his termination should not have come as a surprise. This group also took issue with Dad playing baseball with kids after Sunday service. Apparently, fun and recreation were not appropriate on the Lord's Day.

Two unusual things happened after Bible Way Baptist church expelled him. Two life-changing experiences: one with a prostitute and one with a pastor who impacted his worldview in unpredictable ways.

On Sunday night following a church meeting and the subsequent announcement of his dismissal, my dad walked to his mother's home and stood outside, ashamed to go inside with this news. As he stood there trying to figure out what story he was going to tell his mother, he noticed the dim lights glowing through the window of Sadie's Juke. He figured he might as well buy some time, so he strolled over to take a peek inside. When his eyes adjusted to the dim lights, he saw two couples laughing and sipping beers, noticing in contrast how heavy his heart felt. A few gamblers were shooting dice in the corner at a table as if they hadn't a care in the world. Suddenly thirsty, he decided to sit down with a bottle of soda.

His entire family had been so proud of him when he was ordained and began preaching. It made everyone happy and became one of few things that brought his mother and father into a mutual understanding. That was something special, wasn't it? Preaching in different towns and out in the country, he had been welcomed by many. He had even preached in Savannah when he'd been called on to fill in a sermon for his father, and here he was now, a preacher without a home. He had been thrown out of the church for bringing a marching band to a baptism—for trying to bring a little life and spark into an otherwise mundane service so people could feel the joy of the Holy Spirit in their hearts.

There was an invitation that included a scholarship to attend the International Christian Youth Festival in Buffalo, New York, a two-week seminar where they had been willing to pay tuition, room, and board. He just needed to get himself there, but transportation to and from the conference would cost more money than he had at the moment. He felt all of his plans come crashing down. Without the stipend he received from the church and the money he would earn preaching throughout the summer, he wouldn't have the cash to get to Buffalo in August when the conference was to be held.

He had never traveled outside of the South and he desperately wanted to. His first opportunity was now being taken away. As a Negro teenager in the 1950s, he was aware of the difference between the North and the South. A visit to a northern city held a special fascination to my father and he was aching to go. More than anything, in the life of a young Black minister from South Carolina the conference was an important next step. Prominent Black American Baptist ministers and bishops from all over country would be there. These were the very people representing ecclesiastic districts that were diligently looking for the brightest, most capable young church men who were recently ordained or seeking theological degrees. By attending, he had a shot at obtaining a position as an associate and assistant pastor. He'd been told some young men even found assistance for a seminary scholarship.

So much for that happening now. It was all vanishing right in front of him. Bible Way Baptist members would have stepped up to help pay any expenses for him to go to Buffalo, even if he had the money himself. They certainly weren't going to do that after what happened. Even his success as a traveling preacher was compromised because being a preacher by appointment required recommendations from other churches where one had credibility and contacts.

Grappling with how this had all gone so wrong, he thought back to an epiphany he'd had when he decided to see what it was like for those people working out in the fields picking cotton.

> *"'Colored' schools never opened until all the White folks' cotton was picked. I didn't have to do that, but*

*I'd gotten curious one time and did it. Before noon,
in the hot sun, I knew I was called to preach! And my
cotton-pickin' career ended with me sprawled under a
shady tree praying, 'Lord, I will preach! I surrender!'"*

Now what was he to do? He'd never go back to any cotton field
again, he was sure of that. He could try to look for some odd jobs, but
if he still fell short of the needed amount, who would be willing to help
after his embarrassing dismissal from the church? Nobody, he decided.
He had ruined his future with one careless move.

It was hard to not feel sorry for himself. As he mulled over the grim
prospects, a woman approached his table and sat down. A bit surprised,
my father looked up and recognized her as one of several prostitutes who
worked out of the juke joint. She seemed to be in an amiable mood, and
clearly had enjoyed a few drinks.

"Pretty young Fred Eiken…coats…hehe," she giggled, "whatever
your last name is," she giggled.

He couldn't help but smile, but just as quickly a shadow came across
his face as he remembered the trouble he had caused. He'd never felt
quite so down on his luck. The blues rolling out of the jukebox seemed
to be written just for him in that moment. Dinah Washington in pain;
Muddy Waters crying that his woman just wouldn't do right; and all the
other grief and heartache that could be told on a two-and-a half-minute
recording.

"So, they kicked you out your church, sweetie?" Lady Tee asked.
"Why, those dirty rotten dogs. I am telling you, those church folks are
too much, man, so full of themselves and their high and mighty ways.
Ha! They have some nerve talking trash about the way we treat each
other over here, don't they?"

He thought perhaps she was right. Maybe they were hypocrites.
Even so, name-calling was not going to get him to Buffalo.

"Look here, young blood, I'll tell you this right now, so you pay
attention to me. You want to go on up there in the north to this ol'
church thing? Well, then you go on right ahead, honey. You hear?"

In one swift motion, Lady Tee reached inside the bosom of her dress and removed a checkbook. Borrowing the fountain pen my dad happened to be carrying, Lady Tee wrote him a check after asking how much it would cost to get up to Buffalo.

"Now that place, it's up in New York somewhere, right?" she said. "I don't even know how to get there, but what I do know is this young man right here is goin' up there. Right, Frederick?"

He couldn't hold back any longer. He burst into laughter, and Lady Tee winked slyly at him as if she knew something he didn't.

He woke the next morning, fearing Lady Tee might have been playing him. Could the check be real? Did she have the money to cover it? He decided this was silly and impossible. He would swallow his pride and walk over to his father's house to ask Frederick Sr. to help him get some work for the summer. His mother hardly spoke to him at breakfast, which he was grateful for. He knew she was poised to deliver a lecture about the Eikerenkoetter tendency to try to be too big too fast.

He didn't need that right now, so he finished eating quickly and moved toward the front door to make his escape. But something caught his eye on the lamp table in the living room. There was Lady Tee's check he'd left there last night, pulling all of his attention like a beacon. It was only eight forty-five. He could dash over to the bank and still have time to catch his father before he left to take care of his projects. He reached the bank a few minutes after nine and watched the teller cash the check. It was good. With a mixed sense of gratitude and relief, he tried to digest what happened. A streetwalker named Lady Tee, who the proper society of Ridgeland found repugnant, had put up her own money to help him with his dreams. The whole thing seemed like one preposterous joke. Surely there was some divine meaning in this amusing unfoldment. The church rejected and dismissed him, and a prostitute came along and saved the day. It didn't make sense. Not in a Christian country. Or maybe it did? That juxtaposition became a foundational part of my father's expansive life view and one that would serve him well throughout his career.

When the bus pulled away from Ridgeland bound for Savannah in late August, my dad was there with his small traveling bag. He would meet the train in Savannah that would take him to Buffalo, New York. He had avoided speaking to his father all summer. He didn't want to discuss the church's action so his dad hadn't learned about his invitation to the youth festival. Frederick Jr. was feeling like a man and not a teenager. He had taken a risk and suffered the consequences, but he had worked it out because of who he was and with a little magic from God, who right now felt like his true partner. He had not had to ask his father for a cent to meet any of his own obligations.

His mother had reluctantly approved his trip. She was still distressed about his expulsion from Bible Way Baptist, after which she had been compelled to withdraw her own membership, leaving her without a church home. She now went out of her way to attend various services in other towns or out in the country, where no one knew her shame of the humiliating removal of her son as a pastor. Her fixed belief that only perfect behavior was acceptable came at a great cost. A church of her own had always been her pillar of strength; her anchor in the storm. Every Sunday she worshipped somewhere. But not having her own worship community greatly affected her sense of well-being. It was a severe blow to her self-respect and dignity.

As an unaffiliated young preacher, Frederick Eikerenkoetter of Ridgeland, South Carolina stood out at the festival, making quite an impression with his trial sermon entitled, "How Jesus Has Blessed Me," a theme he took from his memories of his father from childhood.

"Thank you, Jesus, for the good memories that a father can bring. My daddy would sit down to the old pump organ in the parlor and sing and play for Mama and me and my grandmother before she passed on to glory, Praise God. My father would sit down at the organ and play, yes, he would. And he would pour out his good-ness to us. Now just think of the Lord's goodness to you. Because when you think about it, it's already there, just for you. And it is in this spirit that I come before you

today with the help of my Lord Jesus Christ, looking to
share with all of you some of the glory I have received
by simply praising His name."

Dad's delivery was exceptional. His voice was resonant and warm after the lemon juice treatments he had given his throat the night before. He had spent the time to research his text well, and because of that his articulation was compelling. A minister from New York was among those listening. He was quite impressed and took notes of his assessment of the young preacher, emphasizing the importance of contacting him before the festival was over. Dad was beside himself with excitement after the minister pulled him aside and offered him a working scholarship to a seminary of his choosing.

When Dad told him that he preferred going to a regular Bible school, the bishop agreed to support him and told him to pick the school. It appeared he was getting just what he wanted, but time would reveal things to be little more complicated than that.

"Well, I was a young Southern boy. I was thrilled
by all this. It seemed like everything I asked for was
linin' up for me. The bishop was located in New York.
Therefore, I chose a school here in the city. It was a
small Bible institution, and I ended up attending two
different ones, same affiliation, before I graduated. But
the working scholarship? You might say his idea was
heavy on the work and light on the scholarship. That
was something that stretched me to a point I almost
couldn't bear and nearly drove me out of the ministry."

AN EDUCATION IN THEOLOGY AND HARD KNOCKS

Xavier

In September 1952, my dad's four years of formal training commenced at the Church of Christ Bible Institute, where he would be training for Baptist ministry. It was a tiny school, housed in a business office in a midtown Manhattan office building. He wasn't completely satisfied with the school, so for his fourth and final year he decided to make a change and was able to get transferred to the Manhattan Bible Institute. Both schools were governed by The American Bible Institute, based in Chicago.

The bishop was a portly, jovial Black man with significant contacts in Baptist circles around New York. He knew everyone, and he lived well. He was kind enough to let Dad have a small apartment just a block away from Lenox Avenue. The tight quarters weren't anything grand, but they were adequate. Most importantly, they were free.

As the days marched along, he had some unexpected surprises thrown at him. He learned that some, but by no means all, of his fees at the school were being paid. In addition to the stress of trying to earn money and keep up full-time schooling, the bishop demanded my father be available whenever he needed him to type for him, run his errands, and carry his messages. He also frequently required my father to drive for him. It became clear he expected these services as an exchange for his partial support for Dad's school and living expenses.

The bishop didn't have the courtesy to definitively lay out his expectations, so day by day my father could never be sure of what their arrangement was. The agreement began to feel incomplete and rather shady. It had all the appearance of questionable business that eventually led to distrust and resentment. The bishop expected my dad to be his personal chauffeur, so much of the time he needed for study was spent transporting the bishop through Harlem traffic in his luxury automobile.

This was a very tough time for my father. His father, of course, didn't even know where he was, and his mother, who was always scraping by herself, had nothing to give him. In winter, neither his shoes nor his summer-weight clothing could hold up to the cold. Worst of all, he was always hungry, and he seldom had money for food. On the rare occasion he could get away from his obligations to the bishop, he would take the subway out to Brooklyn where one of his mother's aunts lived. Thankfully, she was always happy to see him and would gladly prepare a meal for him any time he could visit. More than anything, he was overcome by a deep sense of helplessness spawned by the idea that he couldn't make it alone in the city. He felt out of his element. There was tremendous competition between hundreds of experienced evangelists in the metropolitan area, making it difficult for a young, ordained minister from the Deep South to earn even a little money.

Associate pastors who had served for years as assistant preachers were coming into the ministerial world at record pace, using storefronts as their mini cathedrals. It was the same throughout Brooklyn, Harlem, and into the Bronx. A fierce environment with battles of who would survive waged everywhere. My father refused to be a part of the ecclesiastical warfare. Instead, he chose to stick to his work with the bishop, even with its many challenges.

Once, the bishop had my father drive him to an appointment at the home of a minister of a very large congregation. The Harlem brownstone was beautiful, and the bishop told him that the minister fancied himself a great chef. He told Dad to wait for him, that it would only be a few minutes.

> *"I sat in the car for at least a half hour before realizing that it was now dinner time and clearly the bishop had gone inside to enjoy a sumptuous evening meal. I was just a frayed-around-the-edges boy minister. He didn't need to think about me. I didn't need a fine meal, at least not in the home of an important church official. My stomach was burning, like it might digest itself. It had been several days since I'd had a full meal anywhere. The little red tobacco can that held my change was down to a few dimes and pennies. Peering into it in the dark, it looked as empty as I felt.*
>
> *Sitting in that car, I suddenly felt a burst of tears well up in my eyes. But I determined not to cry, I just would not let myself do that. I would not give into it. A rush of sadness came sweeping through me at that moment. Here I was, a young man but a grown man, sitting hungry in a car that didn't belong to me, waiting on a man I had trusted, I had believed in, and until then, felt great respect for—sitting there like a dog, really, waiting on its master. And that realization made me angry. My hands clenched into fists, and I felt my jaw tighten, as I pounded the seats with both hands. I stomped my foot against the floor of the car and felt my whole body shake with a growing rage.*
>
> *I waited. And waited some more. Several more hours passed, and the pit of my stomach was filled with hunger and humiliation. I was nothing to anyone, just somebody to sit in a car and wait on the street while kids played ball all around me and mothers held their little kids' hand and laughed at their antics. Young*

men about my age strolled past me with pretty girls on their arms. They were all dressed up in their best and on their way to parties or dances, going out for some fun. I thought of the small holes in my shoes that made me sit always with my feet flat on the floor wherever I was and felt more shame. Even my underwear was covered with patches I'd sewn on myself when holes wore through. My socks were a bunch of stitches too, my attempt to repair the fabric that could no longer hold itself together. I had one decent suit of clothes, but the summer-weight fabric drooped in the freezing weather of New York. The slacks I owned were shiny in the seat, because I'd worn them and had them pressed so many times. And my sport coat was so baggy in the elbows, it was embarrassing to me to be seen in it.

When the bishop came strolling down the stairs of the house, he was patting his belly, just the way I'd seen people do in the movies. He was grinning broadly, a happy man without a care in the world."

My father vowed to never treat people like this when he came into some good money. Dad's generosity became legendary. Anyone who hung out with him ate well. Anyone who happened to be with him when he went into a clothing or shoe store was assured to be gifted a suit and a pair of shoes. He loved to share his abundance and see the joy in people's eyes.

That night, when the bishop got into the car, he told his young driver that he had some typing he wanted done that night and asked if he had a way home later in a way that suggested he didn't actually care what the answer to that question was. It would be a long walk for him, but my father assured the bishop he could get himself home. The bishop complimented him on being able to take care of himself and stressed how important it was for a young man to be able to do that. My father replied that he was just starting to learn how important it was to take care of himself. What the bishop didn't seem to realize was that his thoughtless and inhumane behavior toward my father were my father's primary lessons in that.

> *"Well, it was coming to me loud and clear. I was certainly catching on to the importance of looking out for number one in New York City. But for the rest of that particular night, I walked around with my backbone, as the boys on the corner would have said, ticklin' my belly button. I didn't have two nickels to rub together but, boy-oh-boy was I hungry! Not even enough fare to get to Brooklyn to my aunt's for a good meal. So, I slung my little summer jacket over my shoulder, and I walked. When you don't have a lot of options you just keep putting one foot in front of the other, and that's just what I did that night."*

He often strolled 125th Street to take in the glitz and glamor of this area, which was like Mecca for Black folks at that time. Near Eight Avenue sat the Apollo Theater. It was a tough area, but like the pull of Sadie's, he was drawn there often, curious about what actually went on there. Occasionally, someone would spot him as the country boy he was and ask him where he was from, and he would proudly tell him that he was from South Carolina, which always prompted laughter.

He discovered it was the beginning of an even more terrible period that got progressively worse, deteriorating to the point that people preyed on each other with the stone-faced emotions of predators in a jungle.

> *"In the South where I grew up, no matter how poor we were, people didn't steal from one another. There was tremendous neediness, but no one would ever think about taking what did not belong to us. You didn't have to worry about locking doors against your neighbor. In my town of Ridgeland, Black people were forced to live together because of segregation, and we forged*

community with standards and systems and codes of moral behavior that stressed the dignity of all human beings.

I thought my experience with Sadie's back home had given me a decent glimpse of the rougher side of humanity. But in Harlem, there were more bars than Sadie's had mosquitoes in the middle of summer, which was a remarkable number. In my walks around the city I saw enough lounges, taverns, cocktail joints, and gin mills to run across the Atlantic Ocean in a straight line."

All of this shaped my father and caused him greater clarity in his visions of himself, rejecting those things he found absurd and repulsive, embracing and nurturing those seeds of destiny inside that he knew would blossom into their fullness if he turned his focus inward to God and away from the world outside.

"My dreams became more vivid than ever. I imagined myself dressed in these outrageous, bright outfits, carrying a jeweled cane, pulling up in my new cherry red Cadillac, the gorgeous whitewall tires spinning to a stop. I thought I looked a little more daring with a small, pointed goatee and a gold tooth put in my mouth.

I'd wake with these imaginings and sit up in my bed just howling with laughter, thinking of how much fun it would be to try that just for a day. But in the darkness, the soft truth would move into my mind, and I knew what I wanted and needed was something bigger than cheap entertainment.

So that same night I decided to keep walking right past Harlem and on to Fifth Avenue by all the beautiful residences. It was the first time I'd done it because I'd always told myself I didn't belong there. Tonight some- how felt different and I told myself out loud, 'Tonight, Frederick Eikerenkoetter, you are going to belong to everything. You are going to be everywhere. You can be everybody because you know how to take yourself there.'

I walked past those big, beautiful apartment houses, their proper uniformed doormen standing watch. Looking in through the custom shades in the window, I could see parties with people bedecked in fine jewelry and tuxedos. I began to enjoy this so much I decided to imagine that I was the finely dressed man looking down from the window at a boy from South Carolina looking up. I imagined myself enjoying the tasty hors d'oeuvres, but just a few nibbles, while I waited to be seated at the dining room table for the main courses. I was inside. I saw myself there.

When I finally reached the Museum of Natural History, I sat right in front of all that massive archi- tecture built by the geniuses of our history. The history of all men. Looking up at the majesty of the building I said to myself, 'Hey, man, the museum is yours! This beauty belongs to you.'

Now, of course I could never say such things to other people. It was enough for me to know. I just kept walk- ing and talking to myself. When I reached the Plaza Hotel at the end of the park, I looked at all the beauty, the fountains, the great clock in front of the Sherry- Netherland, the hansom cabs standing by with their horses, the limousines dropping off happy people with big smiles on their faces. But right at that moment, standing by the Plaza fountain with my jacket slung over my shoulder, I remembered there was a half a copy of the Daily News *in my shoes right then. Even as I stood there looking at the things I wanted in my life."*

My father wanted more for himself, much more—and he was determined to get it. Unlike the bishop, however, he would do so in a way that raised up everyone around him instead of diminishing or demeaning them.

A NEW MAN RETURNS
TO HIS OLD TOWN

Xavier

Dad's last year of study was not without trouble. The American Bible Institute believed that what they considered to be his generally unruly behavior was reason to withhold his degree. But after four years of struggle, of freezing in a procession of tiny rooming houses during the winter, learning the art of pawning his clothes to eat and obtain carfare, after months of study and true discovery, he wasn't leaving New York without some certification that memorialized his years of sacrifice and effort.

In June 1956, my father received a Bachelor of Theology degree. He was twenty-one years old and so disgusted with the treatment he'd received there that he joined the Air Force. Some of the faculty members had conspired with the administration to deny him a degree because of his radical, iconoclastic views that questioned everything, opposing the inner wisdom informing his growing nontraditional religious perspective.

His theological studies had culminated in a final thesis on comparative religions in which he challenged, among other things, the practice of limiting modern day ministers to interpretations of scriptural texts that were fallible. The fact that no one dared discuss or question such interpretations for more than a thousand years made it hard for my father to hold his opinions to himself. He had also rejected the premise of a punitive God, a God who doled out favors to some and punishment to others and expected his worshipers to fear Him. That God is a loving Father who approves of his children, supports them completely, and wants to see them flourish in every way possible was a major plank of my father's philosophy and theology.

As a result of his convictions concerning the Almighty, he was reprimanded several times. In the months before graduation, the admonishments finally culminated into a request for him to withdraw from the program completely and walk away from his impending credentials. The action was instigated in part by the school's dean, with whom he'd had a verbal confrontation more than once. The man went so far as to recommend Dad's permanent suspension and had the gall to encourage the withholding of his degree.

Yet my father did not buckle under to authority figures. He was disgusted by the school's efforts to deny him what he'd earned, especially coming so close to the end of four extremely challenging years of studying and struggling to survive so far from his home and his family in South Carolina. Even so, he refused to quit. The idea of having to tell his relatives and friends back home that he'd failed was too overwhelming to consider.

Ruffled feathers notwithstanding, the school officials finally acquiesced, likely influenced by Dad's reputation for always paying his bills on time and in cash. Several hundred dollars that he owed the institution, which was struggling financially, were due at graduation. He made sure the arrangement was clear: he would pay, and the school would award him his degree he'd rightfully earned. Reeling from the effects of the rough emotional terrain he had navigated the entire time in college, he went straight to a New York City Air Force recruiting office, figuring signing up for a military career might be the best thing after all he'd gone through.

He enlisted, spending two years in the military as a Chaplain Service Specialist (a noncommissioned officer assigned to assist commissioned Air Force chaplains). While there, he spent much of his time in the base's small library reading every book on philosophy, sociology, and religion he could find. He found Norman Vincent Peale, the minister who wrote *The Power of Positive Thinking*, particularly appealing, and read about his approach extensively.

> *"The very thought that my thinking could change my life was liberating. Norman Vincent Peale's concept of God was different from what I'd been taught. His teaching became the seed behind my future mind ministry."*

> *"For as he thinketh in his heart, so is he…"* (Proverbs 23:7 KJV)

When he arrived back in Ridgeland at age twenty-three, having left the Air Force, my father was a changed man. His personal beliefs had evolved, and the innate spiritual ideology that had been germinating since childhood was steadily emerging, taking inevitable shape and blossoming confidently the way flowers naturally bloom when it is their season.

He drove back to his mother's house, convinced that he was now at the initial phase of those boyhood dreams he'd had about becoming a prominent preacher. Still in the tender stages of his spiritual evolution, he embodied fundamental beliefs about salvation and saving souls, but he was inching closer and closer to a strong interest in lifting people up from ideas of lack to ideas of plenty.

The difference was quite apparent to his mother as soon as she saw him. The boy she had raised by herself had learned to mask his extreme shyness with a practiced, refined display of proper speech and good manners. This new version of her son carried more sureness of self and outspokenness, a demeanor born of one who'd experienced tough times and survived. While still eloquent and respectful, he held a distinctly unapologetic energy.

My father had returned to a 1958 South where the separation of the races was a deeply ingrained fact of public and private life. In Ridgeland, everything was segregated: the schools, public transportation, housing, churches, social events, and, tragically, even the town cemetery. Every facet of life, especially any government-regulated institution, was divided into two groups, one for Negroes, another for Whites. Blacks had to belong to the NAACP secretly throughout this period in South Carolina. "Colored" schoolteachers had to sign a sworn statement that they did not belong to the NAACP.

The Supreme Court decision to integrate public schools had happened four years before, but it would take several more years before anyone would see the broad changes that were to happen, with the implementation of the Civil Rights Movement. The objective of the Civil Rights Movement was, of course, integration and equal access to American institutions from which the color of their skin prohibited entrance for non-Whites. An ironic benefit of segregation was a remarkable camaraderie and proud cohesiveness within the Black community. The resilience of the Black church community, opportunities for professional educators, and new businesses that prospered in the Negro sections of towns, were somewhat accelerated by the separation of the races, and Ridgeland was no exception.

One of Ridgeland's few racial convergences that skirted segregation's rules was a radio station owned by Whites but beamed mainly at the Black community. There were few all Black radio stations in the country at the time, so for many years my dad was mostly on all-White radio stations as his ministry grew.

Very much his father's son, Dad's vision extended beyond appearances. He intuitively knew what he had to do to establish his new ministry, even if it meant crossing the color line. Since he knew a business opportunity when he saw one, he went down to the station and met with the manager.

At his inquiry, the station manager told him that radio time was available, and there was a fifteen-minute slot he requested for Sunday nights. Then he looked at him and said, "Well boy, just how do you propose to pay for this?"

My father had saved $241 from his Air Force severance pay, which he used to put out his first fifteen-minute radio broadcast. He assured the station manager that all bills incurred by Frederick J. Eikerenkoetter would be paid promptly, and they would be paid in cash. From his first exposure on the air, people wrote him about their needs, which ultimately, he condensed into four categories: money needs, health and healing needs, relationship problems, and the real desire for spiritual understanding. Money needs was what he heard about most. He personally answered every letter in the beginning.

The radio broadcasts were an overnight success. He figured out the formula that worked for him, mastered the art form, and his stream of incoming mail steadily increased, and people started to recognize him around town in Ridgeland.

He'd reached a point in his life where he felt content with little emotional or mental strain. It felt good that his days were relatively uncomplicated, and he was reasonably well compensated. He felt free for the first time in his life. As much as this was possible for a young Black man in a rural Southern town in the late 1950s, he was a free man. He managed his own time and didn't report to anyone but himself. He had plenty of money and paid his bills on time. Beyond that, there was plenty of food at the meals he shared at home with his mother.

He was an undeniably good-looking man and always made an impression, with a minimal, but expensive wardrobe that he tastefully rotated. Only those closest to him realized he washed his one suit and wore it frequently. He took significant pride in his appearance, but it was secondary to his freedom to function in a way other Black men his age could not. Most of the time, his peers would be scurrying around town in work clothes of some kind or other, hustling to report to a supervisor or boss. During his typical day, you might find my father reviewing his notes before a broadcast or briskly walking toward the radio station in a navy-blue suit made of durable wool, a perfectly starched snowy-white shirt, and polished leather shoes with a wing tip overlay. And no one could miss that beautiful hair. People said he got his shiny, dark curls from his father's side of the family.

He was driving a Chevrolet coupe that wasn't brand new but was in good enough condition to get him where he needed to be. A generous parishioner had given him the car, which allowed him to seek out opportunities for a sharp young preacher to share the Word throughout Jasper and Beaufort Counties, considered the Low Country area. The parts of South Carolina that were closest to the Atlantic Ocean were the heaviest populated because of the rich soils. Further out in the Low Country area, away from the shore, were the smaller inland towns. There, Black families were living where the population was so sparse that proper addresses hadn't been established. Even there, where the ground was often too sandy or stony to yield any decent crop, the land for the gospel was fertile. Whatever hardships people endured, or anguish life delivered, faith in the Word of God never faltered.

Often, there wasn't a local minister to be found, so opportunities for a traveling preacher were ideal. Any large space could be turned into a chapel for church service, whether it was a school cafeteria, a large restaurant, or a grassy field. A competent, inspiring preacher with an open mind and a willingness to hit the open highway could discover sections of the state where Blacks formed a significant population of working poor and lower middle-class folk who lived in homes with space enough to host an impressive young traveling preacher. He was always warmly welcomed.

The radio broadcasts began to provide a wonderful degree of flexibility, allowing Dad to travel out of Ridgeland for weeks at a time, giving him regular access to his devoted listeners but reaching people outside of that audience at the same time. He would plan ahead and tape several new radio programs to be aired each week he would be away. The entire time he was on the road evangelizing, he still maintained excellent public relations with his audiences.

His mother's oft-repeated quote was unforgettable to him, like a mantra branded on his brain: "Son, this world doesn't owe you a thing! You have to 'root hog' or die 'poor pig'!" Dad was not about to let that happen to him. He was a planner and became adept at organizing his time and resources. The cost for his radio time was always paid long before the money was due. His veteran's benefits, which lasted six months, made it easier to stay on top of his expenses, so this was his opportunity to build his reputation as a dependable visiting preacher. His reputation continued to grow outward and preceded him as far away as Northern Georgia. He knew communication with his followers was critical, so he created his own system to personally respond to each letter. He arranged any type of sermon the request called for and got to know the people, learning about their family and their needs. People found his uncanny ability to remember those details extremely endearing, and as a result, he became a favorite for weddings, baptisms, and funerals. As his popularity grew, his revivals were filled mostly by word of mouth.

If called upon by a conservative Protestant family to preside over the service of a departed loved one, his eulogy would be gentle and dignified. From the time he could talk, Rema and his grandmother had him belting out gospel music. The result was a smooth baritone voice that blended beautifully with the Word when called upon to conduct a Baptist homily. Grandpa, who'd played the pedal organ, taught him early on how to step into a glory dance when gospel fervor was reaching a crescendo at the Pentecostal revivals. The most well-known preachers in the South couldn't compete with this talented young preacher whose life seemed to have set him up perfectly for every preaching scenario one could ask for.

Soon, Rema's old house started getting a brand-new look. The kitchen table, whose finish was worn from too many washings, was replaced with a new one with a gleaming oak pedestal. She no longer had to cover up the worn spot on the sofa because a spotless replacement with velvety fabric sat in its spot in the living room. Though unwilling to admit it, she rode proudly in her son's gleaming, simonized Chevrolet to and from school, and was quite pleased that she had a new coat to wear to school and church. When he pondered his path to this point, Dad felt gratified. It was a pleasing life, and he couldn't complain. Then why did he still feel a subtle inner tension? The Civil Rights activity and the resistance to it certainly created a sense of uncertainty, but he was thankful Ridgeland wasn't erupting like other places. Folks in that area wanted to keep the peace as much as possible and weren't organizing lunch counter sit-ins and the like that were going on in places like Jackson, Mississippi and Greensboro, North Carolina. Dad had successfully created a world for himself that might have satisfied him for the rest of his life. Ironically, the realization of that contentment stirred up a spiritual restlessness in him. He wanted more. As pleasant as his life was, he knew there was something else, something bigger which had been gestating from his first childhood visualization. As is often the case with divine discontent, from the outside looking in, Dad's life bore nothing worthy of complaints. He told no one about his growing angst, but within a year of his discharge from the Air Force, there was no denying how thoroughly impatient he had become in Ridgeland.

In the beginning, it was exciting to organize and hold revivals throughout South Carolina and in parts of Georgia, but witnessing the same outbursts of talking in tongues and intense confessions of sin—whether actually committed or simply imagined—began to lose its spark. He became distracted and felt his attention shifting to something else. He just wasn't sure what that something was.

Out of curiosity, he went to hear a faith healer at a small church near Sumter one night. The healer used a young woman to demonstrate his healing power. Once "healed," the woman transformed before Dad's eyes into a smiling believer. Gushing with joy, she proclaimed, "This night the demon from the devil himself has been taken away from me! Thank you, Jesus!"

Although he had no idea what was driving his curiosity, my father felt compelled enough by what he'd seen to dig deeper and learn more. During the next four or five weeks, he made a point to attend any healing services he got word of. Each of the healers demonstrated a rudimentary knowledge of psychology, focusing primarily on the mental states where unwanted physical states are originated and maintained. He was compelled by the idea that the healer was simply a conduit, or channel, for God to assist those who were not in a proper state of mind to be able to advocate for themselves.

One Saturday evening, he entered a steamy tent to join the gathering of people hungry to be healed. As he settled in to watch the demonstration, he saw the healer raise his hand up ceremoniously, lowering it to the bowed head of a believer. Cupping the crown of the kneeling man's head, he called out the command to heal.

"Be healed!"

His voice resounded throughout the tent, followed by a stream of rambling prayers. Something began to happen. The preacher shouted the command once again.

"Be healed!"

The man's torso and head quivered. His back started pulsing with heavy, ragged breaths that escalated into a deep, low moan that the audience not only heard but felt, ending in a loud crescendo that resembled a wounded animal.

"Jesus is the resurrection and the light!" cried the healer. "Let His light fill your eyes! Can you see that light? Let the Savior bring you the light to your eyes this minute!"

Healer and believer were locked in a dance of the Holy Spirit. The man's face shone with a radiance reflected by the healer's passion to restore the man's vision,

Pouring every ounce of himself into it, he shouted, "I'm asking every man, woman, and child to pray with me! Get on your knees and call out to our God in Heaven to restore this man's sight and let his eyes work again. Help us, Jesus! Help me to help him! We praise your goodness, Father God, and ask you to heal this man now!"

They all raised their voices in prayer, even those in wheelchairs, on crutches, with maimed feet, hands, and arms, and several who were blind, pouring out their faith into the anticipated miracle.

At this point, the healer held the man's face tightly in his hands, their sweat running together under the hot tent lights. The summer heat and the crowd of a 150 people created an almost mystical setting, carrying on a passionate ritual to invoke the Spirit of God to purge the disease from his eyes.

Suddenly, a scream went up. He had seen the light of God! A ray of light flashed in his barren eyes. The crowd howled with excitement and approval.

That wasn't the only miracle witnessed that night. Onlookers watched with delight as another man tossed his old crutches aside and clambered up to hug the prophet singing hallelujah while he danced with glee. When it was over, the people headed toward their vehicles still crying and shouting out praises of joy.

Dad drove along the Savannah River toward Ridgeland, reflecting on what he had witnessed. Sure, country folks held healers in high esteem, but were they just superstitious and gullible? There was a part of him that wondered if these supposed powers of healing were a blend of ignorance with some old-fashioned good luck.

Then his thoughts went back to when he was ten years old, sitting in with his mother at the State College in Orangeburg, in one of her rigorous undergraduate courses to fulfill her yearly state teacher certification. He remembered hearing a discussion about psychosomatic disorders where science had discovered the connection of the mind's beliefs to physical manifestations in the body. The instructor suggested it was a proven phenomenon that emotional states like hope and fear could produce changes in a body.

Pondering scientific explanations of why the phenomenon of healing existed, healing scriptures kept flooding into his mind, and he couldn't ignore them.

> *Jesus said to Jairus, "Don't be afraid; just believe, and she will be healed."* (Luke 8:50 NIV)

True faith healers believed they were communing with the power of Jesus as reported in the Bible to heal people. They saw themselves as conducting Christ's power, and their faith was so strong that those who believed with them became part of the field of the Holy Spirit where miraculous healings could happen. They took Jesus literally at his word that "the things I do shall you also do." Jesus gave them that power.

These memories, combined with all he had seen, fascinated him. However, the whole notion of healing people was pretty uncertain. Yet his curiosity was piqued, so over the next few weeks, he spent a fair amount of time researching the topic in Ridgeland's library. If he was going to follow this calling to help others heal, he was determined to not fail them, himself, or God.

Meanwhile, the radio shows were working, and my father's ministry was growing fast. He rented a small office in an old wooden warehouse building his father owned. Each day he would go through the mail and read through the requests of people who had specifically asked to be mentioned on the air. He wanted people to know he heard them and understood their pain or predicaments. During his broadcasts, he took the time to acknowledge the kindness of the people who had supported his ministry with a donation when they'd passed the collection plate. He was grateful, no matter how small or large the donation was. He thanked others for offering a bed or a meal in their homes when he was traveling and evangelizing. He'd send greetings of kindness and love to the shut-ins, and shared words of comfort to assuage the grief of those who had recently lost loved ones. He was a voice, a presence, offering spiritual support.

Dad's broadcast was reaching people near and far. In a small house fifteen miles outside of Ridgeland, there was one person in particular, a lonely widow named Willeasa Martin who, inspired by my father's radio broadcasts, would ultimately become a catalyst in his destiny.

Depressed from her husband's recent death, and with her gout worse than ever, Willeasa rarely left the house. The radio gave her comfort, distracting her enough to slip into slumber.

One night a voice came out of her radio and pierced through her sleepiness, stabbing her mind with a clarity she could feel throughout her body.

"I can help you. If you'll just listen to what I have to say, all your problems can be solved. Illness can be relieved, if you just know how to go about it."

She immediately realized this was the young preacher her friends had been raving about. Time and again, she had heard about the young man from Ridgeland, what a great preacher he was. That night, the words on the radio resonated with her. She could feel the sincerity in his voice, and also heard the strength of a good Southern boy who had been disciplined right. One who cared enough about his community and others to do God's work. Just listening to his kind words made her body feel better and her heart a little happier. An idea came to her.

One evening, my father was filing away the letters he had received from listeners, and one letter seemed to call to him like no other had. Willeasa Martin wrote that she was terribly lonely, yet her debilitating gout kept her trapped at home because it was so painful to move her body. It was stealing her happiness, because it was the one and only thing that was keeping her from doing the very thing that meant the most to her in life.

"I would so much like to go up in Boston, where I could see my people who live there," she'd written. "I've got the money. I don't need a handout. But maybe the hand of God might help me just a little bit to make this journey. Would you pray for me to get better, Reverend Ike?"

This letter got his attention and he found himself reading it multiple times. Traveling somewhere new. Boston. An exciting new city full of new people. Maybe it was a place to go to and happily return home. Or maybe a place that would make one want to stay forever.

Dad's training for the Chaplain Corps of the Air Force had called him to travel to Wyoming. He'd never been west before, to cowboy and ranch country, where there were miles of rolling open vistas and rugged mountains. He thought back to the excitement he'd felt then. There was something particularly adventurous about going all that distance to a place he hadn't yet been. It had felt daring and special.

He couldn't shake the desire he felt when he thought about new horizons. Was he comfortable here with his ministry that was just beginning to show the fruits of his dedication? Sure he was. The house that was more beautifully furnished, the car he felt proud to drive, the quality clothing he wore, all evidenced his success and dedication. So why did it feel like it wasn't enough? With all of this good, he somehow felt his future included more. Growing old in his mother's house, never having seen the world, grated on his soul, making him feel restless about his destiny.

Was it that destiny that guided him to focus on a certain woman named Willeasa Martin without even knowing why? Could he have had any idea that the decision he would make through this unlikely encounter would reverberate through the rest of his life?

For Willeasa, nothing seemed to be working. She'd tried Epsom salt soaks and a myriad of medicines the doctors gave her, but the aching in her feet and ankles was relentless. While she was ashamed to admit it even to herself, the idea of asking the Lord to take her in her sleep had crossed her mind a time or two, though not before traveling to Boston to see her sister and the three nephews whom she had never met.

Almost twenty years earlier, her sister Bessie had moved to Massachusetts. Bessie had had it with the South and its "cars full of crackers chasin' Negroes off the road at night and runnin' down and killin' my husband." She'd left and promised never to return. Now in their teens, Hershell, Joseph, and Willis were not allowed to come see Willeasa either. She'd only seen photos as they had grown up through the years. Bessie had forbidden the boys to ever set foot in any part of the South. She reasoned that if Aunt Willeasa ever expected to see them, she could make her way to Boston and stay with them. Willeasa had planned this trip for quite a while, putting a little money away here and there. Over the years, she'd saved a tidy little sum which she'd kept in the bank. The only reason she hadn't yet made the trip was that her painful feet would never let her travel that far.

> *"I made a firm decision to use my radio time to accomplish this healing through the Holy Spirit. It was all whirling around in my head. I began visualizing until I started seeing a woman whose legs were swollen and keeping her in terrible pain. And I'd rehearse my broadcast there in my room at home by myself, shouting it into the mirror when my mother wasn't at home,*

uttering scriptures and saying all kinds of prayers, working myself into a sweat as I declared this woman healed! I wanted to get a head start with God to make sure he would help this woman heal!

Well, the day came for me to go into the studio and tape the show. I was so nervous, just shaking all over. Didn't even know this woman, but I figured that if I could see her in my mind with the gout, then I could see her again in my mind without the gout. The fellow at the station who was responsible for organizing the radio time slot rentals looked at me when I came in and said, "Eikerenkoetter, are you all right? You need some water? You look like you're 'bout to pass out!"

I had prepared these special little notes for the sermon I was going to record, those included all my announcements and the speech I was going to give for Mrs. Martin's gout. But when I got in there to make my tape, I just threw all that stuff away and launched right on into my message to 'a very dear lady out there who is sick in her limbs.'"

A few days before, Willeasa received a note in the mail letting her know that Rev. Ike would be praying for her in her hour of need on Sunday night. She moved to her bedside radio slowly and carefully, feeling a solemn reverence that something important was about to happen. She turned on the radio and prepared herself, listening to a couple of silly ditties about cleaning fluid and hair tonic, wishing they'd just get to the program. Knowing her tired body might drop off into sleep if she laid down, she layered pillows against the radio on the floor and sat up on the edge of the bed, attempting to get comfortable with her feet propped on the pillows.

She wasn't willing to take the chance of missing this special prayer Reverend Ike would be speaking over her.

The moment finally came. First, the familiar music, a buoyant Southern Baptist choir singing a gospel number full of cheer. A happy feeling started to come over Mrs. Martin and she clapped her hands with the rhythm. She could tell something was already happening and she said out loud, "I swear this room is fillin' with the light of the Lord!"

As if right on cue, immediately came the voice she'd been waiting for: Reverend Ike himself, offering salutations to all his faithful listeners.

"Greetings to all of you whose hearts are heavy tonight, to those who are shut-in, for the sick and suffering…" He continued on, promising to raise the spirits of the downtrodden. *"And,"* he said in a voice that became more powerful with each word spoken, *"I want to say hello to a very dear lady out there."*

The moment he uttered her name right there in the glow of the bedroom Willeasa shrieked as if an intruder had just stepped out from behind the drapes and her heart started thudding in her chest.

"Someone's in the house just callin' me!" she shouted. "Yes, yes, glory, the boy has brought the Lord in to see me. Hold me, Lord."

Something came over Dad and he tossed his text and entered a spiritual and emotional state he had never before experienced. Grabbing the microphone, he yanked it out of its holster and began to pace. He stretched his arm toward Heaven, his chest rising with it, and holding microphone against his lips he began to channel the divine message that flowed through him.

> *"I want you, Willeasa Martin, I want you to kneel down by your radio, kneel right down and pray with me. Can you do that? I want you to call God, call to him with me and say, 'God, is it time for me to walk naturally again? Lord have mercy! I want you to tell me, Praise God, for this is the time! Please kneel down, Willeasa Martin, open up to the Lord and bear witness to the wonders we know he truly can perform. Thank you, Jesus! Because some of you just don't want to accept that I know what I'm talking about. Now you might be thinking that because I'm young and rather good*

*looking, it causes you to think that my head is empty.
But I know what I'm talking about, hear? Yes, Lord.
And I say to Willeasa Martin, darling, if you don't
want that gout to mess with you anymore, you tell that
gout that the Good Lord has sent word for you tonight!
Yes, ma'am, He has sent word in His mercy for that
gout to be gone for good! I want Willeasa Martin to
kneel. And put a hand on your radio, darling. Reach
out and hold that place these words are coming to you
from me and receive these words! Touch the radio! And
I don't even want to hear from Willeasa Martin until
that gout is gone. I'll be looking every day in my mail
for a letter that says, 'My pain is over for good, and my
heart is filled with joy, I say filled with the blessings of
our Lord, Jesus Christ!'"*

Sweat pouring down his arms and onto his hand, my father watched a droplet fall onto the large mixing dial on the control board as he slowly faded into the sweet sounds of the choir merging with his voice as they finished the broadcast with a joyful, hand-clapping gospel song.

Minutes later, outside at the station parking lot, my father leaned limply against the front fender of his car feeling completely depleted. The broadcast would not be on the air for another three days, but he sensed the throbbing vibration in his head was a sign that he had successfully scaled an incline that had taken him to a whole new level in his life. The stakes were high here and he knew it. Would it work? Maybe not, but he had to take the chance. He had to give his all, with the gifts God had given him. No one had pressured him to do it, no threats or expectations from his mother caused it, nor intimidation from his mentors. He was in charge now. The new Frederick Eikerenkoetter II was emboldened by an iron will, chiseled to perfection by a lifetime of challenges, disappointments, and setbacks he had endured and overcome.

Willeasa Martin desperately wanted to follow the wonderful Reverend Ike's instructions and kneel, but the pain in her arches wouldn't let her. Yet in the golden glow of her room, as Dad's words flowed from her radio, she was so deeply moved by these personal instructions that the best she could do was to get those angry feet near the voice coming from that radio. She rocked herself backward on the bed into a reclined position, and pulling upward on the lower part of her nightgown, she slowly forced her feet into the air until they were braced right up against the radio's wooden frame. She was gasping from the pain spreading from toe to thigh but willed herself to stay focused on that voice.

Reverend Ike spoke against the acquiescence to pain, saying there was reason to believe that discomfort could be diminished with faith in the power of the Holy Ghost that was with her now!

"Lord, it's worth it to try because I hurt so much and I've been all alone for some time now," Willeasa said aloud. "Lord have mercy!"

For several days following the dramatic event, the pain intensified. Willeasa hurt so badly all she could do was lay in bed the whole day, wondering if anyone was ever going to pay her a visit. Wasn't there a single friend who might be thinking of her and come by? No one did, but something started to change one evening when she got up from her resting position in bed. Cringing when her feet came closer to the floor, she stood but something was missing. The pain. Where was it? Her feet didn't hurt too much. She looked down, fully expecting her heart to stop and death to devour her. But there was nothing but calm. She was still here, alive, but with hardly any pain. She stared at the swollen and cracked feet she'd become used to seeing, but they weren't hurting nearly as much as they had before.

Slowly, she began walking across the room, gingerly placing each foot on the floor, one after the other, and expecting the electric sparks to fire all the way to her thighs. It didn't happen. Before she knew it, she was in her kitchen, where she dropped into a chair near the sink. Running the cool water, she filled a glass and drank deeply. Enjoying the refreshing sensation, she realized with a big grin that nothing hurt. Her feet were still there but the angry pain in them was gone. Her feet were at peace with her for the first time in many years.

Just a few days later, she went to the clinic to see the visiting county doctor.

"Look at your feet, Willeasa, the swelling has gone down a lot!" the young doctor said.

"Yessuh, it has," she replied. "Feel better too."

"See? Didn't I tell you to just be patient and eventually the medicine I gave you would do the trick?"

When she left his office, she was laughing to herself. She didn't need to let him in on her little secret. Those pills he had given her made her sick to her stomach and went straight into the trash after the first time she tried them. She knew the source of her healing and her heart felt happy, light, and free because she was headed to Boston and her family.

Willeasa Martin was finally able to travel to Roxbury to meet her three nephews and see her sister. Bessie was at first disturbed about her long journey from their native South Carolina because of her sister's problems with her feet.

"Why, that sickness is all over, child," Willeasa assured her. "There's a young minister down there in Carolina. He led me through a radio healing treatment and the Lord cured me of my gout! I'm fine, honey!"

Shortly after her remarkable recovery, Willeasa Martin sent a letter from Boston to my father. Deeply moved by her miraculous healing, her sister's church asked if the young preacher might come to Boston to bless others in the congregation.

Dad was astonished. Boston was a prominent city of great historical importance, with many cultural institutions and a tradition of churches and worship leaders that went back many years. He traveled to Boston after receiving a train ticket and assurance he'd be paid a fixed sum for his appearance.

SUPERNATURAL MIRACLES AND HEALINGS

Mark

There was a deep, mystical essence to Rev. Ike that many people missed, particularly as he became more famous and flamboyant. Glitz and glamour aside, from his early years of ministry, it became apparent that he possessed an undeniable quality that some might call a supernatural healing ability. As he explored the phenomena more deeply, he discovered through his own work in the realm of healings that the miraculous healing abilities of Jesus and the Apostles as told in the Bible chapter of *Acts* was not limited to a short time in history 2,000 years ago but could be activated by passionate believers who recognized that *with God all things are possible* (Matthew 19:26 NIV).

He had firsthand experience with events that defied any explanation in the natural world. At only thirteen years old, he'd kept a boy from drowning in a creek because of a vision he'd had in which he'd seen a boy crossing a creek, falling in, and drowning, but knowing he could have stopped it. The vision was powerful, and he hadn't known what it meant until he was down at the creek a day later and he saw a boy attempting to cross the water on a dangerous, narrow, rickety piece of wood. Looking out over the creek the feeling came to him so strongly that this was it, this was the boy in his vision. Scared to death, he started calling to the boy again and again, pleading with him to come back and come back now! He later told his father, "I couldn't tell for sure if it was the same boy in my vision, and I wasn't even certain it was my own voice calling to him, but I knew I had to get him back. I convinced him to come back, and I knew without a doubt I had saved his life."

Frederick Eikerenkoetter told his son then he was going to become a preacher because he knew what that vision meant, and he understood what happened there that day. He reminded him of the words in John 16:13 (KJV):

> *When the Spirit of truth is come, he will guide you into all truth: for he shall not speak of himself; but whatsoever he shall hear, that shall he speak: and he will show you things to come.*

While visions that had a supernatural quality weren't unusual, some of them were shared and some were part of his private spiritual journey. There was one particularly powerful experience he shared that happened to him as a young man before he went off to Bible college. At his grandmother's memorial service, while reading from the twenty third Psalm, he experienced God in the form of the voice of Jesus rising from the Bible and speaking every word of the Psalm directly to him.

His uncommon connection to the divine and the spiritual healing anointing born from that connection is the very thing that started to draw tremendous notoriety throughout South Carolina and launched his meteoric career as a preacher. In the early days of his pastorship, it was his ability to do extraordinary supernatural healings that caught everyone's attention. He gained a reputation for healing conditions which were seemingly impossible to heal. Life threatening disease and life destroying conditions like tuberculosis, alcoholism, drug abuse, cancer, crippled limbs, stroke, deafness, blindness, hemorrhoids, deformed lungs, and broken hearts were being healed and done away with permanently after an immersive experience in the spiritual vortex created at Rev. Ike's healing meetings and revivals.

I had the pleasure of interviewing over a dozen of these people who were touched by Rev. Ike from the beginning. People who are still alive and well after receiving miraculous healings decades ago, facilitated by him. They have sharp, vivid memories of Rev. Ike and still rave on joyfully about all of their experiences with him as well as the healing experiences of many of their friends and neighbors. Several I spoke to are almost centenarians. Mary Ward is ninety-two; Star Cleo is eighty-seven; Rev. Thomas is ninety-eight, yet the light they received, which they largely credit to their own supernatural transformations facilitated by Rev. Ike., has sustained them through long and happy lives. The saturation of Divine energy that occurred during those events resulted in real-life testimonials of recovery, restoration, and maybe even a resurrection now and then.

By 1959, Reverend Ike's Sunday morning radio was taking the community by storm. Each Sabbath day from 8:00 to 9:00 a.m. in towns all over South Carolina, people would clear their schedule to tune into Black Gospel Radio WGBP and hear a new preacher with a new message. His Hour of Blessing quickly became a hit.

In a time when so many were looking for upliftment and TV wasn't yet available, pretty much the whole Black community in South Carolina would listen in. Few in the community could read and almost no one bought newspapers. If you peeked into the average Black family's home during Rev. Ike's preaching hour on radio, you'd see everyone had dropped what they were doing and were listening to him with rapt interest. He had a natural talent at commanding attention of those seeking new possibilities, and they wanted to hear all that he had to say. In the day-to-day sameness of finding work and getting by in the South Carolinian Black communities there wasn't much happening of great interest, so locals were elated to be both inspired and entertained by a master who facilitated their healings, happiness, and breakthroughs in prosperity.

Back from the military and ready to preach as a full-time evangelist at age twenty-four, Rev. Ike began his ministry as a traveling preacher. Even in the Deep South where you'd find pastors young and old alike trying to share the word, Rev. Ike was unusual. There in the Bible Belt, he was a bit of an anomaly. He'd show up and deliver a sermon full of unorthodox enthusiasm paired with a message that was different than they'd heard before. Once people caught wind of it, everyone wanted to hear this unique preacher for themselves. They wanted to find out firsthand if he was telling the truth. On the radio broadcasts, he would announce when and where he'd be preaching at the local churches. As he gained more attention and his following grew, Rev. Ike would broadcast the shared testimonies of the healings that were taking place with the church attendees and those stories began to capture everyone's attention, creating a burning desire in so many to hear him live. He began to expand his reach to counties all over the state and beckoned all who were hearing him on the radio to come out to his Healing and Blessing Revival Meetings to "see for yourself."

Rev. Ike packed every church at which he was a visiting preacher for seven continuous night services starting at 7:30 p.m. and never ending until the wee hours. He was up on stage preaching, teaching, and singing his heart out for twenty minutes and then again in between the time that every person was healed. He taught them to understand God was within, and that by changing their minds they would change their lives. He inspired and taught people that they could create the life and lifestyle, healing and health, and a better future, simply by deeply transforming their thinking according to the admonition of the Apostle Paul to "*be ye transformed by the renewing of your mind.*" (Romans 12:2 KJV)

It was common for young traveling itinerant evangelists to stay at local ministers' homes while they preached. It was difficult to find a hotel that welcomed Blacks to stay in those pre-civil rights days. A kind, older pastor named Reverend Richard Bostick saw something special in Rev. Ike and wanted to support his work. He and his wife Josephine welcomed him to stay with them in their home. It was right in the Bostick home at 1809 Duke Street, Beaufort, South Carolina, that Rev. Ike's first services were held, and his ministry officially began. His name and word of his amazing supernatural healing powers and abilities immediately spread like wildfire.

One day, Mrs. Josephine Bostick went to see her good friend Cleo Stokes. "You have to meet this preacher man!" she exclaimed. "He is something else!" The two ladies had been close friends for years and always shared a dream of serving God by changing people's hearts and healing them in the process.

Rev. Ike met Cleo, loved her energy, and recruited her to join him, Rev. Bostick, and a decent gospel-playing guitarist named Mike Smith as a traveling evangelist group. Cleo became the soloist headliner at Rev. Ike's evangelistic revivals. She knew every song Rev. Ike wanted sung and even helped him write new songs or create new lyrics for his old favorites. Before long, Rev. Ike named her "Star Cleo" and soon enough, all the locals called her that too.

Word spread of this talented troupe of traveling ministers, and in a short time, he and his small team were invited to every church in the low country and on each of the neighboring islands.

Cleo was in her element! "We were working seven nights a week in one church and then moved to the next. The congregants loved us and followed us from church to church. Witnessing that outpouring of love for us from their congregants, the pastors were frequently jealous of Rev. Ike and his colossal abilities."

After exhausting nights of preaching, Rev. Ike invested his days praying, studying, and visualizing the phenomenal results he would have at his evangelistic healing and blessing meetings. He lived, breathed, and moved with intention to create the most profound results. He did not date or socialize, concentrating all his mental power on studying and living in the presence of God to prepare for and deliver majestic, life-transformative church experiences for his followers. He was living his dream. All the attendees felt his love for them. They all loved him and his deep desire to serve them, and they could not stop talking about how great his ministry of healing was.

Cleo recalled those days fondly. "At night, our team was preaching up, teaching up, singing up, and healing up a storm. Rev. Ike told them healing would come from within—with their faith. He looked into each of their eyes and seemed like he could see their soul and the healthy divine person within their sick and diseased bodies. He'd lay his hands on each person that came through the prayer and healing line. He used God-power-and-presence to wake up the spirit in people. Individuals who'd been sitting in wheelchairs for years felt his healing touch and heard him proclaim for all to hear 'God in you can walk' and the people would get up and walk. People hobbled in on crutches and he told them 'Drop the crutches and walk to me!' and they did. He could see the God in each of them and he expected them to exercise the power of God in them with faith. People threw away a lot of crutches, canes, and walking sticks. They would line up in what we called a prayer/healing line and do whatever came out of his mouth. If they believed, they were delivered. We were all young, energetic, and full of let's-do-it-God-powered-spirit."

Rev. Ike's studies taught him that everyone latently has healing potential that God gave them. He woke them up to the presence of God's healing power and potential. Most individuals have never been asked to use their intrinsic God-given gifts of healing themselves and others. Rev. Ike got the audience to be of one collective, healing mind. Together, they generated amazing life-giving vivacity using the presence of God that became a united, collective healing force. He created, cultivated, and curated an atmosphere of healing energy that everyone got swept up into and it worked. The undeniable testimonials during each service proved it. The ministry expanded in proportion to how successful he was at convincing people they had to be a part of their own healing. "Listen, it takes more than a prayer from me," he would say. "You've got to change your mind first. You've got to help me do something here. I'm praying, yes, but you got to do something as well."

> And Jesus said unto him, "Go thy way. Thy faith hath made thee whole."
> And immediately he received his sight and followed Jesus in the way. (Mark 10:52 KJV)

Congregants came in droves, believing and feeling the expectancy of healing, because they heard the messages on the radio or TV or through the "grapevine." They didn't need to know the science or the spiritual practice, they wanted instantaneous healing results, and many got them immediately. The faith the audience had in Rev. Ike was very much like the woman in the Bible story of Mark 5:25–29 (KJV).

> *And a certain woman, who had an issue of blood twelve years, and had suffered many things of many physicians, and had spent all that she had, and was nothing bettered, but rather grew worse. When she had heard of Jesus, came in the press behind, and touched His garment. For she said, if I may touch but His clothes, I shall be whole. And straightway the fountain of her blood was dried up; and she felt in her body that she was healed of that plague.*

People believed that he was who he claimed to be. When they came by faith to the right person, in the right manner of unfaltering belief, they each received a healing.

"I remember when we began our evangelistic crusades in about 1959," Cleo recalled. "In the beginning, Rev. Ike only owned one pair of black shoes, one pair of black pants, and two white shirts. In the low country, it was strange, but he did not wear a tie, which was customary in churches in those days. Not wearing a tie was a 'no-no!' Men did not go to church without a tie and a jacket out of respect for God. But Rev. Ike sweat so profusely that every night he had to return home and immediately wash, wring out, and hang-out his shirt to dry so it would be ready for the next day's services. No one owned a washer and dryer in our neighborhood. His shoes would be soaked with water from his sweat, and he prayed they'd be dried and ready by the next day. We did not have any air-conditioning, because it was expensive. We smiled through the humidity because we were doing God's work. Rev. Ike kept saying, 'We are being about the Father's business!' We warmed up the audience with my solos like 'God Specializes in the Impossible' first and 'I Am Looking for a Miracle' as our second song. Rev. Ike was a great baritone singer, and we sang most of the other songs together. Mike would add his talent with his guitar accompaniment. We would morph the words to fit the healing needs of each church and individually each congregant as he worked his spiritual healing anointing. Everyone came to hear, learn, and employ his previously unheard healing and blessing messages. He encouraged healing and asked the audience to participate in sending healing energy to every other attendee that needed and wanted it. He also asked them to accept and be open to healings, if they were in need. He literally changed their mental and spiritual state of consciousness," proclaimed Cleo.

Everyone came for a healing and almost everyone got one. Rev. Ike shared his healing miracle abilities, and his fame grew. As it did, so did the number of nightly congregants. They started packing the pews at 5:00 p.m. to hear him start speaking at 7:30 p.m. Word spread that it was an experience and event that couldn't be missed. *He* was a once in a lifetime experience. Rev. Ike's attendance exploded, filling every congregation, and if you got there anywhere close to starting time it was standing room only with people pouring out the front door of the church and peering in the windows. When he'd announce the next church he'd be at, the telephone lines would be burning up with local people calling all their friends, neighbors, and relatives, all essentially saying the same thing: "You have to hear this young healer and get healed! You have to go with me tomorrow night. I want us in the pew early to make sure we get a seat. I am told there will be standing room only unless we get there early."

Cleo laughingly recalled, "Our original car we traveled in was a beat-up 1956 Chevy with four gears in the floor. It had such a noisy tailpipe that people could hear us coming or going. Frequently, after church was over at one in the morning, it wouldn't start. We parked, if we could, near the top of a hill. We'd ask fellow congregants to push the car and Rev. Ike would pop the clutch to get it to start one more time. It always did. I guess we were prayed-up!"

Rev. Ike loved to create sermon titles that caught everyone's attention, like his famous sermon called "Don't Step on My Blue Suede Shoes," that he delivered the first time to the Methodist Church in Sheldon,

South Carolina. The title was unique, catchy, and totally different than the hellfire and brimstone all other pastors were preaching in the late '50s. Elvis's song by that title had become the number one hit that everyone was talking about and ultimately became a rock-n-roll classic. Rev. Ike was quite adept at catching the temperament of the times. Not your normal Bible Belt fare. Some of the unusual titles that intrigued people to turn out were: "God Is Sick of People Not Understanding the Real Jesus"; "Little Boy Don't Blow Your Horn"; and "There Is No Telling What God Can Do!"

Between the titles, the music, and his new message of personal power through God, Rev. Ike set up the conditions to make healing miracles happen. He created an atmosphere of many attendees that melded into one coherent and unified mind and heart. He held that image of the person in his mind, heart, and knowing. He saw the truth in them. This invited the person in need of healing to raise their personal resonance and personal consciousness to that level, provided it was congruent with their highest good to have the healing manifested. He was able to hold onto the will of the person's own Higher Self, and if they were ready, boom! Together, they touched the hem of the garment of the Almighty and were made whole. None can resist the virtue issuing forth from the Christ nature (the divine force within healer and the one being healed), once their soul accepts it.

This often happened beyond the conscious awareness of the person, but Rev. Ike always explained their miracle to them in terms of the activation of the power of God within them. It was that, not the preacher, healing them. He explained that he was merely a coach and conduit.

The more churches he preached at, the stronger his own belief in his healing ability became. When individuals got up to give their testimonies, the audience members' belief systems were transformed. These were not distant examples of some person being healed, these were their own friends, relatives, and neighbors. People who knew each other and had lived through one another's trials, pains, and challenges. The healings were authentic. The attendees became true believers and got well immediately. Rev. Ike proved to them how powerful they were personally to heal suddenly, to change, and to transform.

"In the beginning in 1959, he asked us to do church immersive events where we presented seven nights in a row at one church. People all experienced big immediate changes and no small changes. We witnessed people who got their vision back and hearing back. Tumors were shrinking. People on crutches broke out of their old patterns and were walking and living a new and better life. He got drunks to be sober. He got addicts to stop using drugs. Some people literally jumped out of their old wheelchairs. People that witnessed these healings, they followed him from church to church," Cleo said, as she ruminated through those years. "He broke old systems of sickness and turned breakdowns into breakthroughs, and with full health and longevity. They gained a new energy that stayed consistent in their lives."

Inside himself, Rev. Ike grew in the understanding and feeling the experience of what Jesus did. He felt the truth of Jesus's words:

> *Truly, truly, I tell you, whoever believes in me, the works that I do, he will do also and greater works.*
> (John 14:12 ESV)

He was literally waking up in his visionary prayer of being a healer and creator of prosperity. He took his calling quite seriously. It was everything to him. He taught that everyone was to be included. He pierced the veil of spiritual understanding. He was personally overjoyed in these church environments of love, inspiration, and absolute gratitude. It gave him numerous opportunities to be uniquely himself, and people felt his joy and gratitude. It was that genuine love and dedication that kept them coming.

HEALING TUBERCULOSIS

Mark

Rev. Ike could facilitate the healing best when he entered into warm, friendly, accepting, and eager Pentecostal-like church audiences. That was what he had night after night.

"The people who came were like excited little kids on Christmas morning—ready to get the best surprise. Each expecting the gift of Rev. Ike's healing touch or words on them or their loved ones," Cleo reflected. Expectations were extraordinarily high. Word was that this preacher man had 'The gift of God to heal.'"

Henrietta Robinson had been told by her doctors that she had incurable tuberculosis. She had suffered with it and for years had been living at the Memorial Hospital getting sicker and sicker. Medicine didn't have an answer and doctors gave her no hope of survival.

Henrietta knew Christ healed the incurable, the lame, the blind, and the sick 2,000 years ago, but hadn't heard that anyone was currently doing it. After hearing testimonial after testimonial about this miracle man, she decided she was going to contact Rev. Ike and attend his healing and blessing service. Doctors had already told her, "It is almost over, Henrietta, set your house in order." She had nothing to lose.

Henrietta arrived on a stretcher, carried in by four strong men. She could hardly breathe. Rev. Ike told the congregation, "I am praying and asking you to pray for her healing with me now. I want you to rub up God's healing energy in your hands, focus all your healing attention, and we are all going to send it forth into her body and heal her now. Everyone raise your hands up and send her God's complete infinite healing energy now!"

The congregation immediately stood up and raised their healing hands, sending out collective love, compassion, and healing energy. The energy was palpable.

Rev. Ike said to Henrietta, "God in you can breathe fully and completely now. Take a breath! Take another breath!" She did. It was slow gasping at first, and then after a few moments, she began to breathe in with deep, wonderful, and complete breaths.

"I can breathe!" Henrietta shouted. "I can breathe! It is wonderful! I can breathe!" She raised up and off the stretcher, glowing with radiance like she had seen God himself. She hugged Rev. Ike and then everyone else within reach, thanking God and Jesus.

Everyone in the place was jubilant, crying tears of joy and thankfulness. A miracle had truly happened in front of their very eyes. Disbelievers quickly and quietly became believers.

Henrietta lived healed and healthy for the next twenty years. The doctors said it was impossible, it defied medical understanding. Rev. Ike said, "God can do the impossible, including what medicine cannot do. After all, God made the world and you and me. So it stands to reason that the divinity in you is not sick and can never get sick. I reawakened her divine, healthy, and whole self."

"Rev. Ike's story exploded throughout South Carolina," Cleo remembered. "Every church wanted Rev. Ike to come and perform his healing miracles. Everyone heard that he was anointed with divine healing power. Rev. Ike was relaxed, yet you could feel his supernaturally powerful energy. His phone rang off the hook. He was catching on like wildfire. Pastors from big area churches like Ebenezer, Mercy, Memorial, and others wanted him and they wanted him yesterday. As things improved, our transportation upgraded to a used blue Cadillac. We were tired of that beat up, uncomfortable, worn-out old Chevy, but it had gotten us faithfully to many meetings."

HEALING CHRONIC PAIN, STROKE, AND CANCER FOR ONE FAMILY

Mark

Although Mary Ward turned ninety-two years old on January 6th, 2021, her memories of her healing experiences with Reverend Ike are still fresh and vibrant.

"I was sick with terrible stomach cramps. I was bent over with abdomen pain that wouldn't stop. The doctors said there were fibroids in my system from my former menstrual cycles, which caused pain," Mary recalled with emotion. "It was 1963 and friends told me to hear this intelligent, good-looking young traveling pastor talking that night preaching at a church on Helena Island, South Carolina. I desperately wanted to heal from these serious female issues that caused excruciating pain, so I went. After preaching that God could heal anything and everything for almost an hour, Rev. Ike said he wanted everyone who was sick or in pain to come up to the altar. I was in the front row and moved fast to be first in line. I could feel Rev. Ike was anointed with the healing power of God. He had all of us put our hands up in the air and raise the healing energies in the room. He was singing with Star Cleo, a song called *Reach Up and Touch Jesus*. Cleo kept singing and Rev. Ike began guiding us."

"Put your mind on Jesus, reach up and touch the Lord.
As he goes by, he is never too busy to hear your heart cry.
He is passing by at this moment, right now and right
here. Reach out and touch Him, as he goes by."

"I believed in my whole heart, soul, and mind that I could touch Jesus. Just after that, the pain was all gone, never to return, thank God. I never, ever again felt that pain!" Mary exclaimed.

Years later, Mary would intervene on her grandmother's behalf to save her health as well.

"After Rev. Ike had moved to New York and was going strong at United Palace, my grandmother was diagnosed with what the doctors at the Catholic Hospital in NYC called inoperable cancer. They had given her too much radiation trying to save her. I told her 'You are coming with me to hear Rev. Ike and get well, like I did.' I took her to hear him at United Palace. She got healed and saved by the Lord through Rev. Ike's healing service and lived to be 101 years old. We have longevity in our family."

Mary discovered that Rev. Ike wasn't through intervening on her behalf.

"When I was told by the heart doc that I'd had a stroke two years ago at ninety years old, my family took me to the hospital. The hospital kept me in that room for a week. One night, I felt Rev. Ike's healing spirit with me in my hospital room. I know he was there. I asked God to heal me and He healed me completely, again. Everyone was amazed. My heart doctor said it was impossible, I didn't have any sign of a stroke anymore. I got released on the spot and went home with my family.

"I worshiped with Rev. Ike whenever he came to United Church in Beaufort, South Carolina. I listened closely to what he promised. He told people, 'When you die, I will see you again. Wherever I am, you'll be in Heaven with me. I am a servant of God. I am a man of God.' I am glad he put that awareness in me. I know I'll see him again."

HEALING A HEART MURMUR AND HOLE IN LUNG

Mark

Gary was the son of a fifteen-year-old girl who got pregnant, delivered her baby, and then gave him up to a woman who took in orphans. She was known by all who loved her as Nana. Gary was born a preemie and had to stay in the hospital until he grew to a certain weight so he could be released into Nana's care. But he had some serious health issues.

"Nana wanted me to live," Gary Richardson told us. "She would do whatever it took to make that happen. She had an invincible and unstoppable spirit. She loved caring for her adopted orphans. She loved us and brought us up right.

"When I was three months old, the doctors told my Nana I had maybe six months to live. I had a heart murmur and an inoperable hole in my right lung. Nana made the decision to take me to the United Palace to be in the presence of a man in touch with God's healing power."

When they arrived, the church was packed, overflowing with attendees. To them, it looked like all of New York City was in attendance. Holding a three-month-old destined-to-die orphan baby, Nana courageously and without invitation stood up and interrupted the entire church service, proclaiming for all to hear, "I can't wait any longer, this boy is going to die unless you pray for him and heal him, Reverend Ike. You have God's healing power. Gary needs you to use it today and heal him! The doctors say he has less than six months to live with a hole in his right lung and a heart murmur. You are our only hope!"

Rev. Ike could see her love for this child, feel her pain, hear her fear, and believed her faith could be the magic elixir to make this healing happen. "Please bring Gary up on stage right now."

"Rev. Ike prayed with the congregation over me," Gary reflected. "He asked the entire congregation to stand, rub up and raise their hands, sending healing energy into my little three-month-old body.

"I have been told many times by many people who were there that day that healings were breaking out all over the church simultaneously. No one who heard Nana's heartfelt pleas to keep me alive could resist helping me. Her passionate pleas, I am told, were unforgettable."

When Nana took Gary to the doctor the next day, the doctor said, "There is no more heart murmur. The hole in his right lung is healed. Whatever you are doing, keep on doing it."

Those six months have turned into fifty-plus years.

HEALING A FISSURE

Mark

Nana had glaucoma and was going blind. She had a driver's license and a car but did not want to drive with her failing eyesight. Nana enticed Eva by inviting her to be our chauffeur. Eva had just gotten her learner's permit and was desperate to drive.

Eva had a chronically painful protruding hemorrhoid. She was deeply afraid she was going to have to have it cut out, so she agreed to drive us to United Palace for its opening first service on Easter in 1969. Nana made sure we got there three hours early, because she planned to sit prominently in the front row with myself and Eva.

Nana, her surrogate mother, said to Eva, whom she called Tiny, "This morning we are going to get your brother Gary healed." Nana asked Tiny to drive the family of orphans all the way to this new church, United Palace, that was having its grand opening service. As a defiant, independent teenager, Eva said, "I don't want to go see some baggy-pants minister!"

With the agonizing protruding hemorrhoid, Nana was afraid Eva would be in too much pain from sitting for over an hour.

Eva shared her recollection of driving Nana to the United Palace for church that day.

"When I was fourteen years old, I read an article that impressed me. The article said *We are each an individualization of God.* That idea and thought stuck with me. All of a sudden, I am sitting in the front row with Nana and Gary at United Palace and the first thing that I hear Rev. Ike say is 'We are all individualizations of the spirit of God.' I was mesmerized. I looked around the church that was packed with young people like me. That made me comfortable and feel like I belonged there, and I was safe. The young minister was handsome. He was elegantly and perfectly attired, not like all the other stodgy ministers with baggy pants I'd seen before. I sat there riveted and realized I was having fun listening to his message and feeling somehow my life was already changing.

"When the service was over and I was driving us home, Nana says to me, 'Tiny, are you feeling any pain? How are you sitting?' 'There is no pain,' I answered. 'I don't feel anything protruding anymore. I know I am healed.'" The miraculous thing was, I didn't do anything except engage in his healing energy. He never laid his hands on me like he did Gary. I sat there totally amazed, wondering what happened. I realized I was pain-free and well. Rev. Ike created a contagious healing atmosphere. He was never told to heal me. He did not know that I had a protruding hemorrhoid. It just happened. I was no longer bleeding, and the issue and the bleeding never came back because I believed what he was saying.

"As a young child I had been through a lot. My real mother did not like me, she totally rejected me, she repeatedly spanked me for no reason at all, and I was seriously depressed. She liked my seven brothers and talked to them all the time, but never to me. I had even tried to kill myself. I used to ask myself how could a God in the sky not see what was happening to me? Then Rev. Ike said, 'God is inside you and can heal you now.'

"I believed it. Rev. Ike said that day during his sermon that when we had forgiveness in our hearts, we'd be healed. Again, I was an impressionable teenager, and I felt I could trust him, so I mentally forgave my birth mom for all the pain, hurt, and rejection she had for me. It worked. I got healed. When Reverend Ike looked me in the eye, I could feel that he could see my soul. It wasn't scary, it was just his abilities that were Christ-like.

"From then on, if the church doors were open and Rev. Ike was there, so were we. Our family became very close to the Eikerenkoetters. As an adult, after I had worked for years in the insurance business, I became an executive assistant and traveling companion to Mrs. Eikerenkoetter. When Gary grew up, he became Rev. Ike's chauffeur and personal assistant, and Nana was the Eikerenkoetter family's cook. We all loved, admired, and respected each other," Eva noted.

"Whenever Rev. Ike came off the stage during the main service, he was headed directly to the healing section of the church. I knew that people would be getting up out of their wheelchairs and canes would soon be piling up. He'd pray over them, touch each individual, and say to them, 'God in you can walk. Now let God in you rise and walk,' and they would just forget about their ailments, get up out of that wheelchair, and walk across the front of the stage. He would take canes from people and just hook them over his shoulder. It was amazing that crippled people would stand up and walk forward with him. They could feel the presence of God in Rev. Ike waking up the presence of God in them. Frequently, when these miraculous healings happened, Rev. Ike would be swept up in the moment and start spontaneously dancing in the spirit. He was so happy!"

HEALING A HOMELESS, WHEELCHAIR-BOUND LADY

Mark

A homeless lady wearing tattered clothing rolled into church in a wheelchair one Sunday. She waited in the healing and prayer line, and when it was her turn, she said she was poor and didn't have a place to live. The reverend and the congregation prayed for her.

> *"Let me hear everybody say: the healing is already happening.*
> *The healing is already happening.*
> *Now, just you folks over there in the special healing section, I want you to yell up here at me and say: my healing is happening right now. Let's hear it.*
> *My healing is happening right now.*
> *Turn and shout it out at this congregation and say that. Shout it!*
> *My healing is happening right now!*
> *When God rises in you all of your sickness, all of your enemies, everything that comes against you, just breaks up and breaks down and flees away into its native nothingness. So, come on, let's do what the Word says;*

the Word is simple: let God arise, let his enemies be scattered."

The following Sunday, the woman showed up again and she'd had a complete transformation. She walked in; the wheelchair was gone. She was nicely dressed, and when it came time, she gave her testimony. She told of how God and Rev. Ike healed and transformed her. Having heard Rev. Ike she changed her thinking, her mind, her soul, her body. She had gotten out of the wheelchair, found a job, and went back to work. She was happier, she announced loudly and proudly, than she'd been in years. It was breathtaking to witness, and the audience gave her a standing ovation.

GETTING SOBER WITH GOD

Mark

Cheap, homemade bootleg whiskey was made everywhere in the South, as America was coming out of prohibition. During Prohibition, no legal alcohol consumption was permitted from 1920 to 1933. In the deep south it had become a common practice for people to make their own booze. They frequently overconsumed and became alcoholics.

Star Cleo claimed that Rev. Ike converted more drunks to become sober than any other preacher ever.

"Word got out and the wives of alcoholics brought their drunken husbands to hear Rev. Ike. They appreciated his talent at doing then what seemed impossible and even inconceivable to most folks—inspiring alcoholics to get and stay dry and sober. On Rev. Ike's Sunday morning radio broadcasts, he'd tell people to 'Put a glass of water on top of your radio and drink it. It will be blessed by me, and I will help you get sober now. To stay sober, please consider attending my church services this week at Ebenezer Church in Beaufort, South Carolina.'

"Mr. Thomas, a man addicted to his own moonshine and a totally sloppy drunk, came staggering into our service on a Friday night. He'd heard Rev. Ike on the radio preaching on believing in God and being delivered from alcoholism. After hearing Rev. Ike preach that first Friday night he showed up, he was feeling sure that he'd be forever after sober and never drink again. On Sunday, he returned to our church service a different man. He was dried out, dressed nattily, and testified that Rev. Ike cured him of that devil liquor. He *never* drank another drop, and he became a reverend. Reverend Thomas is now ninety-eight, healthy in mind, living well, and he continues to tell that amazing story here in the Low Country. He says that instead of being drunk on booze, he became drunk on God!"

HOW REVEREND IKE
FACILITATED HEALINGS

Mark

Rev. Ike got his audiences to embody the truth of healing and to repeat affirmations and visualizations that they were seeing happen before their very eyes. It got them to understand that the power of God to heal their bodies spontaneously was waiting inside of them to be activated. They had mind, body, and soul experiences all at once. He raised their emotions with new pictures in their minds to live their future health and happiness now. He got them to lock in on their own wholeness and forget their past pains. He was able to help them tap so deeply and fully into that Holy Spirit within that, by the time they left, they were already emotionally and spiritually connected to a positive future. He facilitated a new state of being and memory signature by instantly filling them with new expectations of what their life would be, branding new images in their minds that stuck.

The quantum physics we study today is truly the scientific explanation of spiritual power and intention in motion, that scriptures and the Master Jesus himself taught. From Reverend Ike, they got a new conditioning of all that is possible, with new self-generated images backed with fervent emotion to anchor the new program of belief deep into the minds and bodies. Like quantum studies reveals, he taught them to expect a new thing and attract a new thing by becoming that new thing already in their heart, mind, and soul.

> *"You deserve all of God's goodness, including health, wealth, happiness, love, and joy. Why do you deserve all of God's goodness? Because you are a child of God, no more and no less. God is rich and healthy. You are made in his image, so your divine self is rich and healthy. You shall not bear false witness against yourself or God, that's the meaning of the Ninth Commandment. You are here to show forth the glory of almighty God. You know that God enjoys being you. We have to forgive ourselves and then, and only then, will God forgive us and make us well, healthy, and whole. Man is made righteously well in the image of God. God made you to be well."*

They were truly "born again" in a way that would last their whole life.

THE TRANSITIONAL YEARS: REV. IKE MEETS EULA MAE DENT

Mark

The energetic aura Rev. Ike exuded, combined with his exceptional knowledge of biblical scripture, resonated deeply with people in Boston. When he was invited to preach, audiences were moved by him in a new way. Women wept at the mere sight of him. Often when people see God using individuals for His glory, they will see the person instead of the Lord and ascribe healings and deliverances to them. Rev. Ike was careful to let people know that he was merely the vessel whom God chose to use. All of the glory and honor belonged to his Creator and Maker, the Lord Jesus Christ. He was cautious about using his powers to heal, explaining to the church folks who came to hear him that those powers could not be used idly. Casually displaying such deeply profound religious experiences could be destructive to the powers, as well as to the people benefitting from them. The small church agreed, and the members decided that he would come back to Boston at the first opportunity his busy schedule would allow.

Some of his old roots to South Carolina began to loosen as fresh roots sprang forth, anchoring him in his new persona as a Boston preacher. Then he encountered a new soul-force which drove those roots even deeper. That force was a young woman named Eula Mae Dent.

Eula had shown up for service at a church where he was a visiting pastor, and nothing had been the same for him since. She was raised in a Pentecostal church in Newport News, Virginia. There with her mom, dad, and six siblings, she went faithfully and actively to church at least twice every week for as long as she could remember. The family never missed a service. They were all active in the church choir, and while Eula never had formal lessons, she had taught herself to play piano at their home where she regularly practiced and mastered it. Basically a homebody, she had never danced or been in a movie house, and she had never ventured beyond her home state of Virginia until college. She was a hard-working young woman who limited her social life to church activities and an occasional movie during her college years.

She attended Virginia State College on a partial scholarship and worked part-time to earn a degree in business education. Her academic excellence allowed her to attend Boston College on a full scholarship. She was the first from her family of seven children to go to college. After she earned a master's degree in special education, she accepted a job with the Catholic Guild for the Blind. She used her degree in peripatology to teach blind children cane travel and sensory training. With her skillful training, they could easily navigate around the school as normal children, learning how to travel everywhere with their white cane. Eula loved what she did, contributing to freeing up the blind to live more comfortably, completely, and confidently. The city of Boston thought the world of her successes with the blind and asked her to take her work from Portland, Maine, to four other cities in Massachusetts, which she did with absolute delight.

Eula loved church attendance so much and found no Black churches in the city of Newton where she was living with a roommate. She eventually moved to Roxbury, Massachusetts, to be close to an active Black church. One evening, Navie, Eula's roommate, invited her to come to her church that had a revival going on with a young preacher from South Carolina. She said there was a nice young minister who Eula would like a lot because he was a good teacher. Eula was happy in her church and resistant to attend another. Navie kept urging her to hear this young evangelist. It was purportedly to be his last night and she felt he was special and extraordinary. Eula relented and agreed to attend on a Saturday night. She sat in the back of the church with her roommate. The place was full to capacity. She could not see Rev. Ike because he was seated directly behind the podium and out of her view.

The church senior minister told the audience about a wonderful healing that this woman had gotten through Rev. Ike in South Carolina. Willeasa had told her sister, who lived in Boston, about this anointed young man through which God had healed her.

"That young man is here with us tonight," the minister said, "and that is the Rev. Frederick Eikerenkoetter. Rev. Ike is here!"

When the pianist on stage commenced playing, it was not congruent with what the audience expected as Pentecostal Southern gospel. The people wanted upbeat and lively music. A church usher, who happened to know Eula and her wonderful ability to play Southern gospel piano with a lively, upbeat feel, came over to her and appealed to her to help this young minister with her musical talent. Again, she was humbled but reluctant, but the usher and Navie urged her to do so.

When she went to the piano, she still could not see the minister because her view was obstructed by the upright piano. When she finished playing, she swiveled her piano chair around to enjoy the rest of the service. For the first time, she saw the handsome young reverend. After he was introduced, he came over and asked her to play in the key of G, which was the key he sang in. She smiled and complied. He told her what to play in his heavy baritone voice and started to sing beautifully.

"I never enjoyed a sermon as much as I did this," Eula said to Navie after the service ended. "Thank you for inviting me. It was a great experience."

"Rev. Ike's sermon was so popular and inspiring that they have invited him to preach in the big church sanctuary tomorrow," Navie said excitedly. "I want you to come with me and hear him again."

Eula agreed. She would go back again on Sunday to hear Rev. Ike preach. He was unlike anyone she had ever heard before.

The next day they again sat in the back. Fortunately, the service was held in the larger sanctuary and their regular piano player was there. As was the custom, parishioners would put their offering in an envelope with their names and addresses. At one point during the service, Eula dropped her glove on the floor and reached down to pick it up. When she popped back up, Navie whispered to her, "Do you know when you reached down, he was looking over in this direction, as though he thought you had gone? He certainly has his eyes on you!"

Eula laughed but did not believe her at all.

Rev. Ike was a young man and there were a number of young people around Eula's age, twenty-three, who loved coming to hear him. He loved helping people who were starting out and had their lives ahead of them. You could feel that he knew this was the most important time to give people his earnest guidance, because they could really make something of themselves if they knew the right principles that could change everything. At the service, he would always ask all of the young congregants to write him and tell him how they were doing and if they had any questions. Even though this wasn't her regular church, and she was just attending with her roommate, Eula felt comfortable with Rev. Ike's caring nature. At her own church, they were trying to entice her to go into the ministry since she was already a teacher. It just didn't seem right. Having been raised in the Pentecostal church, she thought that one needed a special calling from God in order to preach his word, not just to be told by your minister.

"I was a little confused about that, so I wrote and asked him because I wanted an answer as to how he felt about my being a minister simply because someone else wanted me to be. He wrote me back and helped me to understand that nobody outside of me should determine my calling. That should only be between me and God. I accepted what he said, and I was relieved because I did not want to be a minister. His answer to me was a confirmation to what I had felt in my heart. At the end of his letter, he asked me 'are you the lady that had the pink hat on?' That Saturday night, I had worn a big pink hat which dipped in the front and covered my face quite a bit. He also asked if I would send him a picture. I was shocked that he knew who I was just from my letter, because the other young people were all writing him at the same time. I was flattered, but I was not willing to send him my picture. However, I did acknowledge that I was the lady with the pink hat. He wrote me again and told me that he was building a church down in Beaufort, South Carolina called The United Church of Jesus Christ For All People. He was so excited they had broken ground and were getting ready to build the structure. He told me all about the ministry, and how that was going."

Two months later the same church invited him back again. In his typical fashion, Rev. Ike sent letters to everybody letting them know about the upcoming service and he wanted to see them there. Eula and her roommate once again showed up to a packed house to see what this intriguing young preacher was going to teach.

"This time, we sat in the middle of the church because I wanted to get a closer look at him. At the end of the service, I walked outside and parked right out front was a beautiful Cadillac with a chauffeur. As I was about to leave, the chauffeur came to me and gave me an envelope. To me, this was unusual, and I had no idea what was in it, so I opened it. Inside was an invitation from Rev. Ike asking me if he could take me out for lunch. I told the chauffeur I had to think about it for a while and I walked away. The chauffeur followed me, asking, almost pleading, for a response, as he was instructed by the reverend 'don't leave without an answer from her.' He just wouldn't leave me alone and explained that he believed his job might be in jeopardy if he didn't go back with my answer. Naturally flattered by all of this unsolicited attention, I finally said yes, I'd be willing to have lunch with him."

Two days later, Rev. Ike picked up Eula and took her to a fancy restaurant outside of Cambridge on the Charles River. It was the first time she'd ever had lobster.

"Here I was, having graduated with a master's degree, and teaching kids, and it was my first time ordering a lobster! We ate and chatted away. He looked at me with a smile gracing his face and politely asked, 'When are you going to eat your lobster?' Until that moment I had not realized I was just eating the stuffing on top! I was totally embarrassed, and quickly figured out that the lobster was underneath. That's when I started digging into it! He laughed because he could see that I was finally enjoying the lobster tail. Of course, I just played it off like I knew the whole time. The lunch was quite interesting, and we both enjoyed each other. When we finished eating, he asked if he could see me again. 'Yes,' I said, but in my heart, I said, 'Anytime.' And our courtship officially began."

While Rev. Ike had his church in South Carolina, the Boston congregants attending his meetings were begging him to open a church there. He had so many young people who became loyal followers, fully engaged in the opportunity to learn from him. They came to all of his meetings when he preached and corresponded through mail faithfully. He began to feel strongly that he could not leave the sheep without a shepherd. So, after coming back and forth a number of times, he finally decided that he would set up his own church in Boston, Massachusetts. He asked a minister friend, Rev. BJ Wallace, if he would look for a place where he could have meetings. Rev. BJ found the perfect spot and Rev. Ike started his church, Miracle Temple. He recruited Eula to be the pianist, which she thoroughly enjoyed.

"We were dating, but we kept our relationship a secret because we didn't want to stir up any drama with the other congregants," Eula admitted. "With a lot of young ladies attending the ministry who secretly thought the reverend would make a fine husband, our privacy didn't last long. The church community soon got wind of the fact that we were dating, thanks to Sylvia, a woman in the church who wanted to be in the middle of everything."

What Eula liked immensely about Rev. Ike was that he was so inspiring and eloquent. He touched everyone with his insightful, compassionate messages. He had endless fortitude and stamina. He desired to wake up God in each and every individual. He also had big dreams and was en route to manifesting them. Poverty, lack, or limitation was not part of his vernacular. On his journey to wealth, happiness, joy, and success, he wanted to bring everyone along with him. Eula loved his passionate and unstoppable drive.

REMA'S FINAL DAYS

Xavier

Although my father still ministered at the United Church, also known as United Church of Jesus Christ for All People, the nondenominational church in Beaufort, South Carolina, back in Boston he also now had his burgeoning congregation of devoted followers. He was growing in his spiritual depth and understanding of the true meaning of the Bible and his opportunities were growing along with him.

At United Church, Dad was straddling traditional religion and the new spiritual insights increasingly appearing during his prayer and meditation time. He'd integrated into some of the sermons the teachings of the power of their own minds to see if the congregation would appreciate a more complete understanding of scripture as he was growing to understand it. For the most part, however, he stayed as close to fundamentalism as he could. He was also facilitating healings throughout the region, which was a fulfilling aspect of his Beaufort ministry.

The congregation noticed increasingly he was absent, and Beaufort began to suspect they'd eventually lose him. The trips to Boston were happening less frequently because he was spending more time there. While he made sure United Church had adequate leadership in his absence, he failed to communicate his plans to the people.

In the budding, transitory stage of his relationship with Boston, his mother suffered a stroke and spent several months in a private Ridgeland hospital, which he paid for without her knowledge. He traveled from Boston to visit her and ensure that she was reasonably comfortable. As his spiritual ideology continued to expand, he never abandoned his attempts to help his mother transform her life by renewing her mind, no matter how rigidly she held to the mentality responsible for her life's pervasive poverty and illness. When he was explaining one of his new philosophical discoveries to her one afternoon, she began complaining about her miserable condition.

How could he share his exciting spiritual revelations with his Boston congregation and not with his own mother? Cautiously optimistic, he privately hoped she'd embrace the beliefs and be healed, but he could see it was terribly difficult for her to even try to understand what he was talking about. He spoke of a victory over illness, a victory of the spirit. She replied with a list of the aches in her body and the suffering she'd endured.

"You don't have to be sick, Mama," he pleaded. She matched his intensity, insisting that she *did* have to be sick, because she *was* sick. With each visit, the chasm of understanding between mother and son grew wider. Others had picked up on the tremendous tension in their relationship long before her illness, but now its presence was so strong their visits seldom exceeded ten minutes.

Their diametrically opposing views on life and healing dominated their time together. When his mother complained that her life had been a calamitous disaster and that God had inexplicably punished her, Rev. Ike countered with, "No, Mama, that's not true. If you stop saying it, the feeling of it will go away. If you keep thinking negatively, that's what your condition is going to be."

She'd look at him and say, "You need to understand right now, son. That's all there is in life, suffering. Black people were put here to suffer, but we will achieve a righteous place in the kingdom of Heaven."

Her perspective spoke volumes about the sadness of those who succumbed to the pain of generational racial and gender-based abuse.

My father represented a departure from that; his mother was trapped in it. The story of eventual vindication constructed to assuage the pain and help people get through a life of suffering was totally understandable, and the old religion validated that view of the world of the self.

> *"I couldn't stand to hear that kind of talk. Every time I talked with my mother, and I had to sit there and listen to her tell me that she'd carried that old rugged cross through life and she would exchange it for a crown in Heaven, I felt like something inside me was going to explode."*

During one of his visits, my father happened to have a large amount of cash in his pocket following a revival where he'd been paid quite well. It was time for his mother to be outside in the sunshine, so he met her on the hospital patio where she had been put in her wheelchair so she could get some fresh air.

"Mama, I want to do something special for you today to try to take your mind off your troubles."

He pulled out a hundred-dollar-bill and held it up to her. She sat there as though she hadn't even seen it.

"Mama, this is yours. You can keep it. I'm giving it to you as a gift."

She wanted to know where he'd gotten that much money all at one time.

"Mama, I'm doing well as a minister in Boston, making myself a fine living."

"Preaching?" she asked. "You making all that money in church?"

"I'm doing well, Mama."

"How much can you be making as a preacher, son?"

"Mama, my accountant says that last year I made almost thirty thousand dollars."

"Say *what?*" she snapped, the way Southern women do. "You made thirty thousand dollars? Now whoever heard of that? A boy like you earning that sort of money. You get on outta here for tellin' that kind of lie."

"It's the God's truth, Mama. You've got to believe me when I tell you."

She never believed him. "Oh, he's not doing anything special," she would say. "He's like all the Eikerenkoetter side of his family with his big ideas. Them and their big ideas and big minds. Their minds get so big, most of the time they can't tell what's going on."

Despite her staunch beliefs about poverty, Dad said he'd go by her house every so often, and to stave off his mother's martyr talk, he'd put a big bunch of money in her lap. Despite her allegiance to poverty, it sure made her happy.

In 1965, my grandmother's health deteriorated to the point that the hospital released her to spend her final days at home. She sank fast, and late one night, while my father sat reading to her at her bedside, her body slipped back, and she passed on. She died without understanding his determination to become a nationally known figure in the world of evangelism. Her last visit with him circled around it in conversation, with him trying to convince her that his ministry was taking him higher and higher in the world, that he had plans to grow even bigger in the world of religious influence.

Years later, he recalled that his mother's life had been a struggle against confusions and fear. She had been a brilliant woman academically, but in other areas, she had been a hostage to beliefs steeped in the virtues of poverty and the expectations of suffering and illness. When she died, Dad made the funeral arrangements and notified her people down around Savannah and some cousins who lived farther south in Georgia. They selected one of her fine gowns from her old trunk and told the mortician that would be the dress in which she would be laid to rest.

The funeral was quite elegant. Plain, but beautiful in its simplicity. People expressed a lot of heartfelt feelings for Rema Matthews Eikerenkoetter. The preacher acknowledged how hard my grandmother had worked her entire life to better herself. Her family had selected the preacher and brought him up from Savannah. He wasn't someone my father knew well.

The ride out to the cemetery was peaceful, quiet, and went off without a hitch, but my father noticed with some surprise that there were fewer people in the cars headed out there than had been in the church. As the burial proceeded, my dad looked up and around the grave site, and again was puzzled that some of those aunts, uncles, cousins, nieces, and nephews of hers were not there.

Near the edge of a row of those ancient weeping willow trees at a perfect spot out in the country, he witnessed his mother be put into the ground. He watched with so many mixed emotions, as they lowered the casket, and he tossed some pink roses onto it. Then he headed back to the house he'd lived in with his mother for so long. He still had her effects to deal with.

> *"I pulled up to the door of the old place in time to witness a living nightmare. I saw some of my mother's relatives, those very ones that were missing from her burial service, piling several suitcases into the back of a small pickup truck, and driving off in a big hurry as they saw me approach. There was canvas covering the contents of the truck, and it still didn't register. I just wasn't thinking at all, just wasn't prepared for what I found when I entered the house. My mother's home had literally been stripped clean: tables, chairs, her China cabinet, the new couch, her favorite pictures taken from the walls, rugs rolled up and removed from the floor. I rushed upstairs to her room where I found the trunk overturned and completely empty. All her things were gone. The only beautiful things she had. The things she'd saved for so long for when company came.*

> *This pack of vultures had gone scrambling through the house and grabbed everything they could, then raced off down the road, not even stopping when I showed up. I felt sick inside. I thought about calling the sheriff before I realized what an impossible situation this would have*

created. No good would have come from that so instead I walked around the house for several hours, leaning against the walls, then sitting down on the floor, then getting up and moving on again. I've never said which relatives of hers did it. And I never will."

When he was able to think clearly again, my father left without looking back. He took a bus to Charleston and got on the first plane out of there back to Boston.

My father's departure from Ridgeland produced sorrow and a lingering grief in the people who had come to love and believe in him. His exit was made even more melancholy because it is said he left without explanation.

Yet he had to go, just as a caterpillar must eventually leave its chrysalis if it is to have a life as a butterfly. An interesting thing happens during the chrysalis stage. The body of the caterpillar dissolves. Previously dormant cells, often referred to as imaginal cells, begin to develop and cluster to form the butterfly. This is a radical transformation. As a young pastor, Dad's radical transformation was occurring within him while he lived in South Carolina. If someone breaks into a chrysalis while this transformational process is going on, they will find an organic soup of matter, and the process will never be complete. No beautiful butterfly will emerge. Like the fate of the caterpillar that fails to complete its natural progression by becoming what it was born to become, if he'd remained in South Carolina, Dad might never have completed his own transformation. Instead, he might have joined the ranks of the conformist thinkers, never fully becoming Reverend Ike.

Never one to complain about his circumstances, my father internalized his pain, and although he used it as fuel, its presence still impacted him. Rumbling inside Dad was pain from several sources: his mother's inability through her last day on Earth to see him as the burgeoning spiritual leader he was becoming; his father's withholding both financial and moral support through those formative years of his life; and the blatant theft of his mother's valuable keepsakes by her relatives while she was being laid to rest.

South Carolina harbored so many of the sources of life-defining trauma for my father. This was a factor in his spiritual/philosophical task of redefining his life and himself.

While many of the memories Ridgeland represented were like a vice grip for him *externally*, potentially choking the life from him, Dad had known at some level as he experienced all that pain and trauma that something major was happening *within* him. Even though at the time he couldn't articulate exactly what was occurring, he knew it was inevitable. He also knew it would take him places he'd only imagined. What he didn't know was how to explain it to the people who loved and believed in him without the awkwardness of admitting that he had outgrown his hometown. Like an emerging butterfly, he had left the cocoon of the known, even though it meant that the townspeople might incorrectly assume that the turmoil he quietly navigated was disdain for his hometown.

REVEREND IKE PROPOSES TO THE FUTURE MRS. IKE

Mark

When Rev. Ike proposed to Eula, she first thought he was joking. She knew he was the kindest man she'd ever met and thought he was just being sweet until he took a ring off his own finger and put it on hers, expressing his undying love, affection, and devotion to her. She was so absorbed in being with him that she forgot to take it off her finger and return it to him. The next day, when she was playing the piano, a congregant noticed his ring on her finger and mentioned it to her. He gave her a hard time about wearing the reverend's ring and kept probing her for all the details, which she would not give.

"After my husband had proposed to me, they were all suddenly concerned with who I was and where I'd come from. I came from Newport News, Virginia, and they knew nothing about me. I realized what was going on, but none of them knew yet that he had proposed to me, and I had accepted. We had started planning for our wedding when the reverend got wind of the gossipy chatter that was circulating around our plans. He came to me one day and he said, 'Listen, why don't we just go to the justice of the peace and get married now?' Well, a lady always looks forward to a beautiful wedding, yet I knew the behind-the-scenes drama that was happening with church people. I also had to admit it would be less work for me because my family was in Virginia, and they couldn't help me plan the wedding, so I finally gave in and agreed to do it."

She did not have any idea at that time that there were certain other women in this congregation who saw Rev. Ike as a potential marital partner. There were actually quite a number of young ladies who thought he would make a great husband. One of them was the young woman Eula had been kind enough to drive regularly to attend his services. Eula realized they were all hoping they might find skeletons in her closet, but fortunately, there weren't any there.

"So that week, more than a year after we'd met, we packed up and drove to the courthouse in Providence, Rhode Island, where we were married by a justice of peace." They returned to Boston, and the next day, they asked the associate pastor, BJ Wallace, to take them to the airport. Driving along with his new wife's hand in his, Reverend Ike announced to the driver, "Ms. Dent is now Mrs. Eikerenkoetter."

BJ was so excited and overjoyed to hear the good news he almost crashed the car. "You two are going to be so happy together! This is a perfect match! I'm so happy for you!"

The reverend instructed BJ to call Sylvia Johnson at the church right away and share the great news. "Sylvia will make this like front page news immediately. Everyone will know we are married and off to New York City for a two-week honeymoon. When we return, everything will have settled down and we can get back to having church services," he chuckled, winking at the new Mrs. Ike.

They dashed into the airport to start their honeymoon in New York. They toured all the major places like the Statue of Liberty and Empire State building, and stayed at the historic Theresa Hotel. That famous establishment is no longer there but that was the main Black hotel where Martin Luther King and all the other notable Black people stayed when they were in New York.

Once back from the honeymoon, BJ drove them to his house first, where Rev. Ike had been staying before he was married, to get the rest of his belongings to take to Eula's apartment where they would be living.

When they got to BJs house, he and his wife explained how the members had responded to news of their marriage. Some of them took it well; a lot of them did not. Although the marriage was not good news for the church's largely female membership, no one could find fault with his choice. Eula Mae Dent was a fine Christian woman with an impeccable background, and she was from a solid Christian family. After the wedding, Rev. Ike whisked his new bride to Beaufort, SC, to introduce her to the United Church Congregation. They realized that this woman had to be "something special."

MRS. IKE TAKES OVER THE BUSINESS OF THE MINISTRY

Mark

Reverend Ike and his hired helpers had been taking all of his voluminous mail out of the trunk of his Cadillac and attempting to answer and handle it from there. As the new first lady, when she saw how this was being handled, Eula immediately knew a system needed to be created to handle the surge of growth for the ministry.

"Three weeks after we were married, we realized that that little apartment wasn't going to do. We found a seven-room house to move into that had space for an office where we would answer the mail. I turned two of our bedrooms into offices and in the family room my husband set up radio equipment because he was still doing his broadcast. He would make these tapes, deliver them to the radio station, and they would do the announcement letting everyone know when to tune in. His broadcasts aired on the Black gospel channel radio station. We had a Boston post office box so that people who were hearing him on the broadcast and from the Beaufort church congregation could send their correspondence to us. The growth happened so fast! We were getting so much mail that we could not handle it, so I had to hire people to work, and split them into shifts. Some would come from nine to five and the others would come from three to eleven. We grew exponentially. It was crazy in the beginning because I was still teaching for the state of Massachusetts, working with the blind."

Eula organized the operation and started to create a workflow that everyone could follow. Very soon she left the job she loved so she could fully and completely support Rev. Ike's dream.

"What he wanted, I wanted. I loved him, his vision, his preaching, and I was excited about our future of service together. I saw his extraordinary potential and wanted to be a part of all of his ambitious dreams and visions. His destiny was becoming my destiny. Ike had immense and unending fortitude and stamina, it was a joy to my heart and soul. I loved being with him."

When she took over the books, the organization had only $3,200 in its bank account and Rev. Ike had only $200 in his personal account. The two of them discussed it, he threw the assignment to her, and she was suddenly in charge of a growing empire. They had a tsunami of incoming mail, and Eula had to keep hiring more and more people to handle it. She managed all of the mail correspondence and the business part of the operation. The work was hard.

One day, as the house was buzzing with activity, Reverend Ike said, "It's no secret that we are using every room but the bathroom."

Eula replied, "Honey, look in the bathroom." She had a person in there too.

In a short period of time, she told her husband, "We have outgrown our home. We need an office." They both knew it had become essential that she take over handling the business, because he was super busy preaching, teaching, and broadcasting to millions on the radio. Fortunately, Eula had taken business courses as her secondary undergraduate study while in college and was comfortable and competent in her new role.

They rented an office and moved the operation out of the house to the new building that had a large room where they could process the mail. It was better, but again, they quickly outgrew that space. The upward trajectory of Reverend Ike's pastoral leadership forced them to keep expanding their business operations and had them moving for a third time in five years. Eula knew they needed to think ahead into the future this time.

"We outgrew that new office space fast, and we needed to think bigger and anticipate our growth, so we decided to buy this huge building opposite Boston University that used to be an automobile dealership. It was a nice, solid concrete building. We were hopeful that this building would be able to handle the explosive growth of the ministry. So, I continued to manage the business side of things. There was something creative about this part of the work for me."

They had about fifteen employees working full-time. Eula concentrated on operating the church business in Boston, but as the ministry grew exponentially, she had to hire a lawyer and an accountant to help manage the business because it had become too big for her to manage alone.

"I admired how my husband always stayed spiritually well-grounded and centered even as his fame and influence grew. I came to know through our years together that he was larger than life and he was contributing to the growth and development of what eventually became millions and millions of fans, students, and church members. He was young, strong, and making a mighty and purposeful difference."

Rev. Ike began to do large evangelical rallies around the country. While he was away, Eula attended to their home, the mail, the increasing staff, the business growth, the pastor himself, and his ever-expanding evangelism. One day she didn't feel quite right.

"Rev. Ike had been traveling, doing some evangelizing. I remember feeling different, so I went to the doctor and the doctor confirmed it. I was pregnant with our first child. As soon as my husband came back and got settled in, it was time to tell him. We were in the back room, and I was sitting on his lap with my arm around him, telling him how glad I was to see him when I broke the news. You've never seen anyone that happy! He jumped up and was exclaiming praises of thanks! He was completely overjoyed. We both were, because I love children and I wanted to have at least four. He woke up excited every day about it. Unfortunately, nausea started to hit me each morning and I had it almost the whole pregnancy.

I found the only thing that would satisfy me was a grilled cheese and a Coke. My husband was so concerned that he made a rule for all of the workers that came to the house that one of them needed to show up with a grilled cheese and Coke each and every day. If they tried to duck into that door without it they had to go right back out. Rev. Ike made those instructions clear. He wanted to do what he could to make sure I was comfortable. He was so thoughtful that way. He was always concerned about how I was doing but also concerned about how other people were doing. He was a master at caring."

Reverend Ike's radio broadcasts were growing and vastly expanding his reach and his influence, but he kept adding more and more. In 1964, he hit the big time with a radio broadcast that reached out of Boston all the way up into Canada and down into Texas. That caused more growth, and immediate growing pains. Boston was phenomenal for him for five straight years, but he wanted to be all he could be and felt he was being called to something even bigger. Eula stood by his side as he continued to gain big fame increasingly faster.

It was during this time of great expansion that the Eikerenkoetters welcomed their first and only "blood son," Xavier Frederick Eikerenkoetter III, in 1965. While the birth of their new baby was joyful and exciting to them, this wondrous event presented some challenges to the new parents. Eula, who had always looked out for everyone and everything else, suddenly needed to acknowledge her own needs in a time of personal crisis.

"Just after the birth of Xavier in 1965, my husband was out evangelizing in California. As a new mother, I had postpartum depression, commonly called the 'baby blues.' I was having mood swings, anxiety, depression, crying spells, and difficulty sleeping just after childbirth. I called him and he flew home immediately, cancelling his engagements, to care for our newborn and me. It was an act of devotion, respect, and true love that I appreciated so much. His kindness and understanding made it easier to get through that difficult period."

Xavier was baptized during the first part of the service at the Miracle Temple. They also took a trip to New York for a service done by Xavier's godfather, Gene Ewing. As Xavier grew and flourished, it warmed Eula's heart to see the love Rev. Ike had for his son.

"Rev. Ike would record those radio broadcasts he would do in the evening when everything had settled down. Xavier would be sitting on his lap, and my husband would be giving them the post office box number. I remember one day Xavier came in and said, "Post office box fifty." He wasn't even a year old at that time. My husband traveled a lot being an evangelist, and I know through the years that was hard on Xavier, but he loved Xavier so much! From a mother's perspective, Xavier was his heart. Xavier didn't realize that until he was older. If there was anybody in this world that he [Rev. Ike] would die for, it was Xavier. Reverend Ike knew from the beginning our family wouldn't have traditional roles with his evangelical ministry and the business demands on me."

Eula continued to step into her broadening role as the business master while balancing the demands of motherhood and her commitment to her husband's ever-expanding vision of reaching the world as an evangelist who could transform any life for the better.

KATY POSEY

MY STORY WITH REVEREND IKE

t was 1965, and after a long ride from Virginia to Boston, I stood wide-eyed in Rev. Ike's office. My mom looked him right in the eye and laid down the law on how she expected things to go.

"I'm leaving my daughter here with you and your work. She is only fifteen years old, and I trust you to take good care of her."

My sister Eula and her husband Rev. Ike had their new growing ministry in Boston and the business side of it was becoming quite demanding. Eula had just given birth to my nephew Xavier, so they asked our mom if I could come and stay with them. I absolutely loved my sister, and Virginia—where I lived with our parents—was not as progressive as Boston. Mom and Dad wanted the best for me, and they liked the idea of me going to Boston to get a good education.

Right away, I started helping take care of Xavier, helping to manage the office, and singing in the church choir. We lived together at 66 Columbia Road, Dorchester, Massachusetts, in a 5,292 square foot home with five bedrooms and three baths. Rev. Ike was a mentor, big brother, friend, advisor, counselor, and ultimately my employer for almost fifty years. He practically raised me. I called him "Dad."

Our little church seemed to have a special draw that attracted people who eventually became famous. Donna Summer began actively attending our church in her late teens. Her friend Lawrence Bagwell, a well-known Boston DJ, inspired her to come. Donna and I discovered we attended all-girls schools next to each other and ended up becoming close friends. She dated Lawrence, who played the piano at church, and I dated his buddy Archie Foxworth, who was our choir director. Donna would sing at the church as a soloist sometimes. The two of us would go out with our boyfriends to Steuben's to eat, talk, and laugh, which was such fun. I definitely think of those times as the good old days at Miracle Temple.

Donna grew up to become an international superstar singer and songwriter, known around the world as the Queen of Disco. Lawrence Bagwell later became a famous concert pianist in Boston. We were surrounded by talented people, and it was wonderful!

One of the sweetest gestures Rev. Ike ever made was to take me to my senior class prom in 1967 because I didn't have a date. He'd never been to his own prom, because he couldn't afford to, and he would not let me go alone. He was a perfect gentleman. He gave me a corsage and treated me like royalty. We arrived in the Rolls Royce, and he was dressed immaculately. Everyone loved his fun nature and humor. He made each of us feel comfortable to be in his presence. He loved being with all the young people.

Miracle Temple was bursting at the seams. It was a big relief when we were able to move into our large new office complex at 910 Commonwealth Avenue in Brookline, just down the street from Boston University. We started out with a more typical Pentecostal service. After his sermon, Rev. Ike would pray for people and miracles were wrought. So many miracles.

Rena Blige had a salon in her home, and she had invented a special hair solution she started making in her basement that she had Rev. Ike pray over. She ended up buying a salon on Blue Hill Avenue, a big shop with seven stations, and her business expanded beautifully. There were so many of those kinds of miracles and praying for people to be healed. The miracles flowed at Miracle Temple.

We went from being on a single radio station in Beaufort, South Carolina, to being on WIOD radio, today called iHeart Radio, starting about 1968. Radio was inexpensive in the '60s and very successful for our needs of attracting congregants. We went from a few letters per day to hundreds. Rev. Ike expanded his radio outreach, broadcasting on even more stations, and we started having thousands of people per service arriving from all over. It forced us to expand through three different offices and keep hiring people until there were about seventy-five employees.

Originally, we answered each letter with a custom response. When the volume became overwhelming, we had to create a form letter to handle the overflow. Reverend Ike had our team extend our hands and pray with him over the prayer cloths and the blessed oil before we sent them out.

Rev. Ike prayed over us, and we prayed over whomever called, because many people needed help. One day, a young man called, and he was stuttering so violently I could not understand him. I asked if I could pray for him on behalf of Rev. Ike and the church. He agreed. To my utter amazement, he started speaking clearly and has ever since. It was a miracle. Many times a day we would hear of the miracles wrought because of our ministries' work.

Always being concerned with our protection and safety, the reverend ultimately had me carry a gun, with a permit of course, and jokingly called me "Pistol Packing Katy." One time I heard one of our car alarms going off, so I ran out and fired the gun into the air and the person attempting to steal one of the church's cars vanished without a trace.

I had the privilege of wearing innumerable hats—culminating in becoming an ordained minister of the Boston church. When it was time for me to go to college, Rev. Ike said he'd fund my education, but first I had to attend one year of computer school. I missed my friends at first, being a year behind them in school, but later I saw the wisdom of his decision. He wanted to make sure I had the skills to be on the cutting edge of technology advancements.

Rev. Ike and my sister were both workaholics. One time, I remember he sang to his beloved wife, "You're One in a Million" and we all cried because our hearts felt the love between them.

Toward the end of his life, he needed to see a doctor. I encouraged him and he refused. When I went to see him days before he would die, he said, "I am going on to the other side." God and Reverend Ike knew he was being called home.

BEYOND THE MIRACLES
AT MIRACLE TEMPLE

Xavier

I t was at the Miracle Temple the ministry for which Reverend Ike would become known worldwide was launched. He arrived in Boston having established himself as a faith healer. The Miracle Temple became a center for healing as well as exploring deeper spiritual principles. There, he dove into what he called "spiritual psychology" and began to present new ideas about God and humankind that were not locked into the traditional religious protocol, theology, or ecclesiasticism that my father knew were missing the fullness of biblical truth in its unfiltered form.

In many ways, Miracle Temple was a bridge from the traditional theology my father challenged to the mystical wisdom that was now being substantiated by written material from spiritual pioneers, with whom Dad was becoming increasingly familiar. His experiences at Miracle Temple took him from an introduction to healing power to a profound awareness that sometimes amazed even him.

Within months of his arrival, word of his healing gift moved rapidly through Boston's large Black community, spreading beyond the boundaries of Roxbury and Dorchester. Hundreds began to show up at his meetings, and he felt the calling so strongly to facilitate God's healing power. At each meeting, he would anoint them with holy oils and firmly grasp the heads of those needing a healing, channeling the tonalities of speaking in tongues.

The spirit of those meetings was intense and real, and he would find himself carried away in the frenetic pace of the service. At one meeting, my father shocked himself when he pulled an elderly lady from her wheelchair, flooded her hair with holy oil, and commanded her to walk. She hadn't walked for twelve years, but miraculously she walked that night.

The timing of Dad's move to Boston was ideal because he had recently become interested in the doctrine of Christian Science, a religious philosophy and organization founded by Mary Baker Eddy that was headquartered there. As a young South Carolina evangelist, he was reluctant to preach the gospel of Baker Eddy or her mentor Phineas Quimby, said to be the founder of New Thought. This progressive movement articulated much of what my father innately believed but had no precedent for in the religious tradition he had been reared in: that God was everywhere, spirit was the totality of real things, divine thought was a force for good, and right thinking had a healing effect.

From Baker Eddy and Quimby, as well as the writings of Norman Vincent Peale, he could point out the weaknesses of doctrine he now understood were aspects of his bible college difficulties. The spiritual teachings of these lesser-known teachers aligned greatly with the burgeoning spiritual wisdom that compelled him to challenge the Baptist proclamations of Hell and damnation. Although as a bible college student, his feelings were real and his arguments had been filled with logic, he'd lacked sufficient substance to back up his arguments.

In retrospect, he realized he'd waged those battles because the bible college's teaching process and dogma allowed no space for exploring the deeper meanings of scripture and how it applied to his faith. Discernment guided his expanding spiritual base, which went beyond intellect. He was a country preacher with a growing awareness of a universal consciousness and in touch with spiritual and emotional mysteries. He felt tremendous gratitude and responsibility that God had offered him a glimpse of these mysteries that others often could not see.

Since the beginning—through the healing services, the revival meetings, and mass baptisms he had been officiating around South Carolina since he was fourteen years old—my father knew he had a gift that attracted people around him to explore, deepen, and evidence their own spirituality. One of the aspects of this gift that utterly intrigued the people around him and sparked them to see themselves and their reality a bit differently was what the old folks around Ridgeland called an ability to physically encounter those whose flesh you did not touch except for healing or baptism: "the power." A person with the power could reach across chasms formed by centuries of doubt and pull others toward them with a spiritual force some found completely irresistible. It was my father's intention to show them how they participated in this and were active agents in the process.

In Boston, Reverend Ike's growing prosperity was accompanied by an inner voice constantly repeating *You can go further*, words that became a litany as well as a challenge for him. But where would *further* take him? While New York City might have seemed a natural place for his kind of ministry, he had suffered in New York, and he'd vowed to himself that he would never be seduced into returning. He conceded that an occasional visit to study the New York City based ministries of Father Divine, Prophet Jones, Mother Horne, and Daddy Grace might not be a bad idea. Besides, my mom happened to be fond of New York City.

He had discussed his vision for expanding the ministry with her, but he never discussed any ideas about acquiring wealth. She had been raised among people who believed that God gave them the exceptional health they enjoyed and the small but comfortable house they lived in. They worshiped with unshakable faith, and God provided. Mom did not immediately buy into Dad's ideas about God and the power of the mind. She never accepted the idea of God as a man in the sky, but it still took her a little while to accept her husband's concept of God in you. She analyzed his message for herself, and gradually, his convictions became her convictions.

The Miracle Temple had hundreds of loyal contributors who attended each week. Their devotion and adoration of my father was something he appreciated. He loved being able to inspire them to new levels. But a couple of hours to the south was New York City, where there were thousands of people needing enrichment of the soul. New York's Rockland Palace surfaced as a natural choice. An old warhorse of a Harlem dance hall, it could easily and comfortably accommodate a crowd of a few thousand.

Dad had done some preaching in New York as a bible college student while also working a full-time job as manager of a religious articles store in lower Manhattan. His energy-sapping bishop's assistant position had drained away much of the free time he had. Still, he'd preached on the evangelical circuit as far away as New Jersey and Connecticut, but the results were not encouraging. Although he tried hard, in those early days as an exhausted student preacher he hadn't been able to arouse a crowd like he had in other places.

Now nearly thirty, he was older, wiser, and significantly more mature. His healing services in both South Carolina and Boston had tested his mettle and he'd learned to handle extremely intense crowd situations with finesse. His intimate knowledge of the Bible was quite impressive and incited enthusiasm with many church folks. He had a nice baritone voice that had pretty decent range, and he could fall into a natural, fluid harmony with the best choirs. All these skills that seemed pretty impressive on their own were a basic requirement in Black evangelism.

However, it took more than that to impress church folk in New York. To stand out in any competitive arena, particularly evangelism, you had to be exceptional. You had to be nothing less than a star. Reverend Ike was, unequivocally, a star. He had carefully designed for himself the sort of public personality that projected both attractiveness and arrogance, not always in that order.

By the middle of the 1960s, my dad was becoming one of the best-known Black evangelists in America. Under his direction, and with my mother's business acumen, the Miracle Temple in Boston was a flourishing success.

Mom made sure that everything was kept in a state of readiness for her examination at the Boston headquarters. Nothing escaped her attention.

In New York City, a schedule of services was organized, and Dad began to make appearances at the Rockland Palace ballroom that were drawing excellent crowds and a solid, regular flow of cash contributions from a deeply loyal congregation. Back then, he used to conduct individual consultations with members of the congregation to help them sort out their problems. He met with parishioners one by one. There would be lines around the building filled with people waiting for their opportunity to sit with Dad, pour out their hearts about what was wrong in their lives, and get advice from him on how to get things right.

When he determined that most of the consultations centered on three main topics—money, health, and relationships—he shifted his message so that he wasn't just helping them navigate problems but actually teaching them to take control of and transform their lives. His desire to genuinely help people go from poverty to wealth, from illness to health, and from dysfunctional to harmonious relationships fueled his ministry. My father loved people.

He conducted scores of individual consultations and then delivered a sermon. Eventually, he had to curtail the consultations because he simply could not continue conducting them while also managing all the other aspects of the ministry without wearing himself out.

Mom had become quite concerned. "We discussed how depleted he was getting from trying to keep up with all of it and he decided he would no longer do private consultations and henceforth would only preach to save his energy and perfect his sermons, making sure they were categorized to people's core needs."

New York was proving to be so successful, in fact, that he was able to hire a former fundraising specialist, Sandra Lane, full-time to organize his gospel meetings and appearances in the New York metropolitan area. A driver named Bravet Gaynor was hired from his corps of volunteer ushers at Rockland Palace. Gaynor would ultimately prove to become such a reliable employee, in time he become a key man on Dad's personal staff.

Amid the flourishing ministry, in the Spring of 1965 certain elements of the church membership began objecting openly to my father's preaching style. It became a major problem at Rockland Palace. At that time, he was integrating into his services some of the teachings of pastors like Quimby, Baker Eddy, Peale, and other science-of-mind philosophers to supplement his text for sermons. He had studied how Quimby, disillusioned with his medical treatment for tuberculosis, had recovered through the power of the mind and its ability to heal the body. Dad was drawn to Quimby's conviction that God is in us, willing us health and happiness. That through observation, intuition, a spiritual awareness of Jesus, and embracing the love Jesus taught we could awaken to our own spiritual reality and heal anything. Quimby taught that Jesus strove to teach people the living principle of the embodiment of Christ in them that could correct man's errors, forgive his sins, and heal his disease.

My dad learned about how Mary Baker Eddy, one of Quimby's students, had experienced her own self-healing from chronic childhood illnesses. He found Baker Eddy especially fascinating because of her disavowal of predestination, and her discovery, through reading the Bible, of the ability to follow Jesus's example and heal herself, which led her to formulate and found Christian Science. Dad devoured her seminal book, *Science and Health*, in which Baker Eddy asserted that the healing works of Jesus were divinely natural and repeatable. At the Rockland Palace, my father's talk of God's presence in the mind, rejection of negative concepts, and the exalted status of every human being, didn't sit so well with many religious traditionalists, who tended to be older folks. Like his mother, they had accepted the classic belief that faith was a matter of struggling endlessly to please a powerful and punitive God who placed burdens on the weary so they would prove themselves worthy of Heaven. They could accept that Jesus performed miracles, but they couldn't accept the truth Jesus taught that they could do the same. It was as though they were blind to the words in their own Bibles.

Verily, Verily I say unto you, he that believeth in me,
the works that I do, shall he do also; and greater works
shall he do; because I go unto my Father.
(John 14:12 KJV)

Reverend Ike's ministry continued to grow and gain popularity across New York's Black Bible Belt. As with other new ministries pressing forward to establish themselves, his was tested by a group of dissidents pushing for control. They decided he was not emphasizing the devil enough in his sermons. He responded calmly that he had a new vision to present, and there was no space for a devil who was in control of every bad thing that happened, from a windstorm to how much food one got to eat. His new emphasis would be on man's glory rather than on humanity's failures. This was a wholly new approach than that being stressed in most other churches.

His loyalists backed him in his new theological direction while the doomsayers quietly left. Afterward, things smoothed out, and the meetings, message, and churchgoers were harmonious. Apart from his frenetic pace and the fact that Rockland Palace was not exclusively his to use, the ministry was in fine shape. Basketball games were also held there, and it was challenging to schedule his meetings in between them. This began to present greater issues until it started to put a strain on his ability to operate, so much so that he found it unacceptable. Rev. Ike wanted his own place in New York.

With services in both places now, Mom and I would travel from Boston to New York on the weekends after she'd managed the office during the week. While it was an exciting time in many ways, it was also a somewhat lonely time for my mother because my father was away so much. That travel, which became ongoing, had repercussions on both the marriage and our family life.

The Miracle Temple in Boston also had occasional discord, which became more pronounced after Dad's decision to relocate to New York. My dad was a strict autocrat who ran his business with no consultation with anyone but God, and there were times when people just didn't like it. While his loyalists in Boston resented his plans to relocate permanently to New York, the increasingly larger New York crowd couldn't get enough of him. These decisions, while of his choosing, weren't easy on my dad. He felt guilty leaving his parishioners in Boston who had been so loyal and faithful. Another element that added to the drama was the group of Boston's younger Blacks who openly expressed hostility toward those who reputedly ripped off the poor, and they considered my father to be in that club. He struggled with his decision to leave and launch in New York, but he'd outgrown Boston.

Since he needed to be able to preach anywhere, Sandra Lane purchased equipment and a large vehicle that would allow him to use his own sound amplification and lights where necessary, creating an entirely portable and self-contained ministry. The original intention of the mobile preaching set-up was merely to supplement his preaching at the Miracle Temple in Boston. But soon enough, it became clear to Dad he could more than hold his own in the Big Apple.

By the late sixties, Dad was conducting monthly meetings on the West Coast, including at the Cow Palace, a large sports arena that seated more than 12,000 people. While there, he directed his team to find a venue in New York that could accommodate the growing number of people showing up for his meetings.

Sunset Theater, a block from Apollo Theater on 125th Street, became the new space, and Dad started having services there on weekly basis. He now had control of the scheduling, but it was much smaller than Rockland Palace. Each week, the place was jammed. People came early to get a seat, and hundreds would serpentine around the block trying to get in. It was immediately apparent that Sunset was much too small. Given overflowing crowds and no venue big enough to fit Rev. Ike's audiences, he sent Dr. Alfred Miller out to search for a suitable locale. Dr. Miller was his new associate pastor and ultimately became the Dean of the Science of Living Institute. Miller was a renowned musician, minister, and teacher who eventually took over the preaching duties whenever my dad was not in New York to preach.

Dr. Miller was finding it difficult to find a venue that would accommodate the thronging crowds that were showing up each week. Then one day he discovered one of five of the Loew's Wonder Theatres was for sale. A vaudeville palace built in 1929–1930 that had become a movie house, it occupied a city block on Broadway and 175th Street in Washington Heights, New York. Dad had his team negotiate the financial aspect, and sight-unseen my parents bought it with a small mortgage for $650,000. Loew's showed their last movie, *2001: A Space Odyssey*, before turning it over to my father's ministry. Dad renamed the building the United Palace. He preached his first sermon at the church he created there which he called the United Church, on Easter, 1969.

The place, which could seat 3,500 in the general auditorium and balcony, was packed. It was an ideal location, because in addition to the spacious auditorium, the block-square complex had space for offices, rooms for auxiliary services, and storage areas.

The theatre had great basic bones, but it was run down, in disrepair, and dilapidated. Mom and Dad hired the best rehabilitation people, decorators, well-known specialists, and restoration people in New York. They restored it to its original beauty and beyond, so it would again be a palace. All of the gold paint was redone, costing a million-plus just to repaint all the walls. Some artisans came from Italy and Romania to apply their old-world techniques to the restoration.

A pyrotechnical team had previously rented the theatre and their flames had burnt the organ flutes, making it unplayable. The organ had to be rebuilt into working and playing perfection. My parents were willing to invest millions of dollars to restore the venue to its original glittering, ornate, Old World opera house condition.

Now that they were firmly planted in New York, and the eminence of the growing church was undeniable, they bought a new home for $350,000 in Rye, New York with eight bedrooms, five bathrooms, and plenty of garage space.

When I was six years old, my dad insisted that I go to Sunday school at Dr. Raymond Charles Barker's First Church of Religious Science in Manhattan because he didn't hold Sunday school at his church. Dad wanted his son to have the advantage of an early understanding of what they believed to be the spiritual truths in the Bible and its principles as a living philosophy. Mom faithfully drove me every Sunday into Manhattan to attend Sunday school.

I have warm, loving memories of my early childhood in our Boston home on Columbia Road, where I would have been three years old or younger, of Dad getting down on the floor to play with me, singing to me "the bear went over the mountain…"

As I grew, it was normal for me to mostly be without my father, seeing him once in a while, weekly at church, or some combination of these. I grew accustomed to it to the point that I often cringed when he came home because the three beeps of the Rolls horn out front signaled the end of my peaceful normalcy. Dad was always "on," and the older I got, the more annoyed I was by that. He was frequently on the road evangelizing, from coast to coast.

While the implementation of my dad's plans put a lot of business and parenting responsibility on my mom, she understood him at a soul level and always made it clear she stood behind his goals and dreams.

"He was an avid Bible student throughout his lifetime. He dreamed and planned to appeal to the masses and help them out of poverty and lack and into plentitude and being all they could be, having all they could have, and doing all they could do. He needed me to do my part to make those wonders happen. I came to know through our years together that he was contributing to the growth and development of what eventually became millions and millions of fans, students, and church members. He was making a mighty and purposeful difference."

His audiences continued to increase, and my father's dream of filling up the twenty-thousand-seat Madison Square Garden gained a sense of urgency. He wanted to do it, and he felt strongly that he could. Once he put his mind to something, it was a done deal.

Now a media phenomenon, my dad's work caught the eye of prestigious academic institutions like Harvard Medical School, which invited him to participate in a Faculty/Fellow Colloquium in May 1973. A letter from the Harvard Department of Psychiatry explained that the colloquium, offered monthly, was a meeting at which the faculty and fellow met with a renowned guest to discuss the guest's work. They had heard a great deal about my father and wanted to learn more about him and his work.

Fortunately, there were some journalists whose professional standards did not deviate from their obligation to objectivity. Several reported on my father's success from an unbiased perspective, approaching their coverage of the increasingly popular charismatic evangelist with a refreshingly open mind.

Other articles in *The New York Times Magazine*, *The Pittsburg Press*, *The Atlanta Journal*, *The Atlanta Constitution*, *Daily News*, *New York Post*, *The Boston Globe*, *New York Amsterdam News*, and *The Sunday Times* (London) included similarly glowing reports about Dad's ministry.

Importantly, my father's work included his determination to help Black people know the truth about who they were and *whose* they were. He helped them see themselves in a far more positive light because he knew it to be the foundation for their ability to improve the way they lived. By using the power of their minds with affirmations, visualization, and speaking their good into reality, Black people attending the United Church experienced health, happiness, success, love, and prosperity like never before. An unintended benefit was that some of the stereotypes held about Blacks were being dispelled, domestically and internationally.

Werner Baecher, a famous German television personality, filmed a documentary on my father and his ministry in the 1970s. He reported that people in Germany thought of Blacks in the US as impoverished, but after visiting the United Church at the United Palace, his opinion changed. Clearly, not all Blacks were living in ghettos. My father was working to change the stereotypes about Blacks that were held not only by White people, but by Blacks. He was doing this by preaching what he called the Science of Living principles, including the impact of positive thinking and belief in oneself.

Once applied, those principles would work for everyone, not just Blacks. But they were having a greater and greater impact on those my father was reaching with his ministry.

MRS. JESSIE MILLER

OUR STORY WITH REVEREND IKE

One of our best friends invited us to see the most outstanding preacher in New York performing at the famous Sunset Theatre back in 1966. Just before he went on stage, we were introduced to Rev. Ike, who was so gracious, kind, and thankful that we came. The auditorium was filled already to overflowing with standing room only He brought us up on stage to sit and watch the show of shows. He was uniquely original and different from anything Dr. Miller and I had ever seen in the Pentecostal churches. We were overwhelmed by the excitement of the crowds. During his sermon, he was talking against voodoo, witchcraft, spells, and alcohol abuse. Audience members were coming up to the stage and throwing bags, trinkets, spells, witchcraft tools, and junk up at his feet, which he had taken out and destroyed immediately. Many of his attendees were from the Caribbean Islands and carried with them erroneous thinking and belief systems. He wanted to teach them the spirit of God, wealth, and well-being, as opposed to spells and voodoo and other superstitious beliefs they'd been exposed to.

My husband Dr. Alfred Miller and Rev. Ike really hit it off. They had an immediate appreciation of one another and started discussing deep topics right away. Rev. Ike spotted Dr. Miller's unique talent and sharp mind and asked that they continue their conversation of the possibilities of working together. They began to spend many hours each day forming a plan and imagining what they could do evangelistically and with the best and biggest church attendance in NYC. They loved talking and exchanging ideas about how to build, expand, and grow the church. The countless hours they spent working together left them energized and inspired them to continue to stretch their limits of possibility.

They discussed the work, preaching, and philosophies of Dr. Norman Vincent Peale, Dr. Robert Schuller, Mary Baker Eddy, Dr. Ernest Holmes, Dr. Raymond Charles Barker, Dr. Eric Butterworth, Oral Roberts, Dr. Billy Graham, and other giants of positive thinking. They traveled together to experience all these folks that were still alive and sharing their wisdom. Together, they transitioned the congregation from voodoo into Science of Mind thinking. Dr. Miller became the dean of the ministry. He brought in and trained Dr. Jiggetts, developing an entire staff. If Rev. Ike could not go to a seminar or retreat that was important, he sent Dr. Miller and staff members to go. He was always eager to have them report back how they could implement it to make the church grow, improve, and prosper.

Rev. Ike was evangelizing in early 1968 at the Cow Palace in San Francisco, California. For eight weekends in a row, he successfully filled all 16,500 seats, with Dr. Miller assisting him by leading the choir and the music ministry. The ministry outreach was so successful in San Francisco that they invited our baby son, Alfred, and me to join them in California. It was impossible to not feel the electric excitement of this booming ministry. It is there that I met Mrs. Eikerenkoetter and their son Xavier for the first time. We all got along so wonderfully that Dr. Miller and I asked the Eikerenkoetters to become Alfred Jr.'s godparents and they accepted.

Rev. Ike got word that the famous landmark Loew's Theatre in Washington Heights, New York was available for sale. Immediately, he asked his wife and Dr. Miller to go back to negotiate and buy it, which they did. Dr. Miller was smitten with the Wurlitzer Organ, which rose out of the floor, having been built during the height of the movie palace movement in 1929. They bought the building and refurbished it into its original glory.

Dr. Miller was equivalently Rev. Ike's right-hand man. When Rev. Ike was not there to preach at the Palace, Dr. Miller was always ready to fill-in with an extraordinary sermon, getting many congregants into right thinking and back on the right path. Additionally, Dr. Miller helped found the Science of Living Institute to train other ministers.

Rev. Ike asked me, a certified yoga instructor, to start teaching yoga at the Palace. It started with one class a week and became so popular that I had to teach twice a day, six days a week. Then the reverend asked my husband and me to start hosting cruises for the congregants. They were a fabulous success, as everyone loved traveling and seeing the world together.

At that time, Rev. Ike formed a Board of Directors and a Trustee Board for the church. Dr. Miller was the first one invited to join. Rev. Ike made everyone sign resignation papers in advance, with the understanding that he could and would use them at his own discretion anytime he wanted to change. They were not dated until he chose to remove them. Most people were extremely hard-working and loyal, but when running any organization there will always be some challenges, and Rev. Ike was masterful at preparing ahead for those challenges.

What a wonderful blessing it was for us to connect with Rev. Ike and the Eikerenkoetter family at the beginning of his incredible ministry at the United Palace. It was an event that God surely brought together.

DR./BISHOP ROBERT JIGGETTS

MY STORY WITH REVEREND IKE

In the fall of 1969, I received an invitation from my friend and colleague Eddie Taylor asking me if I could provide piano accompaniment during the services at the United Palace the following Sunday. Eddie was the musical administrator and main soloist at Rev. Ike's church. Eddie and I had worked together at other concerts for a well-known entertainment company. He knew my abilities and talents as a classically trained and well-educated pianist. Knowing I was already booked to play until late Saturday the night before, I refused. Then Eddie told me the service wasn't until 3:00 p.m. That didn't sound too bad, and I agreed. At that time, I did not know who Rev. Ike was. I had never heard of him.

On my drive to the church, I got totally lost. I ended up by West Point Military Academy in West Point, New York before I figured out that I had missed my turnoff to get to the church. By the time I got there, the church service was over, and thousands were pouring out as I was coming into the church. I had never seen anything like it before.

Eddie was boiling mad at me for being late. In spite of his irritation with me, however, he asked me to come back the next Sunday.

Rev. Ike heard me that first time, and he was delighted with the way I played. He came up to me at the end of the service, said he loved my performance, and told me the team was leaving immediately to do an evangelistic crusade that night up in Philadelphia. He entreated me to join them that evening. I didn't know it at the time, but Eddie was smoldering over in the corner. Apparently, Rev. Ike had taken Eddie aside and told him that he personally was asking me to travel to the crusade. Little did I know that Eddie wanted me *only* playing at the church, and that if anyone should be invited on crusades, as far as Eddie was concerned, it was him, not me. Eddie made it clear he was miffed and told me so, but fate was already in motion. I was now off on a crusade and soon to be traveling around the country. We both realized it was Reverend Ike's decision, and only mine to say yes or no to. I got swept up in the momentum, feeling like something great was happening, and gave Rev. Ike my emphatic agreement to come.

To my amazement, thousands of people showed up in the Philly audience too. In my first day of instant immersion into the life of Rev. Ike, I could clearly see this man had magnetic attraction power. It was an enchanting experience, and I played my heart out.

Sandra Lane was one of his key helpers, running his many crusades around the country. To gather ushers and helpers before the services started, she would solicit volunteers by asking people who came early to the service, "How many people want to do something for the Lord?" A couple dozen people would come forward; they would become the ushers. "Do you really want to work for the Lord?" They'd agree, and Sandra would quickly organize them, giving them the big buckets to fill with tithes and love offerings.

When it came time to ask for the offering, Rev. Ike was a master. The ushers would pass the buckets by the people, and they would fill them. Often, Rev. Ike would say, "Bring your offering down here to the front of the church. I want you to give what you desire, but don't ask for change." We finished after 10:00 p.m. and were back in New York sometime after 1:00 a.m. It had been a bustling day, but I was glad I'd participated. I caught a true glimpse of how dedicated and truly hardworking Rev. Ike was. It was very exciting.

The reverend was so hot at the time with his Blessing Plan and his spiritual red prayer cloths, everyone wanted one. They would hear him initially on the radio and would desperately want to experience him live. He was a super-star showman. In the meantime, Eddie was still grumbling and felt like Rev. Ike had stolen me from the job he'd picked me for.

Rev. Ike and I had good camaraderie. At the many crusades as we traveled, worked, and had meals together we had private time to talk, think out loud, and discuss his visions for the future. He asked me about my church affiliation and was delighted that I was attending church where he was previously a pastor. I was rooted in the same Pentecostal church movement. He liked that I was a classically trained professional musician who could read music, play all the gospel tunes by heart, and lead the choir and the soloists. It also impressed him that I was able to lead and conduct the orchestra. He knew without a doubt he and I had a divine appointment to come together when he discovered that I was teaching seventh grade history, social studies, and teaching Black history as an adjunct professor at Seton Hall University.

In the early days, I was kind of hesitant, and thought it was just a job, because I didn't know anything about Rev. Ike or his ministry. My original goal for my life had always been to become a dean or administrator in higher education at the collegiate level. As Rev. Ike and I became more acquainted, and he laid out a grand vision of what he wanted to do, I realized this was a rare opportunity to put together my two loves: working with the church and education simultaneously. I could get paid to do what I loved, and it blew my mind. I knew then he was on course to do something extraordinary, and that was when I truly committed myself to him and his ministry.

When he shared his vision for his organization with me, it was big, bold, exciting, and he offered me tremendous opportunities to advance. I began to share with him all I'd learned from helping to build other churches. I told him to have a stable and growing church membership, he had to have a Sunday school for kids, and an educational and business department. He had a vision of starting exactly that and asked if I would consider running it. I was thankful for the invitation, flattered, and even a bit surprised by it. His goal, he said, was to eventually have a Bible Institute.

Rev. Ike said he wanted me to start with the Sunday school and sent me out to study at different educational churches. He trusted me to do it with care, good thinking, and excellence. I never let him down, organizing the teachers, the classes, writing the training materials, creating a music department, and innovating the Science of Living Institute and its curriculum. I wrote the Sunday school study guides, the textbooks, and got them printed. With some good people to help me, I created the structure of the institute. I divided the classes by age groups and we had everything a Sunday school should have, including a youth Sunday school, a youth choir, and a regular choir. We did plays, provided a nursery, and even created a great summer school program.

The Sunday School Guides became quarterly booklets. It was easy for me to take Rev. Ike's sermons, edit them to perfection, add questions into them, and make them ready for publication. I used a format I had learned as an educator, and they were so successful for us that eventually Rev. Ike took over the writing of them. Ultimately, Boston headquarters liked them so much they took over and published almost all his sermons as study guides. Students were happy to buy them because they were rich with information.

Our Business of Living classes became so popular we averaged about 700 attendees per class. We educated people on Fannie Mae mortgages, insurance, accounting, stocks, investments, money market accounts, and how to buy and sell properties. We taught people how to be prepared to live and to die. Those classes were taught mostly on Saturdays. Rev. Ike cared deeply about being a resource in multiple ways and lot of people accumulated a good amount of wealth as a result of our extensive class offerings.

Rev. Ike and I formed a strong connection. He knew he could unfailingly rely on me, and I respected his indomitable spirit and determination to change lives for the better. One day he asked me to play at a huge crusade in Dallas, Texas, followed immediately by one in Houston. I flew into Texas and stayed there working all week, which threw my normal teaching schedule completely off. I started missing lots of my teaching classes because he wanted me to be there to play at all of his evangelistic crusades.

Twice, I remember having to remind him that I was a professional musician and educator and not a staff helper. The first time, as we got ready to come into the auditorium Rev. Ike said, "Here, carry my bag." I looked him right in the eyes and said, "I'm not carrying your bag. My mother told me don't ever carry someone's bag." He carried his own bag. The second time, when driving to South Carolina, he wanted me to drive the entire trip. I said, "I'm not driving for you." Ike ended up driving.

Rev. Ike was the show by himself. We'd often fly out on Friday night to do a crusade in San Francisco on Saturday and come back in time to lead a church service at United Palace on Sunday. It was exhausting, and since I was still teaching in New Jersey, I would miss teaching school on Monday. The next weekend we'd do the same thing in Los Angeles and be back to the Palace on Sunday. It was a grueling schedule that he handled without balking. While we were doing crusades all across America, at that time Atlanta, Georgia was a hot spot, and we went there often. Rev. Ike would always hire local crews at each location to film the services. Media people were there to cover all of our events.

We packed Macon Coliseum in Georgia every time, which had 9,252 seats. People would travel in from the neighboring states of Tennessee, Alabama, Florida—basically the entire Southeastern region of the United States. Rev. Ike was the live show you didn't want to miss. When he showed up, people were drawn to the ministry event like a rock concert and couldn't resist attending. His charisma, coupled with our advertising, was an unbeatable combination that had the attractor factor working.

His unique, electrifying personality raised people to new levels of excitement, and nobody wanted to miss a minute of it. He taught things the traditional churches didn't teach, like that they could get out of the ghetto and prosper. There was a restlessness and a lot of movement in the '70s. People were searching for Black leadership and Ike was one of those lightning rods. But he was one-of-a kind because his wasn't political like other Black leaders commanding attention. Rev. Ike talked about green power, rather than Black power, and leading your life from a place of self-love and self-discovery rather than angry militancy.

As I came to know Rev. Ike's teachings, I became the resident pastor of the Palace, speaking on his behalf when he was absent in the '70s and early '80s. On one occasion when Rev. Ike was in Europe, all flights back were cancelled. While all the media said he'd show up and preach, he could not return in time. He called me to fill in and I did a great sermon in his absence with appropriate apologies. I also evolved into being the administrator of the Palace complex. Rev. Ike liked to keep giving me new titles. My ordination papers come from The United Church of Jesus Christ for All People which was still the head ministry. I was ordained to do the things that needed to be done at the Palace. I moved from administration and education into ministry. I was even asked to do funerals and weddings. Rev. Ike worked harder than any other preacher I had ever seen. His endless energy, insights, and style packed houses. He was an effective, tireless worker. He would preach on Friday night, Saturday night, an 11:00 a.m. service on Sunday morning, and again at 3:00 p.m. Sunday afternoon. He also was so strong and focused on his mission to help people that he held a mid-week Wednesday night service. The people loved him and couldn't get enough of him or his teaching and preaching messages that were a joy to their hearts and souls. He promised a lot and delivered even more.

By 1972, I had established my own church in New Jersey with the reverend's consent and agreement. He helped me in many ways to get my church started. He was proud of my church and announced its opening at his church services.

New Jersey church services were held at 11:00 a.m., then I would race to United Palace. I would often bring my choir to perform because they were excellent. Rev. Ike appointed me the dean of the Bible school and started calling me Dean Jiggetts. A lot of people actually thought my *name* was Dean Jiggetts!

One day Rev. Ike pulled me over to see a big stack of correspondence from Africa. They all said the same kind of thing—"Rev. Ike, please come to Africa. We need you!" He made it clear he wasn't going to just run to Africa with all he had going on in the US, so he sent me on an exploratory mission.

I went on an Apostolic mission in 1975, flying into Ghana, Senegal, and Liberia. They had all listened to Rev. Ike on their short-wave radios and came to love him. Our show was broadcast throughout Africa from a powerful station in Brussels. We launched thirty satellite churches in Africa.

Rev. Ike had risen to a high level of prestige when he was hosted at Madison Square Garden in New York City. This was a big deal and it meant everything to him. Performing to a sold-out-crowd at Madison Square Garden was front-page news, especially for a preacher. The venue seats 20,789 people and all the biggest shows, sports events, and celebrities performed there when they came to New York.

Eddie Taylor was Rev. Ike's key person running this incredibly important event. At the last minute, Eddie walked up to Rev. Ike and said he had another gig that he planned to do that night and he wouldn't be working at the Garden. Disappointed, Rev. Ike fired Eddie on the spot. He called me to step up and make this happen. I had been at countless crusades and knew the drill. It's like the song we'd always sing that urges us to, "*Rise, shine, and give God the glory.*"

I was so honored to lead the prayer and meditation that day that I had a new suit custom made for the big event. With excitement and thankfulness, I stood on the iconic Madison Square Garden stage watching Rev. Ike thunder to the audience, "Everyone's mind is programmed to something. Unwittingly, most of you have been programmed by religion and the welfare system to a mind full of poverty. I don't want you to get your pie-in-the-sky-in the-sweet-by-and-by, I want you to have it *now* with ice cream on top!"

It was a smashing success! Out of that one service he was able to cut four or five services for radio and TV broadcasts. It was an experience none of us would ever forget.

Mrs. Ike and I always had the greatest relationship. She is quite an amazing lady, but not at all out in front, and she likes it that way. Rev.

Ike also kept her away from the limelight for her own protection. He was quite the figure and there were threats on his life. Keeping her and Xavier more invisible was a wise decision.

There were people who followed the reverend or came to the church who had mental and emotional problems, so we always had security at the church and around him personally. There was a lady who lost it one day and broke out every window in the educational building. Another woman with a history of mental problems was found standing naked on the roof one day. She somehow found access to the roof from the upstairs dressing room and the police had to get her off the roof. A lot of people would show up and insist that Rev. Ike was in love with them. He loved all people with a God-love and wanted them to know it. If he said in a letter, "I love you, you are special to me," as he did with all people, a few might take it romantically. Some who couldn't get to Rev. Ike would try to get to us to get them to the reverend. They would say something like, "He told me he wanted to meet me. He told me to meet him at the Palace." Or they might claim, "God spoke to me. I had a vision." They had all heard something from God telling them they had to get to Rev. Ike.

Other ministers criticized Rev. Ike because of his nice cars and nice things…but they were the first ones to run out and buy themselves a Mercedes Benz when they got enough money. They were hypocrites. It wasn't like that with the accomplished ministers. Rev. Ike would privately have telephone calls with all the most famous televangelists of the day: Dr. Norman Vincent Peale, Dr. Robert Schuller, Oral Roberts, Rex Humbard, and more. They all knew and respected each other. They didn't squabble like the lesser-known ministers. In private they all got along with one another.

Rev. Ike taught me a lot for which I'm eternally grateful. He was a door that was open to me. I learned what to do and what not to do from Reverend Ike. 1969 to 1980 were super busy and fulfilling years where I was working, performing, teaching, and preaching with Rev. Ike. I must admit, I loved every minute.

A SPIRITUAL MONEY MASTER

Mark

R ev. Ike never wavered in his teachings that untold wealth is yours to have. It is like having an unbreakable safe that contains extraordinary treasure. All you must do is have the right combination, and once you do, it becomes easy. The fortune is yours! Statistically, you'll never figure out the combination to a safe on your own. You need someone to share that information. This right combination was perfected by Rev. Ike, and much of it shared for you through his teaching and right here in this book. The vault of your mind contains that "safe," and I know from personal experience the combination you'll learn as you journey through this book. It will lead you to exciting new places.

When I took ownership of Rev. Ike's illuminated wisdom, I took my unmanifest wishes and created riches! It's a gift he left for everyone who is willing to receive it.

Rev. Ike personally studied all the self-help-action-writers and the American spiritual masters of money. In our many conversations together, he would quote them to me chapter and verse. He had a mind like a steel trap. Once he learned something, it became his to share with others.

My friend always immersed himself in what he wanted to master in the early days, attending, and helping do tithe collections while listening intently and learning the words and wisdom spoken by the greats, preachers like Dr./Rev. Billy Graham, Oral Roberts, Dr. Robert H. Schuller, and A. A. Allen, and John Wesley, who was worth over $200 million, which would be about $2 billion today. Wesley was a minister and the founder of the Methodist Church denomination whose words became etched deeply into Rev. Ike's psyche and practiced in his life. "Gain all you can by earnest industry. Then, earn all you can, save all you can, invest all you can, and then give all you can."

Rev. Ike never gave up on his dream. He chose to believe in the unlimited good of God creating through him even more than he could think to ask for. He never second guessed the words of Christ who reminded us throughout the New Testament that it wasn't ever God who limited our money supply, but our own inability to understand and accept what has already been given.

He knew that our mental imaging, visualizations, and affirmations creates our future reality and experience, allowing us to claim what has already been provided. He was able to lock in on exactly what he wanted to the total exclusion of what he did not want. He knew that life was energy, and taught, "Where the energy goes, money flows—and attention creates our future." The nexus of that was his own self-image, which he defined in unequivocal terms.

> *"I am a green American. The only color of power in the US economy is green power! I am an UN-HYPHENATED American—NOT African American. I was BORN IN THE USA…"* (as he sang the tune)

He mastered and taught Biblical principles of wealth creation and added the wisdom of the greatest prosperity teachers of the century like Dr. Napoléon Hill, author of *Think and Grow Rich*, who he frequently quoted that, "Thoughts are things."

Starting at age fourteen, Rev. Ike was a prodigious preacher, speaker, thinker, writer, media maven, self-publicist, TV and radio broadcaster, and was original in his voluminous work output for six decades of his working life, up to his transition. I'll never forget attending this talk he called "You Can Have It." I believe it was the first one that Rev. Ike started selling as a brand-new audio recording. It was triggered by a newspaper journalist from the *Chicago Tribune* stating bluntly in an accusing tone to Rev. Ike, "Why are you always telling people that they can have what they cannot have?"

Inspired and irritated, it provoked this sermon:

> *"Who is that guy to tell me and my people what they can and cannot have? You know, people are good for telling you what you can't have. People are good for telling you what you can't be. People are good for telling you what you can't do.*
>
> *God only knows surplus. I'm talking to you about how to have surplus instead of shortage. Isn't that a good idea? It's probably a revolutionary idea, and there are several places in the Bible where Jesus multiplied a limited amount of food to feed thousands."*

He was fired up. If that reporter had shown up in his audience that day, I have a feeling he'd have been blushing by the end of it because Rev. Ike was about to tell him what was what!

Rev. Ike was a pioneering trailblazer. He intuitively knew he must re-think erroneous interpretations of scripture and pierce the veil of understanding. He overcame the centuries of misconceptions and corrected the principles so that all could know the truth and divine nature of themselves, to tap their own abundance and joy, and to be truly set free.

EVAN INLAW
MY STORY WITH REVEREND IKE

My father was at a friend's home where we lived in the Bronx, N.Y. when he saw a picture of Rev. Ike on his buddy's coffee table. "That's how a minister ought to look!" he remarked. "That's the man that I want to minister to my family!"

I was their seventh child, born in 1966. My mom was only twenty-one years old and Dad was twenty-five at the time. We started attending Rev. Ike's church faithfully in 1970, becoming close friends of our minister. Dad worked construction and drove a taxi, and using the prosperity principles that Rev. Ike taught, was able to buy us our own home. I grew up under the principles, philosophy, and teachings of Rev. Ike. He became such a great friend to our family that he drove over in the Rolls Royce to bless our new home and join us in our happy celebration.

My entire family would participate in all-night prayer vigils with Rev. Ike. We'd start by blessing everyone on the planet, then individual countries, America, New York State, New York City, its five boroughs, then Washington Heights where United Palace resided, and ultimately each one of us.

When we discovered Rev. Ike, there was a crack cocaine epidemic in the Bronx. Our faithful church attendance, singing in the choir, and all the church activities separated us from the dark activity that was happening in our community and made our family a miracle of success, prosperity, health, and happiness. We clearly see today that was not the outcome most of our neighbors experienced with their lives. There is no explanation for the difference other than that we had the right self-motivating philosophy, principles, and church support.

We discovered through Rev. Ike that God was truly inside of us, and with that knowledge, we were limitless. Frequently, Rev. Ike would have us stand up as examples of "If they can do it, so can you."

One of the central themes to Rev. Ike's teaching was the idea that "name means nature." How a person identifies his/her "self" means something. A person can identify as a "child of God" (Son of God) or as a "son-of-a-gun." A child of God is entitled to all the goodness of God, but a son-of-a-gun would get something very different. Name is also "self-identity"—it tells the world who you are. My name tells others who "I AM." "I AM" is God, and what you add to I AM, you become. That's your name…your nature.

Rev. Ike liked to talk about what happened when Saul encountered the resurrected Jesus on the road to Damascus. Saul was knocked off his donkey (representing his human-self, stubbornly refusing to accept the Christ), and Jesus changed his name to Paul, thus changing his nature from a man who persecuted Christians to that of a man whose writings about Jesus ended up in the Bible.

We found that if you relate to, understand, and accept Rev. Ike's teaching, it's only a matter of time before you will change any negative self-perception, any negative self-identification, and you will even change your birth name if it has a negative connotation. Therefore, it was no surprise to anyone in my immediate family when my dad announced that he was going to have our last name legally changed from "Outlaw." Yes, we had some debate about what name we should change it to, but no one objected to changing it. That is how we became the "Inlaw" family.

Rev. Ike inspired us all to believe that we had inborn genius and God inside each of us. As a result, we each discovered our talents and gifts. We became so motivated under his tutelage that all seven of us graduated college. I became a lawyer, passed the bar examination on my first try, and am now a judge in Yonkers, New York.

When I got downsized from my first legal working assignment. Rev. Ike took me to dinner and inspired me to hang out my shingle as a solopreneur. I was twenty-seven years old and looked seventeen. Fortunately, my first client was out of state, from California, and needed me to evict a criminal out of their rental unit. I did it successfully and from there, my legal practice flourished.

One time Rev. Ike got a letter from a prisoner who was not being treated well at Riker's Island. The Prison Ministry was sending him clothes and goodies and the staff was purloining them. Rev. Ike hired me to go there and explain that had to stop. Because of Rev. Ike, this man had resources, friends, and an attorney representing him. From that day forward the man started getting everything the church provided for him.

In his running of the church, Rev. Ike said, "I relate fast to a lot of people on a lot of different levels, and I make the final decisions." When my parents wanted to renew their vows in his church, his staff objected. When I called him, he told me, "Let's do it this Sunday," and we did. He did what he felt was right with God.

In the '70s, he started the Business of Living Seminars, which he mandated the attendance of all church staff to attend. He had lent out over $100,000 in debts, notes, and mortgages that were not repaid, so he cancelled and forgave all the debt obligations. Anyone wanting money was told to go to the Business of Living Seminars and learn to utilize the principles of money. He wanted everyone to learn to be about their "Father's business" and take good care of all their own obligations. We taught all the basics: managing debt, earning more, saving more, investing more, how to use credit positively and correctly, get a mortgage, stocks, bonds, real estate, et cetera.

Rev. Ike had a natural talent for business. He was a good investor and intuitively knew how to multiply their money through investments. Originally, he had Mrs. Ike and their CPA visit five or six New York investment firms. The finance committee chose two, which did well for the organization. After I had been teaching the Business of Living

Seminars for him, he mentioned in passing that the church had wisely invested in the stock market and made a great return.

I was always amazed at the healing that took place during our church services. One of my legal colleagues and best friends had experienced painful uterine fibroids for years. She was in constant pain. She'd tried different doctors and medications, but none did her any good. I convinced her to attend services at the United Palace to perhaps receive a healing from God through Rev. Ike. Although reluctant, she sat with me in the healing section of the church. Before the service Rev. Catherine Yates, one of Rev. Ike's most powerful associate healing ministers, came and prayed for my colleague's healing. When Rev. Ike started preaching, he directly looked at the healing section of the church, waved his hands over them, and said, "Everyone here is already healed!" At that moment, my friend did not believe she was healed or that anything important had happened. She wasn't willing to accept that God could heal in an instant.

Rev. Ike went on to preach prosperity and was talking enthusiastically about wearing a mink coat. She'd had enough. She grabbed my hand and said, "We are out of here." She had a serious money rejection complex. We went out the side door with her grabbing at her stomach as we left. Once outside, she started vomiting violently. A few days after that meeting, her doctor told her that her fibroids had disappeared and she was miraculously cured. She never needed medicine again and felt no side effects.

Rev. Ike was exceedingly well read and traveled. He could speak eloquently and insightfully on almost every subject. When I mentioned I was off to London or Tahiti, he'd tell me where to stay, where to eat, and whom to meet. He taught me to never limit myself. "You are a child of God. All things belong to him, and you are an heir to His Kingdom." He called me "My son the lawyer," when introducing me to other people. He was so brilliant and loved talking to me about the law, telling me he could have been a great lawyer. I loved witnessing how prolific Rev. Ike was. He had countless revelations that he would scribble down and have typed up to be used in future sermons. He was continuously communing with the Spirit.

My life and the life of my entire family was shaped dramatically by this special man who lived constantly by the guidance of God, showing all of us how to do the same. My family and I will love and cherish him forever.

REVEREND JAMES WYNS
MY STORY WITH REVEREND IKE

It was January 1972, and my friend Dr. Alfred Miller asked me to come sing for Reverend Ike at the United Palace Church. That day changed my life, and I think his too. Rev. Ike fell in love with what I could do. I ultimately became the lead singer on all his telecasts and sang every Sunday in church. In addition, I was the building engineer for thirty-six years and had the license to take care of the boilers, the refrigeration, and the sprinkler standpipe and other systems. I was also a licensed electrician, so my skills kept the building functioning and operating well.

I came out of the Church of God in Christ, so my first couple of Sundays at church with Rev. Ike were kind of rough. It took me a while to understand what he was teaching. At one meeting in those early days, Rev. Ike was preaching about going into Heaven saying, "When you are pure spirit you ain't gonna need a long white robe and golden slippers to wear. You probably won't want to be drinking 'milk and honey' because you know that it's a laxative." He roared with laughter. He then comforted me with John 14:1–7 (KJV): "*Let not your heart be troubled.… My house has many mansions…*" and he added, "*God is the Father, Son, and Holy Ghost. You came from spirit, are temporarily human, and will return to spirit.*" His teachings were so vastly different from what I had been taught, but I couldn't argue with it. It was truth. He taught truth!

Our relationship and trust in one another grew strong, and in 1978, I became a resident pastor standing in at the services whenever he could not be there. After he realized I had the ability to fill in for him, for the next fourteen and a half years, I took over the preaching at the services when he was traveling. In the beginning, it was a little intimidating, but I knew what God had done for me through him, so it wasn't difficult for me to just share what I had learned, and the more I did it, the better I became at it. Rev. Ike and I were close in spirit. To this day, all that I am and ever will be was brought out of me by his seeing the truth of me. I was able to capture that truth from him, and to teach and preach it.

There is no telling what God will do when you believe.

Rev. Ike was a good teacher, and he didn't care what he had to do to make you understand. He was serious about people learning the principles. You couldn't help yourself once you learned them. It was in your heart, and you had to be a winner!

Many people misunderstood the reverend. They thought he was a fancy preacher grabbing up a whole lot of money, but it's not true. The truth is, he had gone through enough poverty to say there has got to be a better way. God showed him and taught him a better way. I had also gone through severe poverty in the deep South. He and I were both from South Carolina and knew deprivation, poverty, and bone-chilling cold from the time we were born. We would talk together about how the homes we grew up in had no insulation. The wooden sideboards had knots and we'd stuff them with rags to stop the cold wind from penetrating right through us. Each of us remembered piling on two or three blankets and quilts just to sleep through the night.

We remembered our families always being in school and trying to advance. They were always in school because nobody could afford to go to college like kids do now. His mom and mine both taught throughout the school year and then went to Orangeburg State College to get their master's degrees during the summer and dragged us right along with them to college. We both understood our respective poverty was meant to be. It gave us experiential awareness that one gets only by going through difficulty. Yes, we suffered, but as a result, we emerged out of poverty and helped our families with all their financial and medical needs. Rev. Ike inspired millions of others to rise out of poverty, lack, and limitations of all kinds. He sincerely taught everyone the truth of themselves and what they could become, like he did with me. He had the anointing of God on him. People could feel the spirit of God coming through him.

Once he called and asked that my daughter Yolanda and I meet him at the church at 5:00 p.m., just the three of us. It was one of our defining moments. We started privately to sing together, then he started crying uncontrollably. Reverend Ike put a lot of pressure on himself and took care of so many people. Whatever was troubling him, we released it together. Whatever was pent-up inside of him came gushing out, and after he cried it out, he said, "I want to thank you. Thank you so much." It was like the Spirit came in and had him release whatever was heavy on his heart. We all felt the anointing of God, we were all taken up in spirit, and all of us were crying together. We were spiritually close like that. Whenever Rev. Ike was working in the healing section of the church, I spontaneously knew what to sing. Songs like, "He Touched Me and Made Me Whole Again" and others like it, some of which we originated. Occasionally, he'd burst into song, and I'd just follow his lead. We recognized the power of the anointing and energized it. People were truly healed.

One time, Sister Ruby came with her husband Bill, who was distressed because she had completely lost her memory. Rev. Ike prayed, sang, and laid his hands on her head. Ruby's memory returned 100 percent and stayed for twenty years, until she died.

There came a time when I needed a new home, so I decided to ask him to loan me the money to buy the best home in Brooklyn, New York for my family and me. It was a large home with twenty-one rooms. "If I buy it and you can't afford it," Reverend Ike said, "I will get it back and have to sell it and we will both feel bad. You can manifest it with your own self-determination-in-action using all the principles that I have taught you." The house was owned by a church deacon. One day I was driving to work, and I heard the Lord's voice in my head as clearly as I hear yours. It said, "Go there now!" I said to myself, "Lord, if you want me to go, I will, but please meet me there." When I arrived, the wife had recently had a stroke and was sitting on the front porch. She called the Deacon out. I told him politely that I wanted to buy the house. He said dismissively, "Son, you can't afford this house. This is a mansion."

At that exact moment, a young lady emerged from the front door calling, "James Wyns, how are you?" I didn't recognize her at first, then I remembered. It was Cecilia Jones from Summerville, South Carolina. We went to school together. That was the Lord meeting me at the house. She greeted me with such warmth and enthusiasm that when I came back to the house, I was warmly welcomed by them. She had been working with them for eight years, and two months after she introduced me, she was transferred to a different location.

She said to me, "The Lord had me here until you could get here." I was hired to be the caretaker of the property for the next eighteen years. When the Deacon died in 2006, he left in his will that I be given the opportunity to be the first person to purchase the house. I paid cash for it by selling my other home. I had it appraised in 2018 and the value was now worth many times what I paid. Praise the Lord. All that Reverend Ike told me came to pass.

In the early '90s, I retired and had my own church ministry with about sixty people. We were feeding about 350 people a week. One day, Rev. Ike called me at the church I worked at in the Bronx. He said, "Son, I need you."

I asked, "When do you need me?"

"Yesterday!"

I didn't know he was sick at that time because he didn't say so. I closed my little church down and went back to United Palace in 2008, about eight months before he died. I stayed on until December 2018.

The reverend and I were, and still are, one in spirit. He taught me the principles and philosophy and I love sharing all that I know with others. He has appeared in my dreams many a time since he passed away. When it happens, it seems so real, like he never left. The last time it happened I dreamed we were at the church, singing our hearts out and having a great time. It was so real I didn't realize until I woke up I was dreaming.

He gave me a gift of self-determination to understand my own resources. I could never, no way no how, forget Reverend Ike. I could never stop loving him. Never. I'll take him with me wherever I go, in the Spirit. I'm always celebrating his spirit every day because he brought me to the place I needed to be.

THE CHURCH RESIDENCES

Mark

As one of the most beloved evangelists in the country, Rev. Ike was traversing the entire US, coast to coast, multiple times throughout the year. And of course, his own gigantic church community in New York, which drew audiences from a large swath of the East Coast. It became essential to have church offices and residences in various locations. The travel and logistics were already grueling for Rev. Ike and his team. As the ministry grew, so did the real estate holdings owned by the church.

After the United Palace was purchased for the United Church services in 1969, the Eikerenkoetters knew they needed to get serious about finding a church office residence nearby. Mrs. Ike had been going back and forth regularly from Boston to New York, with Xavier in tow, but it was becoming more apparent she was needed more often in New York, and they certainly needed more family time.

"I was running the office in Boston and then trying to be at the church in New York," she said, "and it just became too much."

At the house they had rented at 100 Central Park West, they had assembled a small staff. That apartment was used primarily as an office, so naturally the staff was around all the time. Rev. Ike lived there as well, and his wife and son would join him on the weekends. They took any

155

opportunity they could get to go search for a church office residence in New York but hadn't found one that was right. One day, Rev. Ike said to his wife, "I'm a little weary of looking at houses, why don't you and Xavier go out with the real estate person who wants us to see a place in Westchester County?"

Fitting family and staff in one apartment the way they'd been doing had become rather trying and they needed the bigger space. Plus, Rev. Ike needed an environment conducive to having periods of private, quiet time, preferably with nature around, because that was the way he would receive his best ideas to inspire his followers.

The realtor had something specific in mind for them to see that day. He drove Xavier and Mrs. Ike to a place called Greenhaven. It was known as the home to notable stars in the film industry like Martin Scorsese, and Peter, Paul and Mary who lived across the street from the very house they would be looking at.

Mrs. Ike was eager to see if this one might fit the bill. "As we were driving along, I saw this little beach, and this English Tudor sitting up on the hill. The minute I looked at that house that first time, settled among the lovely old trees with views of nature surrounding, I knew this was it. The location was perfect! I hadn't seen it inside, but as we approached and turned into the driveway it felt like this is where we belong. After looking through all three stories that contained nineteen beautifully designed rooms, there was no doubt in my mind or heart that we needed to get this house, but I didn't want to act overly interested to the owner or realtor. I knew that wouldn't help our negotiating position."

Back home from their house-hunting excursion, Rev. Ike was eager to know what his wife thought. "Hey, how did you like the house?" A big smile came to his face as he listened to his wife describe how strongly she felt about the house. He wanted to go see it right away. When they toured it together, he too was thrilled with the location and the beautiful Tudor structure that was large and well-built. "This is our new church residence," he agreed. The owners accepted their offer for $350,000 and the home became theirs. Rev. Ike gazed around the property that would be their new church residence for the ministry that was just starting to move into its greatest period. The nature around it inspired him, and he knew it would provide the perfect environment for him to produce his best work. He could already imagine the office spaces filled with busy church staff keeping the wheels turning for the ministry to reach millions.

As the years unfolded, the reverend and Mrs. Ike invested in a number of office/residences for the church, and those investments became great assets to keep the church operating. A decade after they purchased the Rye, New York residence, they purchased another real estate investment, an office/church residence in Bal Harbor, Florida. That location was primarily focused on the TV production because their new marketing maven, Judy Adler, handled that part of the ministry and she and the company that did the television productions were both there in Florida.

By that time, Reverend Ike was traveling a lot to California, holding huge, sold-out events at the Cow Palace, the Forum, or Shriners Auditorium in Los Angeles, and even big churches like Terry Cole Whitaker's in San Diego. Those events were demanding to produce and required so much work from Rev. Ike and his staff, that they had to have the California office. His West Coast crowds had become as large as the East Coast and the South.

REVEREND YOLANDA WYNS

MY STORY WITH REVEREND IKE

Starting at age two, I attended United Palace with my parents. My dad, Jimmy Wyns, was famous as the lead soloist for Rev. Ike. I can vividly remember being in the nursery in the annex next to United Palace. Rev. Ike was an early adopter of technology, and we had the first closed circuit TV so the working mothers and those working in the nursery would not miss his sermons in the church. They could watch his service simultaneously while taking care of the children.

By the time I was in kindergarten, Mom and I would have to sit in the balcony because the place was jam-packed. We wanted newcomers to have preferred seating. During Sunday school I had learned all the gospel songs like, "Yes, Jesus Loves Me"; "Jesus Loves the Little Children"; "This Little Light of Mine"; and "The Sweet Spirit in Me." Rev. Ike loved my voice, my fearless stage presence, and my ability, like my dad, to elevate joy out of the crowd. He started asking me to join Dad up on stage. His nickname for me was "Sweet Spirit." Soon I was part of the traveling evangelistic team on tour with Rev. Ike singing everywhere. The reverend asked me to learn how to play the piano and keep forever expanding my repertoire. It was thrilling.

I remember one early evangelistic service in Brooklyn, New York when I was about six. Rev. Ike had a refrigerator on stage. He was relating to his confused audience, who believed in strange practices like witchcraft, or a folk belief called "hoodoo." A mojo was a magical charm, usually in a bag, that supposedly cast a spell on the recipient. This kind of Voodoo, which was sorcery, was sold on the streets in the neighborhood and he was sick and tired of people putting their belief in it. He brought a bleeding chicken out of the fridge with blood and guts running and the organist played creepy and scary music in the background. It temporarily traumatized me.

Then Rev. Ike shocked me back into reality when he said, "Oh my Sweet Spirit, please sing my favorite song for me now before this televised audience." On cue, I delivered that uplifting song. The reverend then said, "Now! Bring all that craziness to the altar here and I will banish it forever."

When that service was finished, people got the message that we were done with that kind of nonsense in our church!

As a seven-year-old, I remember singing "Something on the Inside is Working on the Outside." When I sang that song, for the first time in my life, I felt the undeniable presence of God in me. It was a profound emotional and spiritual connection that I had never felt before. I was overwhelmed and happy at the same time. I had conversations about it later to both my dad and Rev. Ike. They told me that I felt the Holy Spirit.

As a kid, I was shy, except when I was singing. Singing brought me into being fully alive and I loved it. While I was good in my school studies, I knew inside that I was supposed to be in music.

By the time I was in junior high school, I came to truly know, appreciate, and use the principles that Rev. Ike taught, like visualization. Early on, I knew that I wanted to be on the honor roll, be among the smartest kids, and make the Dean's list in both science and music. I saw myself in my mind's eye being chosen to be in the Gifted and Talented classes, and I was. I pictured myself walking into school and hanging out with the smartest kids. I wanted to be in that league, and it all happened for me because of the teachings I'd learned from Rev. Ike.

Kids can sometimes be brutal to each other, because they have not learned to have filters. Some students would taunt me, saying that I was part of a cult. I loved singing everywhere with Rev. Ike. I knew the truth about him, so I always defended him and didn't let their words get to me. When I matriculated into the Manhattan School of Music, I chose to study music, voice, and piano, also studying sciences.

What Rev. Ike taught me has lasted throughout my life from childhood to this day and I am in my fifties. I literally visualized being a backup singer for some of the most famous singers in the world. I was a backup singer for Prince for two intense weeks, and I worked profitably with many of the greats like Stephanie Mills and Freddie Jackson. I saw myself happily being a lifelong backup singer making great money, and that's exactly what happened.

I was blessed to have Reverend Ike as my spiritual father, so to speak. He told me to make "lots of money" and also gave me personal recommendations to learn to invest and multiply my wealth. He told me to get my own bank account early in life and see myself making regular deposits. He had me take all the Business of Living classes at the Palace to get a good grasp of building wealth personally and I've been quite successful with that.

He was protective of me, like my parents were. I cherish that I could talk to him about anything and feel safe in all my opinions. When I told him I wanted to do church work for my entire life, except that while I was in college, I felt lonely sometimes. He responded, "Being a minister is a lonely business. Be prepared to be alone." I had to marinate on that statement. He also told me, "In metaphysics, we know all is one. We create everything in our own lives, including our relationships. You are a co-creator with God." Occasionally, when he was teaching me, I would repeat his brilliance back to him, and he'd say, "Thank you. You are taking ownership of this."

While from the audience's point of view, his sermons often looked impromptu, there was nothing about them that was off-the-cuff. It was totally strategized, planned, and well thought-out. He cued us when he was taken over to preach with the Holy Spirit by saying, "The Holy Rollers are here," or "Who let the Pentecostals into church?" He wanted us to know that he would regain control and composure, but plan for a fiery and alive red-hot sermon. It was coming through him clearly right at the moment.

As his tele-evangelistic ministry took off, I asked him why he didn't put the entire church service on TV rather than just a prayer cloth and testimonial show. His wise answer was, "You must meet people where they are. Most need training wheels and are not ready to ride a bicycle yet. If I talk above them, they will resist me, and I will lose them."

When I would work with him, it was amazing to watch him perfectly and professionally edit the big old reel-to-reel shows, cutting them to be on telecasts, radio broadcasts, and in his many publications like *Action Magazine* or the Study Guides.

Frequently, when he was advancing me, I did not feel qualified or ready. He would say, "Fear not, you will grow into the job." He made me resident pastor. I surrendered and was okay but felt more competent as the minister of music. When he made me resident pastor as he was transitioning out of full-time preaching, I didn't feel totally ready. It was around early 2000. I felt it was my Moses moment. I told him I wasn't the right person to build the church because it was built on his personality.

I came to realize that his ministry transcends the church building. It is in you, me, and many, many others. It is an international ministry. The spirit of Rev. Ike lives on, and he has more devotees now than when he was alive.

COUSIN PEARL HEDGSPETH

MY STORY WITH REVEREND IKE

My first impression of Reverend Ike was his loving personality that shined through when I first met him in 1978. I initially had negative thoughts about him and was a little suspicious of his teachings because of my Pentecostal background. Growing up in that denomination we were taught that there was something wrong with you if you liked riches and possessions. Until I met him, my focus was mainly on living forever in Heaven and not to concentrate too much on Earthly wealth. He made me feel valuable, loved, and special. He embraced me thoughtfully right away, which eliminated my fears.

My main role was to assist Mrs. Ike, and I would do whatever needed to be done. There was always plenty to do in a fast-growing church enterprise. My duties were forever expanding, including reviewing the children's church members' report cards to see his or her eligibility to potentially receive a college scholarship from Reverend Ike. He trusted me because he knew I was his wife's favorite cousin. He would call me Cousin Pearl, and this caught on to others, even outside of the family. That name has stuck.

Rev. Ike ran his business with strict adherence to the law, with integrity, and accountability.

Rev. and Mrs. Ike appreciated my always being available to help them in any capacity that I could. With their encouragement and assistance, I was able to acquire a master's degree in theology, May 1997, NY Theological Institute in New York City. His graduation gift to me was something I will treasure forever. He surprised me by telling me I could get anything I wanted. I decided that I wanted to furnish my library with great educational and spiritual books. Rev. Ike furnished my library with Bibles, commentaries, condensed biblical cyclopedias, Bible dictionaries, Spurgeon teachings, Greek and Hebrew books, etc. for my graduation gift.

The most meaningful thing Rev. Ike did for me was to raise my level of thinking that I could accomplish anything I wanted to do.

As a result of working with Rev. Ike and Mrs. Eikerenkoetter, and being employed by them, I imaged myself as the entrepreneur I'd longingly dreamed of. After sharing my vision with Mrs. Ike, she encouraged me to take the leap, which I did. I started an employment agency in 1985 in Long Island City, New York. After two years, I envisioned more for myself by listening to Rev. Ike, and I was blessed to move my office to Park Avenue, New York City, as "Temporary Solutions," employing men and women to work in Fortune 500 companies, as typists, stenographers, proofreaders, secretaries, and other related fields. This business thrived through 1995 until I closed it to go to New York Theological Seminary for a master's degree in Theology. This, I credited to the teachings of Rev. Ike and my faith being elevated as he taught "that I could do what I wanted, be what I wanted, and have what I wanted."

THE IMPACT YEARS

FACING ATTACKS AND HIS CHILD-SELF

Xavier

Every once in a while in life, one experiences an epiphany so profound that nothing is the same after it happens. Life takes on a new layer of meaning and purpose, from which arises a new conviction. Inherent to the nature of epiphanies, it is an illumination that doesn't simply teach you, but it causes you to become someone new.

Dad's arrival at this epiphany during the spring of 1974 was preceded by a mystical experience that brought the young man he had been face-to-face with the man he had become. Prior to this numinous encounter and likely a factor that precipitated it, my father had gone to Harlem Hospital to discuss the medical implications of religious healing at an open forum.

It wasn't the first time and certainly would not be the last, but following his appearance, what was then referred to as "Black militants" attacked Dad, ridiculing his ministry and challenging what he was doing. They called him degrading names and criticized his style. This group of protestors was vicious, and their jeers were all the more cutting because these were Blacks with little knowledge about the impact my father was having on some of the people they were determined to "set free."

Some of these activists had a primarily fight-the-man approach and placed a lot of external focus upon politics and the oppressive social systems operating in America. They felt that because my dad was not doing the same thing, he was out for himself and scamming people. The thing is, my father and these activists were both trying to empower people while coming at the problems from different angles. My father was not politically engaged on the front lines, but he was always privately voting his conscience. He was not walking in protests, but he was pushing hard against the mental, psychological, and even spiritual oppression that had been placed upon Black people for centuries. His focus was on liberating minds and spirits by helping others to do deep psycho-spiritual work. Dad's Black critics didn't seem to understand that he was exhorting Black people to think for themselves in much the same way they were, but with a different emphasis. My father's M.O. was not "fight the man," but "I am the man, and I will exert divine justice by creating my own reality." And, of course, help others do the same. The approaches were not mutually exclusive, and many organizers of marches and protests encouraged Blacks to think for themselves, believe in themselves, and prosper for themselves. Dad did not see a need to be combative toward an external enemy, and he was unique in the way he furthered the cause of Black self-determination.

None of that mattered, because all his critics saw was a flashy, over-the-top preacher man with a fine wardrobe, fancy cars, and expensive jewelry. One reporter seemed particularly determined to expose this "smooth talking con man" preying on poor Black people whom he believed were doomed to lifelong destitution by virtue of their race. Dad wanted no part of equating Black people with poverty and had said as much publicly when he received a telegraph from Black leaders inviting him to participate in the Poor People's March.

> *"I didn't like the sound of 'Poor People's March,' and I interpreted it to mean they were giving Black people a poverty image. They were labeling us like they always do. It became too cliché to be poor people. I didn't like that poor people had become a badge of honor. You've*

got to be careful with your self-image, because your self-image is everything. I saw the danger of poverty and Blackness becoming synonymous, and I couldn't have any part of that. I refused to contribute to that. I don't believe that to be Black automatically means that you must be poor, and you must be proud of your poverty. I believe the opposite of that, and I rejected it from the time I was a child!"

No Black preacher was supposed to have the money my father had. A preacher who stood for the Black community shouldn't be living a life that luxurious. Besides, the fight was for equality, not for getting rich. Dad had no problem with those types of accusations because he understood them. The central argument they held was that if you are rich and prospering, you're doing it off the backs of the poor. My father did not believe that because he did not believe in scarcity. In other words, he saw an abundant universe that had plenty to provide for everyone and the fact that he was claiming his portion of it did not take away from any-one else, even though people who didn't have much money were giving money to his ministry. In fact, he saw that if he was able to inspire the act of giving in a person based on worthy and expansive ideas regardless of their financial status, it expanded their ability to receive because it is a psychological and spiritual opening that creates more space to be able to let more in and hold/host more energy and substance in whatever form is needed. Part of it is that when you're giving, if you're giving in the right consciousness with joy to something you believe in, you're not remaining too attached to what you have, and that lack of attachment means that more can easily float in.

Dad didn't like that poverty mentality bred a we vs. they mindset, whether or not race was a factor. Many poor White people shared the same belief.

As they screamed accusations of selling out and stealing from the very people he was supposed to be serving, my father smiled all the way through it. While his critics' attacks were resolute, he maintained his composure and spoke with his usual elegance. But they *did* get to him.

Dad was deeply concerned about how he came across at that seminar because it was in Harlem, and it jeopardized his reputation with people he felt an allegiance toward. He would never dignify their accusations by responding to them, but he had to be fuming with a desire to set them straight, just this once, because of the venue location.

In other settings where he had been accosted with similar accusations, his reply had been simply, "I know the truth of me." And he did because he performed significant philanthropic work in Harlem as well as around the country. He could have opened his critics' eyes and allowed them to see beyond his external persona by letting them know, for example, that he'd leased two buses for Alma John, a community leader and radio personality, who'd asked him for help transporting a group of performing artists to visit men in prison throughout the state of New York. He could have let them know that he sponsored the Carrie Steele-Pitts Home for Children in Atlanta, where he visited and inspired the children and staff as well as donated money and vehicles for their work. He had made countless donations to children and adults to help them continue educational opportunities. He never did broadcast anything about his acts of generosity because he wasn't interested in impressing anyone, and he did not believe in grandstanding at the expense of others. He gave back, and forward, in abundance.

This group of Blacks with an angry, militant attitude toward anyone who didn't agree with the narrative that they were oppressed by a force outside of themselves never saw the excitement spread through Harlem residents whenever Dad was there. Or perhaps they did and that fueled their resentment toward him. There was always a cluster of people who emerged from hallways, the corner store, a neighborhood bar, and the laundromat down the street to see him. There was no hostility anywhere in the atmosphere. In Harlem, it was clear my father was loved, and the feeling was mutual.

My father was able to walk through Harlem with respect, because the people there knew how hard it was for a Black man to transcend racism and the self-imposed limitations so many of them succumbed to. They celebrated freedom vicariously through him, and they loved him for always saying that nothing was impossible. He reminded them of other great Black men who had made it and still loved them, like Joe Louis, Jackie Robinson, Sidney Poitier, and Muhammad Ali. He was a star who had risen above the fray and was shining light toward them, exhorting them to come and join him.

My father's early years in South Carolina, his experience living across the street from Sadie's, the unforgettable generosity of Lady Tee, and his near penniless wanderings across the boroughs of New York City made it easy for him to stroll through Harlem with confidence and total safety. He was unafraid. He genuinely liked to visit, and the people could sense his authenticity, even clad in his designer threads.

> *"Of course my life is an exaggeration, I know that, because that's the only way I can fully get my message to Black people. It's the only way they are going to know how much there is really out here, and that's to see how much a man like me can accomplish. And I've accomplished a hell of a lot. But how much is left for anyone who wants it? Plenty. Black people don't see it, so I make sure they see it. They could build a life in this country the likes of which has never been seen in the history of mankind. Because Black people believe and their belief is powerful, Black people are not so cynical as some others we have in this society. They're a sincere, trusting people. Black people believe the American dream. Black people, so many of us, don't realize how much at the center of the world's energy capital we are. I want to wake everyone up to that. America—hear me when I say this—America is the greatest country that could ever have been conceived in any God's mind."*

Dad had a genuine appreciation for the people in Harlem and believed he could help them if only he could get them to understand what he understood. That they, like everyone else, were divine, and therefore capable of far more than the drudgery-laced existence they endured.

> *"But these people, the incredible Harlem people, they're smart, they get it, they see through all the jive, man. Once they learn they can do something bigger, they know that it's the social workers, not the bankers who are running a game. Show the banker you can make money, he'll back you. Show the social worker you can make money, she'll cut your welfare check off. So, who's really looking out for you? We can save all this, we can change it all right now. We can raise the standard for everyone, now. I mean it's possible. It can be done."*

Dad was trying to help people understand that the social welfare system they came to depend on kept them in a cycle of neediness. He wanted them to learn to depend on the power of God in them to create true abundance. "Welfare has its place, but don't let it be a resting place." The capitalistic system my dad chose to be a part of was the one that rewarded him for his skills, talents, and work ethic, and he wanted the same for them. The adversaries accusing him of being a sellout had no idea of the mutual adoration between my father and the people of Harlem. Nevertheless, Harlem weighed heavily on his mind after the hospital forum. Maybe he felt guilty that he hadn't been able to reach more people with the truth about their inner power. He had walked many a mile in their shoes—shoes lined with newspapers because of the holes in them—and he had survived. But at what expense?

His private turmoil culminated in a dreamlike experience during a Sunday meeting at the United Church that shook him to his core. Later, he shared it with his executive assistant, Ruth. It was late, the others there had gone to bed, and Dad and Ruth were going over some correspondence. It was a little after one in the morning when a storm came up outside and it started to thunder. Ruth said he seemed a little uncomfortable as the lightning began flashing and hitting the ground, and you could hear the rain pounding against the roof. Dad was the sort of person who could talk and tell stories, and that night the storm had put him in storytelling mode.

He recounted the story of when his mother had tried to rush out into a storm while his father fought to hold her back. There had been a lot of screaming, and he shared the details, including how frightened he had been by the whole episode.

Then he asked Ruth if she'd noticed anything unusual that Sunday after the Harlem Hospital conference, anything that seemed unusual at the service he'd preached that afternoon. She couldn't recall anything specifically, so he shared with her what he'd experienced. As he stood there in the pulpit that afternoon, his mind had filled with gratitude and wonder of all that his life had become. Then he saw a man walk into the church and head down the aisle toward the stage.

Something about the man's walk was puzzling and a bit unsettling, and as the man walked from beneath the overhanging balcony, my father saw a young Frederick J. Eikerenkoetter Jr., maybe in his late teens, in old, worn clothes and shoes that had newspapers sticking out of the soles. He waved up at Dad and kept moving forward.

Until that night with Ruth, my father had never revealed that he'd seen himself. He said that the man he'd *been* came to confront the man he'd *become*. He wondered what he had become and what he was doing.

Ruth admitted then that, thinking back to that day, she had seen a difference in my father's demeanor toward the end of his sermon. She had been standing near the stage waiting with a few of the ushers for the collection to be over when she noticed my dad appeared to begin rushing a bit at the end of the meeting. He moved quickly toward the backstage area once he'd offered a benediction. She found out later that he'd never gone up to his private study, which was a habit he never altered. For the first time since she'd known him, he walked straight out of the United Palace, got into a limo, and was driven to the airport.

A week passed, and nobody on the staff heard from him. If he was in communication with my mother or anyone else, no one knew. Two weeks went by. Then three. Rumors were flying, and a reporter in New York claimed that he had been chased down by the police as he ran naked through Wall Street. It was hard for his staff to deny anything because they had no idea where he was. Six weeks went by, and most people had no idea where he was.

Eventually we learned that Mom knew where he was, but she'd kept it completely to herself. She knew better than anyone that he gave all that he had in each sermon, every radio broadcast, speech, TV show, or interview. Sometimes after intense periods of outpouring the love and devotion he gave, he simply needed to be alone—to be by himself to regain his strength and stamina. During those times he wanted to talk to no one.

Dad had flown to Los Angeles and checked into a small, unknown hotel, the last place he felt anybody would look for a millionaire minister. Nobody looked for him there or bothered him. He was by himself all those weeks. He started penning some ideas for a book that described many of his visions and dreams, how he made them a real part of his life. He wrote about how others could share that knowledge if they would trust him and believe in themselves, and God in them. It was also during those weeks of solitude that he confronted certain things about himself.

> *Jesus was led by the Spirit into the wilderness…forty days and forty nights….*
> (Matthew 4:1 ESV)

That earthshattering visage of the teen Frederick J. Eikerenkoetter Jr., in old, worn clothes waving to him at church that day reminded him to whom the truth of these principles had been given, and of the deep responsibility he had to help disadvantaged people to understand those principles.

> *To whom much is given, much will be required.*
> (Luke 12:48 LSV)

My father returned from his impromptu sabbatical with no explanation to anyone, and he reinvigorated his ministry with the teachings of the truth he had been so fortunate to receive. He didn't hold back. He pulled the old angry God with big gray beard right out of the sky and delivered the true God of love and light into the living spirit of every heart and mind in front of him.

My book-aholic father devoured all the disciplines that were congruent with his philosophy that your mind was the gateway to understanding and enjoying the abundance, freedom, health, and joy that God continually promises throughout the scriptures.

Raymond Charles Barker and Neville Goddard were powerful influences on my father's work. Neville embraced an Ethiopian-born rabbi named Abdullah as a spiritual mentor. According to Neville, Abdullah trained him in what Neville called "real Christianity." Neville spoke of the nature of God and His intimate relationship to each and every person. Dad had been using visualization since childhood, so it was no wonder he was fascinated by one of the principles Neville came to be known for—the power of one's own imagination. Neville taught exactly what my father had practiced since childhood, using imagination to manifest what one wants.

People like Barker and Neville articulated what my father had been practicing since he was a kid. The fire to share these truths fully in his ministry had been rekindled to a glorious blaze. My dad understood that the true locus of divinity was inside the spirit of every living soul, and that divinity was a loving, caring one. Dad had love for people and an awareness of God's presence inside of each person. This renewed relationship with himself strengthened his commitment to give his parishioners substantive tools to improve their lives. The Christian Resurrection wasn't the only resurrection celebrated that year. My father had been reborn. His first meeting back was a Joy of Living meeting where he spoke to a full house, preaching a hair-raising sermon that left people electrified.

Some called it a miracle. Others called it magic. "I have brought you, revealed here before you all today the truth that shall set everybody free who hears me speak and who comes to know the wonder and the glory of mind power that activates the awareness of God in you."

He was pleased to have even those old-line traditionalists he expected to remonstrate surprise him by thoroughly enjoying every minute. They loved having him back, more powerful than he'd ever been, and they could feel the joy pouring out of him. Whatever doubts lingering in the minds of those around him about whether this renewed message of gospel truth would work were shattered when, as usual, it turned out he knew precisely what he was doing. The growth of his ministry from that point was exponential. The era of my father's golden gospel became a 1970s phenomenon.

JOAN CLANCY

MY STORY WITH REVEREND IKE

T humbing through the jobs wanted page in the newspaper, I came across an ad for a church wanting an assistant graphic arts person to help with their direct mail. The job sounded intriguing, like it might be a good match for my skills, so I filled out the application and made an appointment. It was then in 1992 that I met Reverend Ike for the first time. I remember walking into the office/condo in Redondo beach, California, and being awestruck by the grandeur. Having grown up in a humble household in the Midwest, I'd never seen this kind of elegance in interior décor before. It was magnificent and quite flamboyant. He even had velvet chairs fit for a king with a crown above his head.

The reverend gave me a warm welcome and started chatting with me, asking some questions and filling me in on the ministry and its background. I was immediately impressed by his charisma. The complex consisted of several condo units that included a church residency adjacent to an office. Everything was beautiful and done to perfection. As he explained what my duties would be, should I be hired, I became impressed with his big vision for his evangelistic movement. It was thrilling to meet someone so self-assured and passionately on-purpose. Everything seemed to be the right fit for me, so when they offered me the job, I enthusiastically accepted. In keeping with the elegance that was a staple of Rev. Ike's operations, the offices had a dress code for all staffers. We were to dress elegantly, and no sweats were permitted. Additionally, no gum was allowed, ever. The standard of impeccability was set by Reverend Ike himself and whenever he went out, he was always dressed to the nines, decked impeccably to the highest degree of perfection, mostly in perfectly tailored Brioni suits.

The job was purely a nine-to-five operation based in a sumptuous setting of beautiful Redondo Beach. Our early offices consisted of a phone, computers, fax machines, and a few staffers. We were communicating primarily with his Boston and New York headquarters. My role was to help with all the written materials for the church and all the affiliates of the organization. Rev. Ike grew to appreciate my talent, creativity, and thinking. He liked that I could finish all his multitudinous assignments on-time and under budget. On occasion, he had me travel with him to meet people so I could finish even more of his projects and fulfill his promises to parishioners and others. He frequently stressed to me that I would be needed to help manage and help realize his legacy.

During my time there, I learned so much, and grew in my spiritual understandings and convictions. I came to discover that all his offices and residencies had hundreds of books that I had never heard of before. I was in awe. He introduced me to many books on wealth, happiness, spirituality, positive thinking, and he was especially fond of Neville's book called *Resurrection*. He inspired me to read them and ask any questions that tickled my imagination. When we had opportunities to hang out together, he was endlessly patient and wise and had answers to my every question. I was constantly amazed at his knowledge on almost every topic. I felt like he knew so much about so many things, yet his curiosity was insatiable. He was always learning something new that he wanted to share, and I loved the wisdom I was gaining from endless discussions we had through the years. Over time, many of my opinions and understandings were changed to become more like his as I became more immersed in the principles he taught and gained new insights and understanding.

I was given the task of writing some of his copy for his direct mail pieces and other written advertising or promotional materials. Ultimately it became so natural for me, that he said, "Joan, you've really learned my voice and thoughts. You can write in my voice, you have got it now." He came to trust that I understood his teachings and that I knew how to communicate them in a way that was completely aligned with how he wanted them communicated.

Eventually, he would kick off the piece by saying a sentence or paragraph and I could sculpt it together in a direct mail piece that he was almost always okay with as though it were him speaking. He was always generously patient with me and those around him. He wanted to make sure he was taking us forward on this journey with him, that we were all learning and growing in every way. I remember him talking to me specifically about how to handle money.

> *"Don't ever disrespect money or it will disrespect you. Always arrange your money in your purse or pocket in an orderly fashion. Do not crinkle up money or throw it into your purse or pocket with unconscious abandon or you will be rejecting it and it you. Always keep at least a hundred-dollar bill in your purse or pocket. It reinforces your prosperity thinking. Don't ever say I can't afford something; just say I have plenty of money. I release this money with joy. I know there is a never-ending circulation of money coming into my experience to enjoy. I earn plenty of money. I invest wisely and competently. I am giving to good causes and philanthropies that I believe in and know are doing great good."*

Rev. Ike would take the time to privately instruct me in ways that personally helped me grow as a human being. Those of us who worked with him daily came to know that personally, and professionally as a pastor, he lived the way he taught others. I found him to be totally honest, congruent, and living with consistent integrity.

His generosity was beautiful, and he expressed it in the way the Bible admonished: *Give in secret and you will be rewarded openly.* He was proof-positive that this Science of Mind he was teaching works and is the law. Some days, out of the blue, he would say to me to "Get the check book and anonymously donate here or there or pay the tuition of this or that student." It would instantly make a *huge* difference for that person, yet he insisted on no acknowledgement whatsoever. A smart kid who couldn't afford to pay college tuition? Rev. Ike would cover the whole thing. Another kid who was about to have to go home from college because he ran out of money and his family couldn't pay? Rev. Ike stepped in and paid, and his college experience went forward without interruption. There were so many stories like that. He gave so much to so many and refused to be recognized or known for it.

Because he was hungry much of his young life until he was in his twenties, he insisted that all the refrigerators in all of the buildings from which we worked always be full. It was an official house and office rule. Anyone working or visiting could have whatever they wanted to eat, but they must note it and he'd have it replenished promptly. He himself always appreciated good food, probably because of its scarcity in his younger years. His favorite of all was Häagen-Dazs ice cream.

When Rev. Ike had a little time to watch TV, he wanted to relax watching something like the comedy of Chris Rock, which broke him up into peals of laughter, or the clever series called *Doogie Howser, M.D.* In the story plot, Doogie was a child prodigy with a genius intellect and an eidetic memory who graduated from Princeton University at age ten and finished medical school four years later. According to the story line, at age fourteen, Howser was the youngest licensed doctor in the country. I think Rev. Ike liked it because he personally related to it as an ultra-bright youngster who began preaching at age fourteen, and shortly thereafter began to help countless people heal or solve the problems that were brought to him.

Rev Ike had a wonderful sense of humor and liked to do harmless but hilarious pranks on people. We had a staffer named Jeffrey who hated lima beans, so one evening as we all sat down to eat a meal, Reverend Ike had someone prepare a giant bowl of lima beans which was served and placed right in front of Jeffrey. When Rev. Ike announced, "Okay, let's enjoy dinner," the look on Jeffrey's face was exactly what the prankster side of Rev. Ike was waiting for. He howled with laughter before he revealed there were other things to eat for that meal.

Rev. Ike was always planning his next presentation. Daily, he would invest several hours in deep personal meditation, from which he would write his profound sermons and insights. He didn't seem to need much sleep. I know this because eventually I moved to Phoenix and started working for him remotely. At 3:00 a.m., I would hear my fax machine kicking into action and I knew only one person working at that hour: Reverend Ike. When he wrote his final sermon, he'd be faxing me the notes to be printed for the next service. One of his early favorites that he sent to me in the middle of the night was *Get Your But Out Of The Way*. He was so passionate about completely scripting each sermon that by the end of one month we equivalently had enough copy for a complete book. He was spontaneously creative with catchy, compelling titles. Sometimes he'd start with just a skeleton idea and develop it until he turned it into one of his masterpieces.

"I am the goose that lays the golden eggs," he would announce to any staffer trying to distract him, give him work assignments, or get him off-purpose in any way. He would not deal in any day-to-day minutia. "I am about my Father's business, so please don't be impatient or interrupt me. I must be free to be creative, preach, and help others."

He was constantly appearing on every major TV talk show. Intuitively, he knew who was "gunning for him" and planned to be critical and mock him or his ministry. He told me after accepting an invitation to be on the popular TV show of one of our former presidents' son, "Watch, he is coming for me, and I am ready. He only thinks he can embarrass me. He can't. It's not even remotely possible." Rev. Ike did a brilliant job, and the interview came off without a hitch. He was so good at holding the outcomes inside of himself that somehow always seemed to manifest perfectly.

Once, when asked about another famous minister imitating him and the Rolls Royces on TV as a new prosperity preacher, he said, "He is teaching the same principles in a different package." Instead of being incensed at someone trying to copy what he was doing, he continued, "I am impressed that he learned it all so well."

He loved and cared deeply for his wife, son, and extended family. They were very important to him, and we all knew it. As a busy evangelist, he spent as much time with them as humanly possible, even though he had to balance that against what we all knew was that burning calling within him to share his work with the world to make a difference for as many people as possible.

Solitary time was important to Rev. Ike to create his best ideas and he loved walking on the beach to clear his head, heart, and mind. Sometimes, when he finished, he would take a brief nap while sitting in the sun, but he seemed to need a minimal amount of rest in comparison to his constant work focus and effort.

He read through four newspapers daily: *The New York Times*, *The Wall Street Journal*, the *Miami Herald* (if he was in Florida) or the *Los Angeles Times* (when he was in California), and *USA Today*. He read just enough to know what was going on in the world but didn't accept the negative conditions like energy shortages or high interest rates into his world. To him, those were external events that could not affect his health, happiness, or prosperity unless he let them, and no one was better at holding his perfect picture of his perfect life and manifesting that vision regardless of world events.

One of the many cherished memories I have of my years with Rev. Ike is when we were in Miami. We'd had a long day of meetings, so he gave me his credit card and told me and one of the other people working with him at the time to go enjoy a nice dinner. He hadn't mentioned anything about being hungry, but we ordered an extra entree to bring back for him in case he wanted something later that night. I knew he loved romance novels he called novellas. On the way back we walked by a bookstore, and I couldn't resist. I went in and bought him four novellas on a lark. When we gave the novellas to him, I will never forget how shocked he was. He said, "You bought this for *me*?" Sure, he had people who shopped for him or brought to him whatever he expected, but I think it was the fact that someone thought of getting him something he hadn't asked for, just because. Such a simple thing, but it made him happy. He said, "No one has ever done that for me before. Thank you!" I could feel that little act of thoughtful kindness touched his heart. It felt so good to be able to give something unexpected to a man who was a constant giver and had given so much to me.

Rev. Ike had a burning desire to help people become better in all areas of their lives and he believed that every person could if they just learned the principles. He would regularly bid farewell with one of his favorite salutations that I love sharing even today: "I'm wishing you continued blessings of good health, healing, joy, love, success, prosperity, good fortune, and unlimited money!"

SUNDAYS FOR THE EIKERENKOETTERS

Xavier

At our Westchester, NY home, Dad had been awake since before dawn. After spending half an hour in silent meditation, he strolled the short distance from the house into the peaceful wooded side of the property where he could commune with nature. We all knew this first half hour was his solitary time of pure silence in preparation for the day. In addition to affirmative prayer, a significant part of his morning ritual included visualizing another spectacular "Joy of Living" meeting in New York. That was what he called his Sunday afternoon services at the United Church. He planned meticulously for each meeting, which demanded intense focus of spiritual and creative energy. What began as my father's process of daydreaming and fantasizing his future as a kid developed into a discipline he would deliberately adopt and make an official part of his spiritual practice. In great part, visualization is what he used to manifest his explosively successful ministry and exceptional life. Nature provided the peaceful backdrop, with the ancient trees that reflected life's magnificent cycles—witnessing more beautiful growth in each new season. This was a perfect setting to prime himself for his day ahead.

On this Sunday morning, hours before he would deliver his sermon, he prepared by closing his eyes and seeing himself smiling brightly as he took the stage, adorned in one of his beautiful custom-made suits, and seeing the congregation in advance, already on its feet, applauding wildly, eagerly hanging on to and absorbing his every word.

During his quiet visualization time, Dad was in a world of his own. As it related to his ministry, he practiced what he preached, which electrified his sermons with authenticity and a passion people could feel. He sincerely believed that he had to model what he was preaching, serving as an example that what he preached worked. "You can't lose with the stuff I use!" he often said. He knew they couldn't because he had repeatedly demonstrated for himself that his Science of Living philosophy worked.

As a youngster, I didn't understand the magnitude of his responsibilities. I only knew he was away a lot doing his thing. He had to be "on" all the time. His radio show was being broadcast to over 1,770 stations, and he did the broadcast from home. In the early days, sitting there with his reel-to-reel and his big booming voice delivering his weekly message, was a regular thing. He sometimes sat me on his knee while doing his recording for the show, and apparently it had enough impact on me that when someone once asked me when I was about three years old what my father's name was, I said, "Broadcast!"

The presence of hundreds, thousands, and eventually millions of people who believed in Dad's message, who wrote to him, who listened to him on the radio, and followed him weekly in his services, seminars, and crusades was the norm for me growing up. People wanted to see, be close to, and touch him. Even those who had a difficult time accepting his departure from the more oldline religious dogma found his message intriguing, and many were there just to see for themselves what all the fuss was about. Regardless of how they came to know him, they all wanted a piece of Rev. Ike.

Every Sunday was showtime, a full-on logistical operation that orchestrated multiple principal parties and their departures and arrivals, crowd control, and technical theatrics. The services at the Palace drew thousands from throughout the tri-state area because there was nothing like experiencing my father live and in person. Services often were attended by people from all over the world, being drawn from his European and African broadcasts. He also distributed his Blessing Plan, Success Ideas, and *Action Magazine* that reached six million people.

Following the services at the Palace, our family's legendary Sunday dinners took place. They were elaborate spreads, complete with servants. Indeed, they were feasts fit for kings, attended by family members, close friends, associate ministers, honored guests from out of town, and the occasional celebrity.

The dinners were held when he was in New York, and not out filling up auditoriums and stadiums in major cities. Rev. Ike had become a household name, being mentioned on popular television shows like *Sanford and Son*, featured in magazine articles, and appearing on popular television talk shows like *The Oprah Show*, *Larry King Live*, *The Phil Donohue Show*, and *The Mike Douglas Show*.

Dad had even been approached to appear in the movie *Car Wash*, but he turned it down because the script sounded too buffoonish. There was no way he was going to subject himself to anyone's comedic attempts at ridiculing him or his message. He saw nothing funny about teaching people the truth about themselves. Ultimately, the producers included a parody of my father in the movie, played by Richard Pryor, to capitalize on his popularity.

Nevertheless, he was clear to keep his focus on the people who were genuinely interested in his message. On Sunday mornings, he maintained a precise, meticulous process for getting ready to see them. From all accounts, the people cleaned up, dressed up, shined up, and stepped up to come to hear my famous father, the one and only Rev. Ike. They drove fine, polished, luxury cars or they rode on one of the many buses from all over the city. They even came by subway to fill up the United Church. Coming to see Rev. Ike was a special thing that both my father and those attending looked forward to.

This audience would also include people who decided to work smarter, not harder, by collaborating on the American Dream. There was example after example of working adults who pulled together to share a mortgage in the suburbs where Blacks could not even live just fifteen years earlier. Dad told them to see themselves living in better circumstances. As a result, many did. There were women who did laundry and men who worked double shifts at their industrial jobs, and then went home to give piano lessons to Black youngsters in ancient Harlem living rooms. People started saving money in several bank accounts because they began to see the truth of themselves, as someone better who deserved more, and their lives reflected it.

For my father, part of getting people excited about the message was getting them excited about church, and people were excited about church at the Palace. Dad was fond of saying his services weren't like those at the regular churches. "We have fun here." And he was adamant that there would be no downtrodden, sad, woe-is-me music like the type performed at the old traditional Black churches he came from. Dad recognized the significance of music, so he made certain the band's instrumentation was reminiscent of the more upbeat old-time gospel, but with revised and enlightening lyrics that reinforced his message.

Now that he was experiencing astronomical success, my father spent an inordinate amount of time maintaining it. Even when he was at home he was working, so we didn't spend much time together. He sometimes summoned me to his living room to have a "chat" with him from behind his newspaper as I sat uncomfortably on the couch. Aside from the Sunday dinners, there were few family meals together. On occasion, I joined him in his suite for lunch or brunch. We weren't your typical nuclear family, something my father informed Mom and me matter-of-factly, assuming we surely understood why he couldn't be the kind of traditional husband and father while traveling and evangelizing. Not while also maintaining his spiritual empire.

The public was mesmerized by my father and his assurances that, by changing their minds, they could change their lives. But I was a typical kid, and by the time I was a teenager, I had begun to resent the whole thing. In his absence, I had shut down my emotions toward my dad. I had learned to stop expecting him to be there for me. I was no longer interested in saying what he wanted to hear or hearing what he had to say. I felt bitter feelings whenever I was around my father. I loved him deeply but felt a constant hurt from not being able to be with him.

Earlier in my childhood, before this bitterness toward him had set in, I was completely used to being by myself, only child that I was, and not having a father to engage with me at home. Once, when I was watching television, he came in and asked if I wanted to go with him somewhere to do something or other. "No thanks," I replied. It was an honest answer from a little boy engrossed in a favorite television program who was not used to being taken out by his father. Later, when I was older, he told me that my response gave him the message that I didn't really want to hang out with him.

It must have hurt him. He had been crestfallen at my response. Nonetheless, that's what our relationship had come to. As I grew older, my disinterest moldered into disdain. Like any other normal boy, I initially wanted my father, but he wasn't there, and his lack of presence in my life had consequences. Although I had two parents, my mother and I constituted our nuclear family. She performed many of the duties typically done by fathers. If she wasn't driving me to my recreational activities, I'd be driven by one of our chauffeurs.

The defiant part of me resented how much of my father's time his ministry consumed. His image was everywhere, except with me, so although I wholeheartedly followed and agreed with his philosophy, I hated his fame because it didn't allow me to have my father. I saw other friends at school who had similar feelings about their fathers not being there for them. Like mine, their busy, successful fathers were rarely home. I was aware that the lifestyle he afforded me gave me access to privilege, money, wealth that he didn't have growing up, and he believed he was doing his best by me. I appreciated all of that, but in my heart and mind, that was no substitute for the emotional connection I craved. He was proud that he provided that way for me and for my mother. Of course, Mom was 50 percent responsible for the creation of the business.

He told me at one point that he was doing all of this for me, because he said, "I don't ever want you to experience poverty." His point of reference was always the pain he felt from the lack of financial support from his father. Grandfather was so neglectful after my grandparents split and he left them to wallow in poverty. It was a seminal experience that wounded my father and shaped his psychology forever. He never was able to fully heal that wound, and I think that was why he wanted me to be a reflection of him…a mini-me. The personal sacrifice and inner battles he had won to become who he was couldn't be lost when it was his time to leave the Earth. He was certain I was born to take over his empire.

Although I'd hear the powerful messages he'd broadcast each week, my bitterness tried hard to block out all his self-love, positive self-image, God-in-you mumbo-jumbo. As an older teenager, it all started to embarrass me. But even then, I was my father's son, and his message did manage to seep into my consciousness, despite my rebellion.

Juxtaposed to this major dissonant theme in our father-son relationship was the harmony we experienced together as spiritual thinkers. From childhood, I read and studied spiritual writings and texts. My father gave me an ongoing assignment of reading daily inspirational pieces from Religious Science's *Creative Thought Magazine* and writing down my favorite passages. I enjoyed this, finding it uplifting. When we periodically got together, he asked me to read them to him, and we discussed what they meant. I did this for years until I branched out into my self-appointed research into meditation and Eastern mysticism.

I grew up understanding exactly what Dad meant when he explained his Science of Living philosophy. I had fully ingested, digested (and sometimes regurgitated) it, by the time I was in my early teens. Our best times together may have been our deep philosophical and metaphysical conversations. I would pull a book from his extensive library and get his assessment of the author and contents, an understanding of the particular nuance of the approach, and how it compared to some of our favorites. We were eye-to-eye this way. I also enjoyed hearing him preach. He was, in fact, quite an inspiration to me as a spiritual teacher into my twenties.

As a child, I even went to sleep by his recorded sermons. He made it clear that his Science of Living, and later, Thinkonomics ideologies, were not theological doctrines but derived from the original Greek word, *gnostic*, meaning "to know." They consisted of his direct knowledge of how the divine moves and operates based on his authentic and personal experience with it, knowledge and experience he urged people to acquire for themselves. He was a model. Dad's intention was to teach techniques for healthy, happy, loving, successful, prosperous living. To accomplish that, a significant aspect of his ministry was helping people to *unlearn* religious dogma that had them believing in a God in the sky. He preached, convincingly, that God is in you, and he urged people to establish in their minds that this loving, infinite God wanted them to have and enjoy all the good they desired.

To get this into the minds of people week after week, my father put on a grand production, the behind-the-scenes of which moved like a well-oiled machine, even on Sundays when there might be a glitch in the system.

Reverend James Harding Council, Dad's associate for seven plus years, would be in full motion by 9:30 a.m., checking with the dozen men and women who were the official church ushers, making sure every one would be there and standby ushers were notified if they would be needed. By 10:00 a.m., he would start his commute to the city. He was responsible for opening and supervising the Sunday school programs, which began earlier than the main service at 11:00 a.m.

Out on Long Island, in the town of Hempstead, Dr. Alfred Miller would be reviewing the musical selections scheduled to be played at the service, sometimes making last minute changes. The timing of the music was important, and if there was a lapse in time, he would need to fill it by either lengthening the introduction of my father or by adding some music.

Ms. Anastasia Jones was a pianist and singer who was delighted to sing solos at the meetings. After navigating the challenging maze of show business and becoming disheartened, things had turned around professionally as soon as she agreed to perform at United Palace. She was so thankful for the big changes in her life she was happy to be there to offer her talents at a moment's notice.

From his phone in Orange, New Jersey, Dr. Robert Jiggetts would have already started coordinating the day with both Dr. Miller and Reverend Council, leading them through a last-minute check on the course of action they would each set into play as the day progressed. You would always see a four-man work team enter the Palace through the stage door with big crates as noon approached, and head directly for the area behind the pulpit. They set up big flower urns, the throne chairs, and carefully unpacked and displayed the crystal table lamps. While this was happening, the sound and media crew would arrive to set up their sound systems and cameras.

Sunday school classes would begin to wind down so all attendees would be right on time for Dad's first appearance of the day at mid-afternoon. At this point, the curtains out front would be closed in anticipation of that moment.

Around the same time, my father might be hosting a noon hour meeting with his ministerial staff. The focus could be anything from a new series of classes for young Science of Living ministers to last-minute arrangements upgrading the sound system. During those staff meetings, it was not unusual for my father to lapse into a lengthy monologue.

He was the first Black minister in America to preach positive self-image psychology to the Black masses within a church setting, and he knew it.

He wanted Black people to be able stop believing they could only be impoverished by seeing themselves, imaging themselves, as prosperous. He had done that for himself and firmly believed—and said frequently—that the best way to help the poor was not to be one of them. He understood just as firmly that once you are outside of poverty, you can help others get out too. He didn't miss any opportunity, even if he was speaking to just a few of his staff right before a service, to help others understand how it all had worked for him.

By 1:20 in the afternoon, Dr. Jiggetts would be downstairs with all the musicians, going over their schedules and reviewing music selections. A typical service might include Brother Coston, the organist when Jiggetts wasn't playing; Coston's wife, who would sometimes be called on to sing solo but mostly backed up the choir; Anastasia Jones, the go-to soloist; the favorite duet for five years, Marlene and Joanne Bennett, who were always up to speed on their numbers; and my father's personal drummer Thomas Odom. His special role was to rhythmically anchor the band and keep time when Dad and others sang.

A car from Westchester with Mom, me, and our driver would reach the Palace more than twenty minutes before Dad's lead car was due, and we would be escorted to our designated fifth-row seats in front while others were still filing in.

The United Palace would often be filled with well-dressed Black people who were living lives they'd previously thought unreachable. My father wasn't preaching to them about gaining equality with White people; he preached to them as though a person's color had no relevance to what their lives could become. Dad told his congregation that they deserved everything they wanted—cars, homes, scholarships, great health, harmonious relationships, everything. He told them to honor themselves and the efforts they made in the world. Dad told them they deserved commendation for their work and for their lives while they were still on Earth, that the minute they took responsibility and created their own life, they would receive all the blessings of God in them.

> *"I'm tired of talking about White. That worn out old cliché, that tired code name for failure. I stopped blaming White folks for things years ago. The minute I realized the White man doesn't control me, I do, then things got a lot better. There was a roadhouse, a little shack of a dining place in Georgia somewhere when I was a younger man. I was driving a year-old Cadillac, had a wad of about $2,500 in cash in my pocket when I pulled into the hash house to get myself something to eat. And they told me they did not serve Negroes. Very polite, but no food for a hungry traveling man.*

With just the money I had then I could have bought this joint, believe me. But I just walked away quietly. I didn't get angry because I knew, from that crazy incident, that I didn't ever need to hate Whitey anymore because I was going to be too busy for the rest of my life listening to the sound of money. What they said or did, naw, it didn't affect me one bit. I started hearing the constant rustle of cash filling my pockets right there in that no-name dusty little Georgia town. I just moved on."

Dad would be driven to the United Palace in the Rolls Royce limo. He once asked a young man who questioned the extravagance of the Rolls limo, "Would it help anyone if I got out of my car and rode a bicycle?" He did not believe that anyone's scarcity meant more for someone else. He believed that when we manifest good, it opens up the gateways wider for all to receive. Reality had to expand to accommodate the fulfillment of conscious desires. To contract one's expression of abundance was to shrink the cosmic gateways.

Dad's awareness of his indwelling God was so strong he sometimes spoke in language that shocked the religious to their core. He was not afraid to refer to himself as one with God saying, "I'm not God Almighty but I'm made in the image and likeness of God, therefore I'm Godstuff." He recognized the existence of God in everyone. Whether they recognized it in themselves was another matter, and my father was on a mission to enlighten humankind of its divinity.

By the time my father would reach the United Church, nearly 4,000 people would be in the fixed seats with more in folding chairs and several hundred more standing or seated in wheelchairs. Dad's teachings impacted people who were embracing the principles he preached and transforming their lives.

These were real people who had taken the leap into self-employment after assuming most of their lives that it was only natural that they worked for others and not themselves. These were real men and women who had started office cleaning businesses, revived old daycare centers and eventually expanded to three of four sites, and brought decrepit old motels back to life with their tireless work ethic. Others had started frozen custard franchises that serviced amusement parks or had flourishing appliance repair businesses. This was a Black community that had been reinvigorated about life and all of its possibilities. All by the man they eagerly awaited.

At precisely 2:30, in anticipation of his appearance, the Palace lights were dimmed and the crowd would go silent. Immediately, a spotlight formed a large circle around exit 29, which was his designated entry point, and a moment later my father would appear, immaculately dressed in a meticulously coordinated outfit including matching pocket scarf and tie, with exquisitely made jewelry that flashed every time he took a step, and a fresh boutonniere pinned to his breast pocket. He'd flash that movie-star smile toward his followers, and the television cameras caught every glorious moment.

"Everybody, give yourself a great big hug," he'd say.

Whether you were backstage, in the lobby, at the furthest corner of the auditorium, or in the nursery area, Dad's rich voice could be heard over the elaborate speaker system. His audience that was 90 percent Black would enthusiastically wrap their arms around themselves and reply as one, "Thank you, God in me!"

For those who could not be present, Dad read their letters. He shared testimonies from people across the US who were practicing mind science and changing their lives. Some had received unexpected IRS checks after shifting how they thought about money. He shared letters from those who had been cheerful givers of the ministry, having come to understand the truth of themselves and having received everything from new Buicks and new jobs to pay raises and sudden inheritances after expecting the God in them to bless them abundantly.

Microphone in hand, he would strut exuberantly along the edge of the stage. "All of you—*all of you*—can change your lives too, if you haven't already done it. All of you out there can have what you want to have."

"Yes, Lord," the audience would reply, almost in unison. "Hallelujah!"

The service would move, grow, and vibrate. Anastasia Jones might offer her most incredible ever rendition of the song, "I Believe," and tears would fill eyes throughout the auditorium. Later, he would lead them through an electrifying version of his favorite prayer-meditations.

> *"I now enter into my secret closet just like Jesus said. Repeat this after me, it's going to change your life forever."*

The people would repeat every word, faces uplifted, eyes closed, lips moving.

> *"I shut the door and I shut out doubt and fear, and I shut in faith and love."*

Often, there would be shrieks, and several women would be restrained from trying to reach the stage where my father sat on his green velvet throne, quietly leading the visualization.

> *"I enter the theater of my mind. I close my outer eyes and open the inner eye of faith where I see myself exactly as I wish to be. I see myself as a healthy person. I have no time for depression. There is no space in me for sadness. I love this God in me. Therefore, I love myself, and I see myself having all that I desire. I see money in my mind, more money than I've ever had before. Thank God for money, for having money, for making money. For money making money, for money, money, money, making money, money, money making money. Money, money making money, making money, money."*

This was a mantra for the purpose of helping people program their minds to receive money. This is the way he did it for himself and wanted to share with them, everything that had helped raise him out of poverty. While some traditionalists and fundamentalists not attending a United Church sermon might think it crass and inappropriate for a minister to invoke the spirit of money, my father said that it was one of the most consistent issues people wrote to him about and sought counseling with him about. He developed that mantra in response to the millions that contacted him in person, via radio and mail, to take care of all their concerns, such as health, happiness, love, success, prosperity, and money. He saw this mantra as covering just about everything. And, yes, money was a part of it.

He concluded the session with the same powerful benediction prayed at all of his gatherings.

> *"And now the presence and the power, the love, the healing, the strength, the best, the prosperity, the success, all the good that God is, go with you, above and beneath you, behind and beside you, within you and before you, and make smooth, beautiful and perfect your way. Amen."*

Dad would walk toward the stairs that led to his upper-level study after stage curtains had closed around him. As happy churchgoers made their way to the exits, empowered for another week of being creators of a better life, he would disrobe out of sweat-filled clothing for a quick shower in preparation for a press conference with yet another group of skeptical journalists. Interviews finished, and after pausing to wave gratefully at a crowd gathered around the stage door, he'd step outside and into the opened door of the Rolls Royce.

More than 4,000 inspired folks would head back to their lives with spiritual tools to navigate the week ahead. While those individuals, couples, and families were leaving the Palace reliving the time spent with Rev. Ike, my father, my mother, and I would make the trip back to our Westchester estate to have our Sunday dinner.

WE RISE TOGETHER

Mark

I can say without doubt that from the time I met Rev. Ike and inculcated the wisdom, philosophy, insights, and principles he taught; my life continued to move in a skyward-bound trajectory. I was a budding young professional speaker when I first came into the United Palace. I gained confidence, poise, and ultimately the stature and influence to attract ever bigger clients, and ever more lucrative contracts.

It led to my realization that people wanted more of what I could bring to them. The idea I had for plotting one's future positively in that journal called my "Sunshine Diary" that I had bravely shared with Rev. Ike in our first meeting evolved into my first book called *Future Diary*, published a few years after I met Rev. Ike. The book was a great success, which I sold from the platform to my growing audiences around the world as I became one of the most sought-after speakers of the time. Ultimately, that led to my opus—the creation of the *Chicken Soup for the Soul* series, which to date has sold over 500 million copies. With that came the opportunity to speak to millions of people around the globe and create a lot of wealth and notoriety.

Rev. Ike was very supportive of me and my work the entire time, and I think he actually felt a bit proud of the fact that he knew his mentorship had helped me soar to the great heights I was reaching. His famous words I'd heard time and time again, turned out to be exactly correct for me. *"You can't lose with the stuff I use...."*

My relationship with Rev. Ike went from student-mentor to mentor-peer, and then to a deep and lasting friendship.

As Rev. Ike's ministry continued to grow, naturally he kept growing with it, and part of that was his desire to reach outside of his current following and tap into new audiences who could receive the unique value and guidance he provided. The first time I booked Rev. Ike was with a speaker's bureau I started in the eighties called "Look Who's Talking." Reverend Peggy Bassett had a church in Huntington Beach, California, with 17,000 attendees, and had asked me if I could book Rev. Ike to speak at her church. Rev. Ike was a huge hit, and since then I had always looked for opportunities to share his wisdom on different platforms. Through my company he shared the stage with prominent speakers and leaders like Dr. R. Buckminster Fuller, Dr. Bernie Siegel, Rita Davenport, Les Brown, Ray Bradbury, Og Mandino, and many others.

I was happy to be a catalyst for those expanded experiences he was seeking. By 1998, I had formed another company called Enlightened Millionaire Institute with two other partners. We held big events around the country to packed audiences of up to 4,000 people. I was extremely blessed to know so many talented speakers, teachers, salespeople, ministers, and leaders, and I felt a duty to share them and their wisdom with my ever-growing list of well-heeled clients. The speakers and my clients would benefit as new ideas would be shared. One of my favorite personalities to book was the incredible Reverend Ike. He certainly had "arrived" at that point in his life and didn't need to do another thing. Even with Ike's profound fame and recognition in the world, he still wanted to touch more people with the message he knew could help them grow. Despite the supreme confidence he carried and extravagance with which he lived his life, Rev. Ike had a special humility that was very much in alignment with the words of Christ:

> *The greatest amongst you will be your servant.*
> (Matthew 23:11 NIV)

For Reverend Ike, this life was about self-mastery through a true understanding of the principles shared in the living Word of the Bible. He knew the learning was never done. He knew he needed to continue studying and immersing himself in the highest thinking that was in alignment with the undeniable principle that we as the offspring of the Creator must constantly pursue the truth to discover within ourselves ever-evolving wisdom leading to a true mastery of living and being. Life would continue to happen and to present challenges. Every day presented the opportunity for new decisions and new choices. He knew that one can get into a comfort zone when things are going well and become complacent in his or her pursuit of excellence.

Though sometimes accused of being a self-serving egomaniac by those who knew of him at a superficial level, Rev. Ike's true essence was that of principled service. His intense immersion into the Bible from infancy exposed to the intuitive young Frederick a clear discrepancy between the gospel promises and how his mother and so many others in the Black community lived. At the youngest age of reasoning he began to discern that their own acceptance of their poor, downtrodden existence was an inaccurate interpretation of God's Word. That liberating truth became galvanized inside of him to a point he became determined to never waver from it. There was only one track of belief for him. You couldn't doubt your worthiness and still have a plentiful life.

> *"You shall not sow your vineyard with two kinds of*
> *seed, or all the produce of the seed which you have sown*
> *and the increase of the vineyard will become defiled."*
> (Deuteronomy 22:9 NASB)

Rev. Ike knew his value. He knew if he provided value to God's people he would be rewarded greatly like a king. He understood the principles and the law.

> *"Give, and it will be given to you. Good measure,*
> *pressed down, shaken together, running over, will be*

put into your lap. For with the measure you use it will
be measured back to you."
(Luke 6:38 NIV)

Even as a wealthy man, he made sure he got paid his fee any time he spoke for my agency or on anyone else's stage. He recognized that value was a circle. You must give value, and you must be willing to receive value. He didn't waiver, because he perceived at a tender age that it was the lack of people's belief in their own value that caused poverty. My amazing friend knew the rewards that were his were in balance with the tremendous good he did by freeing millions of people from the enslavement of their own flawed beliefs. Beliefs that had been perpetuated by church doctrine that presented poverty as virtuous, coupled with a government social system that reinforced mediocrity by doling out just enough to help people survive, but never taught them to excel and thrive. It was one of the topics my friend would justifiably get on a rant about.

He was also the first person to use his own money to pay for a young man to go to college, or help a young pastor fund his expenses as he was getting started. He lived unfailingly by the principles he taught. He knew by him having more, nobody else had less. Having more money led to paying for more publicity, which led to more members, who became more people who learned to create their own freedom and prosperity knowing that they were powered by God.

He spent all those years as a young lad walking back and forth to school because his mom's choice was to live in lack. He made a different choice to live in luxury, and that shift in consciousness had him living in a completely different world than the one in which his own mother had chosen to exist.

I remember talking to Rev. Ike after a church service where he had been sermonizing on prosperity. I knew darn well it wasn't going to be convenient for him, but he told me he was traveling 3,000 miles to attend a Positive Mental Attitude Rally, the kind I talked at around the world. With all he had going on at any given time, it couldn't have been easy for him to juggle his demanding schedule and still make the time to go listen to other brilliant teachers of truth, but he had an attitude of insistence to continue to learn while he was here on this planet. Rev. Ike also had a childlike wonder about the universe and her mysteries. His heart was humble, and he was willing to learn from others who might have a new perspective on the secrets of living greatly. It was that hunger for righteousness that he defined this way:

> *"The right usefulness of your mind is a mandate from God within. Every moment of trial and temptation is a moment to overcoming and victory. In 1 Corinthians 10:13 it tells us, You will experience no temptation that is above your ability to bear. In other words, the very moment that you catch your mind creating opposition, you had better come back into agreement that there is but one presence, one power, one mind, God, the good, divine love, omnipotent.*
>
> *You see, in the one God, every man is God of his own experience. Now, universal or infinite God or consciousness, grants certain privileges and entitlements to individualized mind or man. Individualized mind or man can choose. You have the power of choice."*

I'm not sure I've met another human being in my vast travels who was so diligent in his determination to sculpt his perfect life through the correct choosing of the thoughts and visualizations that would manifest every single dream he had into existence. Using his own mastery of the principles of the words spoken by the Master Jesus and the prophets of old, he extracted the supernatural force within those messages and demonstrated true miracles for himself and others.

GROWING BUSINESS AND ACCOUNTABILITY

Xavier

My dad's success and the expansive reach of his ministry put him on par with contemporaries of his day, such as Billy Graham and Oral Roberts, but as the first mega-media ministry created by a Black man. It was a huge operation, and what helped it grow rapidly on a solid foundation was the meticulous work my Mom did with record keeping. From the beginning she and Dad knew that to avoid any potential legal and financial problems, the organizational records needed to be clean, no--crystal clear. At inception, she made sure that the business ran properly and everything was well accounted for. Her methodology was initially antiquated, but proved to be everything needed for professional accountants to pick up the job when things grew to a certain level.

A stroke of providence brought my parents together with Bradley Steinberg, the man who would become their longtime accountant. Mom and Dad were brought to Brad's attention by a friend who was subleasing part of his commercial space in Boston to them.

The friend reached out to Brad because Mom, who was still the head of business operations for the ministry, was advised by counsel to procure a sharp accountant.

What Brad discovered when he eventually met with my mother was vastly different from what he expected. He'd been told that my father was a local evangelist growing in popularity who received a large volume of mail, often containing cash donations. The pastor based his operation in a leased office where his neat, soft-spoken wife worked every day of the week answering letters and managing the mail and donations.

Full of easy assumptions based on what he knew of disreputable religious entrepreneurs, Brad did not see the point of meeting with my parents

Brad guessed there had to be some sloppy bookkeeping or impropriety similar to what was happening at the other storefront ministries popping up for the last few years in the Boston area.

He was ready to decline a meeting with them, but his friend urged him to speak with my parents because they were undeniably outstanding tenants. They were extremely courteous and meticulously clean. Best of all, they paid their rent early each month. The friend who was subleasing the space to my parents was impressed because, even with the gigantic volume of mail they had received at the building, my parents kept their office orderly and tidy at all times. As their landlord, he didn't fully understand everything they were doing. The nature of their work was a bit of a mystery to him, yet they seemed to be fine people.

Against what he thought was his better judgment, Brad called the office, perhaps prompted by something larger than his doubts. My mother answered and assured him she would be able to supply any relevant documentation to explain all my father's organizational and personal finances.

He got straight to the point. "Who is the accountant or bookkeeper currently handling the business books?"

"We don't have an accountant or bookkeeper. I handle all of that myself," she replied.

"So, I'm assuming you must have some training as a bookkeeper?"

"I do not," Mom replied. "I've always done that myself. I created my own system."

"Do you have the exact figures on what your husband receives in the mail or on-site contributions?"

When Mom remained quiet, Brad assumed she was being evasive due to inadequate record keeping.

"I don't know how she did it but she convinced me to come down to their office. She was a persuasive woman. We sat in the small space that was furnished with only two tables, a desk and chair, and a couple of file cabinets. She showed me around, and then led me to a closet door where paper towel boxes had been repurposed as file storage and stacked neatly in rows. Each one was sealed and carefully labeled. She lifted one out and set it on one of the tables. When she opened the flaps I looked inside and saw hundreds of small squares of paper, tightly folded and stacked in straight, neat rows." Each was organized by date and in alphabetical order, detailing the ministry's expenditures from the beginning. Mom was extremely fastidious and had let nothing slip by her purview. Expenses had been tracked on individual papers with clear, simple notations. Each dime pressed into a parking meter had been logged, citing the day, place, and the reason for the particular expense like "Picked up flowers for sanctuary."

Every mile they had driven for business purposes was listed with the proportionate gas mileage. Every single corresponding name of companies they'd done business with were there, dates were listed, addresses documented, and telephone numbers carefully noted. The whole thing would have impressed the strictest of bookkeepers. Everything down to the staples to attach letters was tracked. Not a thing was left unrecorded.

"Frankly, I had never seen anything like it. She was able to lay the groundwork for the information that could advance and preserve her husband's career."

Brad told them they'd have to give him a little time. It would likely be months before he would have it all entered into a proper accounting system. He dove into the task, getting more absorbed as he worked. His few hours per week eventually became a few days of work per week as he created a definitive structure for my parents to reconstruct and track income into the future. When he needed something else to put the full picture together, Mom was there with every detail. The scrupulous work their new accountant did to get through each and every paper record Mom had prepared informed Brad that my parents operated the business with the utmost honesty and integrity, as well as disciplined accuracy.

Far different from his initial concerns, my parents' new accountant found their entire operation to be financially solvent and impressively growing more prosperous every day. The law of attraction was certainly at play because my father was planning to expand his operation tremendously and would need a modern accounting system a sharp accountant like Brad could develop. He and Dad had not even met, but a destined partnership was developing based on each man's impeccability and how he moved in the world.

Brad began to methodically construct the new books for my father and his ministry, spending more and more time in the small office. By the end of the summer, he was reaching the point where he could turn over the new accounting system he created to my mom and her staff so he could move onto assignments at other companies. It was late afternoon, the little office was getting warm, and he was ready to call it a day. As he was finishing his final task, he looked up, surprised to see a slender, flashily dressed Black man let himself into the office with his own key. Brad was a conservative looking young man with glasses, and based on my mother's similarly conservative appearance, Dad's flamboyant style threw him for a loop. Matching my father's appearance was his gregarious demeanor and his loud, engaging laugh.

Opposing appearances aside, they had an instant appreciation for their respective accomplishments. Brad respected the success my parents had achieved in their ministry while staying grounded and fiscally prudent. Dad was grateful for the accountant's willingness to step in at a moment's notice and dedicate himself to developing a foolproof system for classifying and standardizing their financial information.

Brad confessed to my father that he'd been amazed at his wife's conscientious attention to the smallest details of their business. "She began bringing out the boxes that contained every one of the thousands of letters you received, with notations that stated the exact amount of a donation. She even included the form of the money, from denomination of currency to checks or money orders. Everything I would need was something she had thought through and had organized and available. It was just a matter of sorting it out. At first, I wanted to avoid getting involved. After I saw what she'd done here I was happy to help."

The only real dilemma they had between them was Brad's embarrassing inability to pronounce the name Eikerenkoetter.

"You aren't the first and you certainly won't be the last who has trouble with our name," Dad persuaded him. "As you become associated with me, the way I'd like you to, it stops being that difficult. But for now, just call me Reverend Ike like everyone else."

"Did you say something about being associated with you?" the accountant asked. "Our work is pretty much finished, actually."

"No," my father replied confidently. "Our work is just beginning!"

Brad became an integral part of my parents' team. He faithfully maintained their books, relieving my mom of a good amount of minutia so that she could focus on other aspects of the business. They worked so well together that Bradley Steinberg became General Manager and built out the operational staff at the eventual UCEA (United Christian Evangelistic Association) operations building in Boston that would house the international mail ministry. This allowed Dad to continue generating millions through his work without any concerns for the business.

The United Church at United Palace in NYC was also part of UCEA's multimillion-dollar business that employed a full-time director of education and special activities and a staff of four (including Dad) full-time salaried ministers to serve the needs of the congregation. The church also provided confidential assistance to those having substance abuse problems and their families, a legal assistance fund, and counseling to redirect troubled youth. All the services provided by the church were based on Science of Living principles because the solution to any of life's ills rested in people understanding the power of their mind and their ability to rely on the God in them to guide them.

Proud of the ministry and all its services, Dad explained, "The cost of running this organization is very high. We publish *Action Magazine*, which goes free of charge to a million and a half people twice a month. We buy television and radio time and pay for advertising and the cost of running the organization. We are, I am happy to say, a multimillion-dollar organization, and our expenses are also multimillion."

Dad knew the FBI kept a file on him and that the IRS scrutinized his business closer than others, but he never worried because he knew the books were in order. Adhering to spiritual law meant automatic alignment with all legitimate man-made laws. Even though my father was aware that he was held to stricter standards as a Black man than his White counterparts, that fact was not the motivation for his financial impeccability. He was simply a man of integrity, and every aspect of his business reflected that.

He was always forthcoming about the business, which no doubt astounded some people. Although the church was a religious nonprofit organization that was not required to, he was in favor of churches paying taxes because doing so might get more money into the hands of those who needed it. He made that opinion public in an interview with television and radio personality Tom Snyder, but he didn't want his to be the only church paying taxes. He was ready to pay taxes when the others did too. That he paid taxes on his salary was something else he revealed in the interview, along with the annual figure, which was $50,000 at the time. He knew that some people thought his income was also tax exempt, and he wanted it on the record that he paid taxes like everyone else. His salary was a good one for the time, but of course, he also had a liberal expense account that allowed him to spend money on clothing, among other things.

He had his mother to thank for his organizational skills that, ironically, informed the way he handled money. Although she espoused religious-based scarcity and believed she deserved the poverty they endured, she insisted on structure, order, and cleanliness in their home. His childhood chores and an innate desire for doing things well prepared him for running a multimillion-dollar operation.

His father also factored into Dad's successful managing of his business. He had something to prove to the man who, although quite prosperous, refused to support his own flesh and blood.

And, of course, he had the ultimate organizational and money management weapon: his wife. The Lord had provided him with helpful models and a superb helpmate. Added to the philosophy he'd adopted in childhood and came to understand fully as an adult, it was an unbeatable formula for prosperity.

MASTERY OF THE LAW OF INCREASE

Mark

The Law of Increase was ever present and at work in Rev. Ike's life from the time he began preaching at age fourteen. He saw it operating on every plane and growing in its expression along with him. As he gave his time, talent, and the little treasure he had, the rewards of Heaven started to pour out, first as small victories and rewards, then unfurling a path that continued to cultivate redeemed souls, transformed lives, and a tremendous amount of personal wealth and success for him. He taught that Spirit in you seeks expansion and increase. If we believe small and bury our talents and treasure our lives remain flat.

> *"I am one of the only preachers who preaches money into your pockets. I can then preach it out of your pocket to help you multiply yourself with seed money donations to this church. Your prosperity is not determined by world conditions but by the conditioning of your mind power.*
>
> *My favorite Bible verse is Jeremiah 17:7 and 8. 'Blessed is the man/mind, who believes in, trust in, and relies*

on the Lord/Law of Mind and whose hope and confidence the Lord is. They will be like a tree planted by the water that sends out its roots by the stream. It does not fear when heat comes; its leaves are always green. It has no worries in a year of drought and never fails to bear luscious fruit.'"

From the earliest whisperings in his inner knower, Rev. Ike had a deep understanding that step-by-step he'd master getting congregants to tithe and their lives would miraculously improve.

People of great wealth like J.P. Morgan, Carnegie, Buffett, the Walton family, and Oprah often credit their successes with being active and perpetual tithers and givers. There is an impressive correlation in the world of business titans between giving and receiving. Rev. Ike understood the scriptural foundations to the law of tithing at the most tender age of awareness when he would witness his mother putting a representational number of precious coins in the church basket, regardless of how little they had. As his influence and affluence grew, the cycle of reaping what you sow became undeniably evident in his life.

Weekly, I watched a master preaching valuable sermons eloquently and fervently, always enthusiastically including a message of tithing, inviting congregants into the glorious cycle of giving and receiving as old as time itself. As a result, I personally beheld his devoted tithers prospering greatly—many of them ecstatic to witness in front of 5,000 attendees their personal detailed experience of increase of opportunities, money, and status because they were dedicated givers. I participated cheerfully with others when Rev. Ike requested people with a hundred-dollar-bill or more walk forward and bring it to the stage. It was a money altar call that was inspiring to watch. He demonstrated amazing courage, belief, to keep the flow of giving in his church. Because of that, he was able to offer to his congregation not just a transformational experience of deep scriptural and spiritual learning accompanied by glorious music in a beautiful environment, he also made available to all the Science of Living institute, the Business of Living classes, special children's programs, and so much more.

Haywood Hodges was one of the men I'd regularly stand next to at the weekly altar call. Haywood was working as a building superintendent in New York City, a fancy name for a janitor. He was only earning forty-seven dollars a month in 1972. His wife said in her testimony before Rev. Ike at the Palace, "It was hell trying to live on nothing but fumes every month." Haywood started attending Rev. Ike's Palace church services regularly in the early '70s and listening incessantly to his audios. What he learned changed his mind, life, and future.

Haywood started seeing himself differently through the teachings and began to look for better opportunities. He was offered a job selling life insurance and became an immediate success. He started prospering and couldn't stop telling everyone about his good fortune. Others wanted to join him and prosper too, so he started the Haywood Hodge Life Insurance Agency, hiring and training multitudes of agents to be all they could be and become financially independent.

"Now we have our offices in the most prestigious location in New York City, the World Trade Center. We are doing over eighty million dollars' worth of business a year (in 1975)," Haywood proudly announced to the congregation.

By that time, I had grown my speaking and training business, and my training that taught life insurance agents how to successfully sell was in high demand. I officially introduced myself to Haywood while standing next to him sharing our tithing at the church altar. Later we started chatting and I told Haywood that I train life insurance agents to double their income and triple their time off. Haywood hired me on the spot. I trained all his people for years to each be earning over $100,000 a year within a year, by thinking rich, feeling rich, being rich, and selling at least one policy per working day.

We learned and grew together under Rev. Ike's tutelage and enriched one another's goals. We stood together many a week as dedicated tithers, priming the fountain that continued to pour out to us. We celebrated ours and others' successes over countless great meals together at the Windows on the World restaurant on top of the World Trade Center North Tower, where his magnificent offices were. Haywood wanted to give everyone willing and wanting to work an immediate hand-up because he had tremendous gratitude that against the odds, he had risen from rags to riches. With Rev. Ike's inspired philosophy and teachings, Haywood created hundreds of new millionaires, encouraging them all to attend services at Rev. Ike's United Palace and to join us in the glorious cycle of giving and receiving.

Rev. Ike articulated perfectly that tithing is neither a gift, reward, charity, nor payment for services rendered.

> *"It is one-tenth, or more, of your income. It is spiritually owned by the original Source of all things. The Lord requests that each person voluntarily gives back ten percent to that Source."*

It is up to us to discern the best choice to which we return our tithes that is in alignment with the highest good we and others are receiving in the advancement of the expression of Heaven on Earth. As an adept student of the Bible, Rev. Ike taught that a tithe was originally 10 percent of the flocks, herds, goods, or produce. It was the best of that that was to be given to the Lord. When money became the medium of exchange the tithe became 10 percent of all the financial earnings that a person created or earned.

> *"Tithing is the master's Law of Increase. If you want increase, you have to tithe and keep on tithing. Tithing keeps the tither, the giver, in contact with the Source of All. It affirms that you understand there is a creative and invisible power that is experienced only by the tithers. The fruits of the law are contingent upon the observance of the continuing act and practice of tithing by you! God is the original Source of all things. He gave you everything and only asks that you give back a portion."*

"And all the tithe of the land, whether of the land, whether of the seed of the land, or of the fruit of the tree, is the Lord's: it is holy unto the Lord."
(Leviticus 27:30 KJV)

An astute communicator, Rev. Ike talked about the true purpose and Law of Tithing stated in Malachi 3:10 (KJV):

"Bring ye all the tithes into the storehouse, that there may be meat in mine house, and prove me now herewith, saith the Lord of Hosts, if I will not open you the windows of Heaven, and pour you out a blessing, that there shall not be room enough to receive it."

It was important to the reverend that you believe in the Law of Increase and the Law of Tithing before you give. At one service he thundered:

"Some of you won't believe what I am going to say next. I don't want you to give, unless two things:

You believe you will make a whole lot more, thanks to voluntarily giving/tithing.

You believe that because of this ministry you can become infinitely more successful, prosperous and, yes, rich.

Rev. Ike was the boldest asker for tithes that I have ever witnessed. At one service, he handed out mock checks made out to United Church for a million dollars each. He asked everyone to put them into their purse, wallet, or pocket and meditate on that reality, which would mean that they had earned a net ten million. It was an exciting possibility that raised every congregant's imagination, thinking, and belief into overdrive. It became a reality for a few people who truly believed. Everyone was enchanted with the idea of having overflowing and ever flowing abundance.

"The Law of Tithing is directly related to the Law of Sowing and Reaping.

2 Corinthians 9:6 (KJV) says, 'Whoever sows sparingly will also reap sparingly, and whoever sows generously will also reap generously,' and Galatians 6:7, 'Do not be deceived: God cannot be mocked. A man reaps what he sows.

"It is true in agriculture and in life. It is simple cause and effect preserved voluntarily by the giver. At the front end of receiving, one must first give."

I have my own personal testimony about learning the Law of Tithing from Rev. Ike. Even after having faithfully attended many different churches throughout my young life, I never *got* the tithing message. After hearing the message at United Palace, it finally took on relevance and meaning. I saw that it worked, and I decided to work it. My success, influence, and wealth began to accelerate in every good way. I was so grateful for the blessings I experienced through tithing that I sought out countless stories that demonstrated the power of tithing and wrote a book called *The Miracle of Tithing*. It has gone through numerous reprintings. I have stacks of letters thanking me for sharing the truth of tithing. I must say that I have had mega-churches buy 5,000 copies at a time and give them out to their congregants during fundraising sessions, many of them achieving record-breaking giving by doing so. I wrote the book in the spirit of a giver wanting other givers to know the truth and be set free financially, a profoundly valuable lesson I credit to my dear friend.

Rev. Ike's life was a perfect proof positive of the laws he taught. He started out with little but his wishes and dreams, but by offering himself wholly to God, he obtained life's most glorious riches. Once he received, he turned around and gave again, and kept giving. Everyone who received his largesse was graciously asked to keep it quiet and never mention it. He honored Christ's admonition in Matthew 6:4 (ESV), *"so that your giving may be done in secret. And your Father who sees in secret will reward you."*

I have interviewed countless recipients of his large tithes to different churches and each pastor told me the generous amount given. Rev. Ike walked his talk every day of his life.

He was always sure to remind us of this simple truth: *"Life gives to the giver and takes from the taker."*

EIKERENKOETTER'S WORLD TRAVELS

Xavier

My father knew from a very young age he wanted to see the world. He yearned to see other cultures, and to experience other people and their ways of living. The family took a lot of fabulous trips through the years, and he even had Dr. Alfred and Jessie Miller run cruising excursions that were available to the entire congregation so they could see the world too. Notwithstanding the strain that was present in my relationship with my father at times, some of my favorite memories with him were family vacations.

One such experience was the time Dad's assistant, Terry Hudson, traveled with Dad and me to Egypt, the holy land, and Italy around my sixteenth birthday. It was an awesome trip memorialized in fabulous photos we took. I'll never forget an absolutely hilarious episode that happened when Terry and I coaxed Dad up on top of a camel. We were on the Giza plateau near the great pyramid of Cheops marveling at the awesome splendor of the mystical monuments. There was a man with a camel there offering rides. Terry and I both took rides. The camel walked with a loping gait that engaged every bone in my body, necessitating me to follow his motion in order to relax into my position atop this strange, tall creature that spit and groaned as we went along. When I caught its rhythm, it was a most pleasurable experience. I was in Egypt next to the Great Pyramid riding a camel. Woohoo! It was fun.

When we had completed our rides, Terry and I asked my dad to get on and take a ride. He was adamantly against it.

We kept badgering him until he relented. He hesitantly walked over to the camel that was docilely kneeling waiting for its next victim. He swung his leg over, holding tightly to the pommel, and before he could get settled, the camel stood up, sending Dad reeling backwards, barely staying in the saddle, desperately clutching the pommel with both hands and his man bag under his left armpit. That bag held his cash, checkbook, credit cards, and passport, so I think he would have hung onto it even if bucked off the beast.

Terry and I exploded into laughter, and were doubled over trying to contain it, one step from rolling in the sand. When the camel stood on its back legs, my father swung in the opposite direction with a "Whooooaaaa!" By now we were laughing so hard we could barely breathe.

The camel proceeded to lope around the plain with Dad shouting, "Get me off this thing!" and shaking his fist at us between grasps at the pommel. Youthfully mischievous, Terry and I convinced the handler that the ride should continue. My dad had a once-in-a-lifetime experience on the Egyptian camel looking like something between a drunken cowboy and Don Quixote swinging at windmills. The visual is eternally emblazoned on my mind and still causes me to chuckle.

We used to cruise together as a family. One holiday cruise we took, I flew down to Miami to embark with Dad. Mom, Aunt Kay, and her daughters were meeting us there since they had wanted to board the ship earlier. I have warm memories of this cruise as it was during a time when I was courting my future wife, Annette, and spent considerable time on expensive ship-to-shore calls, checking in with each other. It was a particularly quiet and peaceful vacation and not too crowded, which was just the way both Dad and I liked it.

Another time, our family decided to take a Caribbean cruise during holiday time on a popular cruise line. Dad and I were both a bit reluctant to get on as it was a huge new ship and would hold a giant crowd of people. We both liked to hermit out on vacations and not be surrounded by thousands of rushing travelers. Once on the ship, it was just as we feared: a huge crowd experience with its concomitant raucous activity and noise. We joked with each other about jumping ship. After three days somewhere in the Caribbean, probably in Puerto Rico, in the midst of doing just that completely independent of each other, we met up on the gangway, each of us quietly disembarking the ship with our respective luggage in search of some peace.

We looked up and saw each other and broke into laughter. Like father, like son.

BISHOP E. BERNARD JORDAN

MY STORY WITH REVEREND IKE

One might assume that as hard as Reverend Ike worked to build his ministerial enterprise, he might be protective of his teachings, even averse to letting his pastoral competitors try to scoop up a piece of the enormous pie he had created. In reality, other aspiring Black ministers like me were surprised how unconcerned he was about that. As I got to know Ike, he made it clear that he wanted me to succeed. I felt like he wanted more for me than I wanted for myself and was willing to share his resources to help me make that happen.

Rev. Ike had a remarkable way of encouraging younger new pastors to be their best, even if from all outward appearances it would seem they might be in competition with him. I was one of those young pastors who had a growing ministry in New York City in the nineties.

I was introduced to the teachings of Rev. Ike by some of his attendees who also came to my church. They wondered if I would like to meet Rev. Ike. I decided to invite him to a breakfast I was having, not sure if he would consider taking the time to come. To my delight, he did, and immediately took an interest in me and what I was doing with my ministry. I invited him to come to see my church sanctuary, and he accepted, asking me to ride in the Rolls Royce. He had such a big heart, and from the beginning he seemed to care deeply about me and the difference I was making. We became friends.

Rev. Ike had so many talents, but the one I was most impressed by was his unfaltering ability to maintain a level of prosperity consciousness. I loved how he mastered his mind. He could hold consciousness, to bypass all negative thoughts, doing the work consistently to keep his life in alignment with his highest values of truth, light, and abundance of God.

He would not get into anything that would promote worry or concern. He didn't want to know what the light bill was or any of the minutia that would pull him from the creative realm he lived in. He wanted no concerns that would occupy his space in consciousness. His investment broker handled all of his investments and moved the resources around for him. He didn't go into the details. He lived his own principles of money so well and had been ultra-successful at generating and investing a lot of money. He was so internally complete with money, finances, and property, that he was masterful at just *being*.

Shortly after we met, he began to advise me, particularly with my mail and television ministry. Rev. Ike taught me so many things.

Under his direction, my mail list grew from twenty thousand to over one million names. I was on TV seven times a week. I gained national recognition on BET, Word Network, and others. I had been doing TV before I met Rev. Ike, but with little success.

I came to understand there are three ways to grow a business—product, organization, and customer intimacy. Rev. Ike did all of them well within his enterprise, but the one at which he was an unmatched master was the customer intimacy. He guided my gifts to figure how I could be more impactful going forward. I referred to him as my 3:00-a.m.-friend. He didn't need a lot of sleep and would spontaneously reach out to me, even at all hours of the night after he had been reading up on something I'd done.

He ran his operation like a business, and he taught me to do a lot better with my own investments. He continued to advise me on how to structure and restructure my ministry throughout the years. I appreciated his mentorship and even decided to redo my entire library by ordering all the books Rev. Ike had in his library.

From time to time, choices came up and I would ask him about whether I should do this or that. I once mentioned that I was struggling with the choice of: build the church in the mountains or in the city? He told me I could have my cake and eat it too, that I didn't have to cut off one to have the other.

> *"You can think God can only do this or that.... God can do this **and** that. Build the church."*

Well, he was right. I built it. Eventually I sold it and came back to the city, and then went on to build a big online ministry with thousands of followers worldwide. He was a big help in the beginning of my ministry. I could only look back and marvel at the memory of what he poured into me financially, as well as spiritually. That's why it was nothing for me to send him my tithes. He didn't want to take it, but he knew it was important to receive it from me, so he took it and used it for his ministry.

Reverend Run was a young man when he came to my ministry, broke and bankrupt. He went up the ranks with me from a deacon, to minister, to reverend. I mentored, educated him, and got him back up on his feet. His success took off! He ended up doing the popular *Run's House*, a reality TV show about his family, and became a part owner in Baby Phat, making millions and millions of dollars. Run was so grateful to me he gave me a brand-new Rolls Royce as a tithe for my years of mentorship to him. It was a four hundred-thousand-dollar car. I knew I owed so much of my life and success to Rev. Ike that I turned around and gave that car to him as a tithe. It was the least I could do for my friend and advocate.

Rev. Ike was always working on something new. He wrote his sermons every week. Often, he would write a sermon and fax it to me saying, "This is what I'm preaching on this week."

It was like he wanted me to know his thoughts and share it with my congregations. He was so unselfish in that way. His actions in so many ways made me realize he lived to serve. He loved teaching and preaching about the prodigal son. The prodigal son wasted his life in riotous living and then realized he could return to the father and have the most joyful reunion of abundance, love, and happiness, to finally be welcomed home. This might have been the reconciliation of the rejection of Rev. Ike's own father within himself. He understood these biblical principles were real in a deeply personal way and that one was about himself. He didn't just preach it. He lived it.

Rev. Ike had a big operation, and within that, he had a lot of loyal people that stayed with him for decades. They were committed to him and the work he did to make the world a better place. He was such a giver. He gave and would not announce what he would give you. What a philanthropist he was! I think if someone did the work to figure out how many people he put through school, how many ministries he supported, they would be amazed, but he kept it secret. He wanted no credit and expected no repayment. He had "spiritual sons and daughters." Kids that came into his life through church or other connections; kids who were hungry to learn and grow but often didn't have the financial support they needed to get an education—he mentored all of us. He cared deeply and inquired regularly to find out how he could help. He made it clear that his reward was making the difference for another human being.

At the end of his life, it was hard to see him go. But in his later years he had shared with me that he felt like he no longer wanted to be on the Earth. He was retiring. He was happy and peaceful, but he was done. "I've seen everything I could see," he said. "There's nothing else to experience on this side of Earth. There is no other place for me to go… it's time to be beside the Lord."

Reverend Ike's legacy will always live on in me and so many others.

THE RICHES OF KING SOLOMON

Mark

Gazing over my notes in the green room at Rev. Terry Cole Whitaker's mega church in San Diego, California, I looked up and saw Rev. Ike coming toward me. I jumped up to give him a big hug.

After a powerful day, where we each delivered a talk about prosperity that respectively drew standing ovations, he suggested I come to his hotel and have dinner with him so we could catch up. Later that evening, at the restaurant at the Horton Grand Hotel, we sat down to order dinner. Famished, we both settled on a mouth-watering steak and a bottle of wine, stressing to the white-gloved waiter how grateful these two hungry men would be to get our food as quickly as possible.

Once the issue of dealing with our ravenous bellies was out of the way, we congratulated ourselves on successfully delivering our respective uplifting messages to the excited and appreciative crowd at the prosperity seminar that day. During his presentation, Rev. Ike had mentioned that he'd just seen the traveling King Solomon and Queen of Sheba exhibition.

Coincidentally, I had also recently visited the Solomon exhibit. I learned through the years that Rev. Ike and I were kindred spirits who both enthused about similar interests. Both of us coming from blue collar, humble beginnings, we shared a lifelong desire to raise ourselves up from the station into which we were born. We both had an insatiable desire to learn the secrets of God's Word and the universe that would nourish our minds and spirits. We loved teaching all that we learned and believed that sharing our knowledge would maximize our respective impact on the world.

We sat there enjoying a fine meal and celebrating the life of King Solomon, author of *Proverbs in the Book of Wisdom* in the Bible, who taught the Laws of Living, marveling how thousands of years later, these lessons were still guiding us. The traveling King Solomon-Queen of Sheba exhibit curated from the British Museum of History was an experience that seared many images indelibly into each of our minds and memories.

We both agreed on the silliness of human beings dividing each other into groups based on the melanin on the top three-sixteenths of an inch of their skin that gives skin its color. After all, according to our historical experts, as a White Jewish king and a Black Egyptian queen, Solomon and Sheba saw none of that. They were enchanted with each other and had a great deal of respect for one another.

We shared a common frustration at the atrocities that had been done and humanity divided by these false definitions that mankind creates. We agreed that every one of us is the very offspring of our Creator in Heaven, a spiritual being having a human experience, noting that for two of the most central figures in the Bible, color and race were completely irrelevant. Moses and King Solomon were both White Jewish men who had both married Black women. Both Moses and King Solomon suffered family and religious objections to these marriages.

This wasn't the first time we talked about the fact that God was totally color blind and race blind, and that it was only human fear and ignorance that caused folks to make a fuss about such a ridiculous notion that the tiny layer of pigment on the top of your skin matters one bit. We shared a vision that relished the thought of all relationships being guided by the pure love that comes from understanding the oneness of God and all of His creation.

After our meal, I gave Rev. Ike a big hug and wished him well. "Until next time, my friend."

Rev. Ike had a clear perspective on race and color issues that were being discussed and defined in political realms at the time as they are today. The bottom line was he couldn't stand labels. He wouldn't tolerate the thinking that one should identify with the color of their skin no matter what color it was, because the only thing that made a bit of difference in this world was the color green, the color of money. Beautiful green money, according to Ike, was the symbol of exchange for which all of our efforts, determination, excellence, and achievements would be measured. He wanted all Black people to get past the political narrative that they were somehow disadvantaged because of the color of their skin because by accepting that narrative in their mind and spirit, they limited their own great potential. This was a recurring topic in his sermons because he was adamantly against Black people wrapping their identities around the color of their skin when he knew the only identity they should focus on was that they were a beloved child of the most high God, not a God who was living in some faraway galaxy, but instead dwelled inside of them as His beloved spiritual offspring.

Rev. Ike was steadfast about raising the inner value of each human being so much so that skin color was not relevant in any way to what one makes of their life. He taught a lesson on spiritual regnancy from The Book of Wisdom, Proverbs 20:8 (NKJV): *A king who sits on the throne of judgment Scatters all evil with his eyes.*

> *"A King sits on his throne and knows his spiritual regnancy over materiality, over hard facts, and conditions. Too many read the Bible impersonally. The Bible is written to reveal you to you. The theologians have put all understanding in the past, future, sky, or hell. This verse reveals to you your spiritual regnancy. God reigns over me and my world, therefore I can control my circumstances and hard facts. We are here to be in charge of our life and not allow the world's negativity to control, affect, or dominate us."*

To be regnant means to rule, reign, dominate, or have influence over someone or something. Rev. Ike's life's work was to awaken that power in every man and woman to become the ruler in their own lives by tapping their spiritual gifts endowed by God.

THE FATHER-SON DYNAMIC

Xavier

Earlier in this book, I shared my belief that people choose their parents. The way that dynamic unfolded between my father and grandfather confirmed it and provided tremendous insight in my attempts to understand the same dynamic between my father and me. Ours was a complicated father/son relationship, but make no mistake about it, we loved each other deeply.

A memory that clearly depicts the complexity of our relationship was captured on a professional photograph of Dad and me. When I was around six or seven, he'd gotten a suit custom-made for me that was identical to one of his suits.

"Son, I had a suit made for you exactly like mine, and we're going to take a picture together in our matching suits."

I was very excited. I got the suit, an exact copy of my dad's. The day came, and I put it on thinking about how good he looked in his and how good we were going to look together in that photo with our matching outfits. It was a unique suit with white lace over black with a tuxedo lapel, made by a famous haberdasher Harvey Krantz, which outfitted stars like Elvis, Liberace, and some say Michael Jackson. When I arrived at the church on the day of the photo session, he was wearing a different suit. I was deeply disappointed, of course, and remember feeling dejected. When I look at that picture, I can see in my eyes how sad I was.

That picture speaks volumes about our relationship. My dad was larger than life, and like most boys, I wanted to be like him because I loved him and he was cool. That's how we are wired—we learn how to be men by emulating our closest examples. There was a deep part of me that wanted to be like him in order to please him. When I was a child, one day he asked what I wanted to be when I grew up. I told him I wanted to be a minister, innately knowing it was the answer he wanted to hear. He beamed with pride.

Eventually, though, my childhood desire to make my father happy by confirming his will for me and assuming his predetermined identity for me dissipated, and the issue of what I would do with my life became problematical in our relationship. His expectation hardened into a demand, which I resisted as strongly as he insisted. He was not accustomed to being told no, and he definitely had trouble tolerating it from his son. Although we were not your typical nuclear family, Dad was like other fathers who had a strong desire to see their sons follow in their footsteps. I longed for more of a typical father/son experience as well as the self-determination he preached about in his sermons.

My dad and I were cut from a similar cloth. Our textures were different, and our colors varied according to our individuality. And though our contrasts were sometimes glaring, we both eventually recognized the ways in which we were naturally alike. As a youthful metaphysician, I appreciated his philosophical wisdom, but as his closest biological relation, I resented his inability to see me.

I was proud of him as a man of significance in the world but rued his lack of attentiveness to home life. Like him, I thought for myself and insisted on being my own person. I finally got this through to him one day in my twenties when we were arguing about his desire to crown me Rev. Ike II. I told him that both his ego and lack of consideration for me had gotten out of hand, and there was no way I would continue in the ministry as his mini-me. He grudgingly backed off from that for a time and gave me a little more psychic space.

I understand that it was hard for him to comprehend how he was being inconsiderate of me when he was giving me an abundance of material goods and positional advantages and trying to maneuver me into the place where no one would question me as his successor. Even so, one need not secure a nail with a sledgehammer. He later told me he sought to put this all into place because it was what I said I wanted when I was eight years old. Of course, at eight, I had not yet individuated from my parents, and I was far too young to have developed a sense of what I might want to do in the world as an adult.

He ran with what he perceived to be my vocation choice like a bull trampling through my sensitive psychic garden space. My own will according to the unique destiny I came to this planet with needed the environment and support to grow and flower in its natural way, as opposed to having my developing plants uprooted and grafted onto others. To paraphrase the scripture Psalm 1:3, he used to like me to read in church service from a young age, "*I shall be like a tree planted by the rivers of water which bringeth forth my fruit in my season.*"

My season, not his. I had that right.

"It is antithetical to your own teachings to try and force somebody to be something they do not want to be," I pressed. "Are you a hypocrite?" Then I used his own mantra on him. "'Do what you wanna do, have what you wanna have, and be who you wanna be.' Is that true for everyone but your son?"

That was one of the few times he did not have an answer for me. I appreciated that he thought it through after I threw his own words in his face like a bracing glass of ice water, and he responded with accommodation as much as he was capable of doing, which was incomplete in its application. It takes a lot to redirect a locomotive.

While I was always a good kid, I was not an angel. I enjoyed rebelling against my father. It gave my Aries nature a passionate battle to wage. Having him as a focus of acrimony, a major foil to match wits against, energized me to push away harder and claim my own territory. This is necessary in any child's bid for developmental separation from parents, and it is totally natural in the only journey worthwhile, that of finding one's authentic self.

I feel pity for those who remain forever psychically fused to their parents, never thinking their own thoughts, feeling their own feelings, or living their own lives. It would take me a couple more decades, however, to get to the place of not wanting to fight, to set down my weapons and most importantly, my armor, and to cease being defined by that struggle and entrenched in the habit of it.

Nonetheless, a part of me remained my father's son. I understood the power of thoughts. I successfully waded my way through my teenage angst and rebelled against his desires to have me follow in his footsteps. Similar to the impact his father's refusal to buy him shoes had on his success, my father's failure to spend more time with me fostered a fierce independence that has served me well. My dad transmuted the lack of fatherly provision into a singular drive for success, and I transformed my dearth of fatherly attention into an intense insistence upon living life my way.

Importantly, I grew to understand and deeply appreciate who my father was and what he was able to accomplish. His legacy gets richer with time, not only for the people just discovering him and those who grew up with his message, but also for me. I am regularly surprised at how often I hear of people from varied places, circumstances, and walks of life who have been touched by my dad's work.

People continue to analyze his impact. As an example, in 2011, Harvard assistant professor Jonathan Walton, Harvard Divinity School, authored an essay on my father called "The Greening of the Gospel (and Black Body): Rev. Ike's Gospel of Wealth and Post-Blackness Theology." That he delved into my father's ministry, decades after its heyday, is significant. It's fascinating that he zeroes in on what he called Dad's "professed post-Black identity." He was undoubtedly referring to one of my father's frequent assertions: "I am not a Black preacher. I'm a green preacher. I quit being a Black preacher millions of dollars ago!"

In his essay, Walton mostly falls into lockstep with the critics who accused Dad of preying on the poor. Whether he was pro-Rev. Ike or anti-Rev. Ike is of less importance than the fact that he devoted a significant amount of time to a historical analysis of my father's theology. It was a topic deserving of such time because of the tremendous impact my father had on society at that time—an impact that arguably continues today. It makes sense that people not privy to his thought process and the reasons behind his decisions formed conclusions based only on what they saw and what they heard him say publicly.

Dad knew that the Sunday school classes, more than two dozen adult classes, and children and youth classes were good, but he needed to quickly move into getting his sermon lessons into print form and made available as weekly lesson sheets. A small but effective publishing team that included Rev. Robert Jiggetts (also known as Dean Jiggetts), Betty Vear, Anastasia Jones, and Keith Mitchell was responsible for transcribing, editing, and printing those lesson sheets. The lessons were then made into a newsletter to be distributed to followers from every state.

By 1972, The Science of Living Institute was born as an educational arm of United Church. The Science of Living is a self-image psychology, a philosophy of self-understanding. When people truly understand themselves, then they understand everyone and everything.

Dad broke it down like this: There is really nothing else to understand except yourself. Knowing the truth about yourself sets you free. When you know your own divinity, you know that you are one with God.

It may be stated this way: God is the reality and totality of me. That's putting it personally. You can change "me" to "man" or "woman" and retain the meaning. Here again, we do not want to simply leave this philosophy in the abstract. We want to apply it. There is nothing about the reality of us that is not God. The Master Jesus realized that there was nothing constituting his beingness that was not God, and it is the same truth of every man.

Dad would say that the reality of you is God. When you begin to experience and to express God, then you begin to be God in action. As long as you think *I am man whose breath is in his nostrils*, then you live like man, suffer like man, sin like man, and die like man. But when you know that God is the reality and the totality of you, then you live like God, love like God, act like God, walk like God, and talk like God.

The Science of Living does not address itself to solving problems on the mass social level. It began with the individual, because society can only be what individuals make it. The world can only be what people make it. Until people understand themselves, they are not going to understand one another.

Take the issue of race. When man understands that man, in reality is Spirit, then it will make no difference that one may be White and another Black. There will be no fight over color. When we all know that we belong to the same Source, to the same Substance, then there is no more social or racial conflict. Self-understanding is what each individual needs.

Along with establishing The Science of Living Institute, quarterly study guides were printed and used in the Sunday classes. The old traditional Sunday school classes, where the Bible was studied, were transformed into Science of Living study groups. People attended the study groups to reinforce the ideas that were taught during the Sunday messages. They went to the groups to transform their minds from the old way of thinking—that they needed to suffer and die to get to Heaven—to a new way of thinking—that the kingdom of Heaven is within the heart and mind of every man, and that every man is a Son of God.

Dad was always coming up with creative ideas that would help reinforce these messages and keep them top-of-mind for people so that each day they were reminded to stay in the journey that would move them from living in mediocrity to living in excellence.

Like when he was inspired to create a "prayer cloth." His red prayer cloths quickly became famous among his followers. They were made from full industrial-sized spools of material and Dad would bless them and pray over them by the millions. His inspiration for the cloths came from Acts 19:11–12 (NIV):

"And God was doing extraordinary miracles by the hands of Paul, so that even handkerchiefs or aprons that had touched his skin were carried away to the sick, and their diseases left them and evil spirits came out of them."

He viewed them as a symbolic point of agreement, similar to crosses or rosary beads. He considered the prayer cloths a collective joining of faith through which all who believed could manifest health, happiness, success, love, and money.

Many believed he televised his sermons to make money, but Dad televised his sermons so more people could hear his empowering messages. He and Mom were answering letters from millions of people each week, but it eventually became time and cost prohibitive. Creating the newsletter allowed him to communicate more efficiently to millions by providing guidance on the top three topics: money, health, and relationships.

There were millions of ministers preaching hellfire and brimstone. That preaching was all about what *not to do* to avoid going to Hell, but no one was teaching what we *should do* before we get to Heaven. My father felt that that was his calling. No one else taught that part of life before death. Besides, why preach sin, salvation, Heaven, and Hell to people who were struggling to feed their children and pay their rent? They were already in a "hell" of a fix. Because he had experienced it himself, Dad sincerely believed that changing your mind could change your life.

His ministry was all about having a rich, abundant life by changing the way you think.

REVEREND IKE'S PRISON MINISTRY

Mark

Rev. Ike was a constant giver. He gave of himself in a multitude of ways and felt a deep calling guided by a scripture in Luke 4:18–19 (KJV) which he quoted often:

> *"The Spirit of the Lord is upon me, because He hath anointed me to preach the gospel to the poor; He hath sent me to heal the brokenhearted, to preach deliverance to the captives, and recovering sight to the blind, to set at liberty them that are bruised..."*

He mirrored the message of Jesus in so many ways. Many people were unaware that Rev. Ike formed a prison ministry which helped so many deserving inmates that were truly ready to "repent" and change their lives in positive ways. These stories are basically unknown to the public. Unless a recipient of the reverend's largesse told their testimonial, it has remained unknown, until now.

This all began when one of Rev. Ike's church attendees introduced Janet Potter, a full-time counselor to prisoners at Rikers Island, to Rev. Ike. They liked each other immediately. She invited him to speak to the Rikers Island inmates, and he did so three times, in 1995, 1996, and 1997. He gave inspiring motivational talks for a half hour and then answered the prisoners' endless questions. Rev. Ike loved what Janet did for the inmates. He wanted to be a permanent influence for good for these inmates, so he decided to join forces with Janet Potter as head of his United Palace Prison Ministry.

JANET POTTER

MY STORY WITH REVEREND IKE

There are a lot of people in prison who shouldn't be there. Rev. Ike and I believed that some of these prisoners didn't get a fair chance, which is why he named our prison ministry program 'A Better Chance.' We have so many compellingly stories of redemption which were a result of this beautiful ministry, but I'll just share a few.

There was one young man named Charles who wasn't a real criminal. He was a good, hard working hospital employee with a wife and two children. One day after working two shifts, he was exhausted and fell asleep in another man's apartment. Unfortunately, there was a lit candle on the table. The window was open and blew the candle over. The flame lit the curtain and that started a fire in the apartment. The apartment suffered fire and water damage, but the Fire Department quickly extinguished the blaze. Everyone got out safely, but he was charged with arson and sentenced to six months at Rikers Island.

It was a complete travesty of justice. We took on his case and I was able to help him keep his job because he was a competent and hard worker, the hospital loved him, and wanted him back. At Rev. Ike's recommendation, I called the hospital saying he was on an extreme emergency where there were no phones. We needed to protect him because he hadn't been protected by the justice system. Thankfully, the hospital never knew that he even went to prison, or he would have permanently lost his job. He's never committed anything close to a crime since then and went back to living a good life once again.

Another interesting case we handled was when an inmate named James came to me for help. He looked like death warmed over. I told him I was going to buy him a black outfit for his funeral unless he came back cleaned up, healthier, and ready to change. He was given the messages of Rev. Ike called *Change your mind and change your life*. He got it. It touched him inside. He was ready to be a new man with this new knowledge in his heart. He cleaned up and transformed his ways. Later, after he was released, I got him a city job helping others at Rikers Island. He felt so grateful for what he had received he wanted to do the same for others, so he wrote a twenty-page pamphlet about what to do and where to go, and how you survive when you are released from prison. His transformation allowed him to start down a new path and do well. He found a nice woman and got married. He was able to buy a car, a house, and live a respectable life. He recently retired with a full pension.

John was nicknamed "AMTRAK" because he stole everyone's bags from above their heads on the AMTRAK train while they were reading or sleeping. John took whatever was in their bags and was gone like a flash, rarely being caught. The judge said John's police file was so big and thick it looked like an old time New York City telephone book. The judge told John that if he came before him one more time, it wouldn't be Rikers Island he would be going to, he would be off permanently to the "Big House," as a lifer doing hard time. That scared AMTRAK straight. Wanting to be truly repentant, he came to me for counseling and to work with our church's prison ministry. Through Rev. Ike's teaching and mentorship, we transformed his thinking, his life, and helped him get a city job. While there, he married a fellow officer and became a clean-living and hard-working citizen.

I worked at Rikers Island until I retired in 1999. The prison ministry was dedicated to helping qualified inmates who were about to get released, with no place to go, who had no families or other help to get them relaunched into society. Our focus was to transform their thinking, get them work, and arrange for their housing. Rev. Ike chose to name the program A Better Chance because he said, "God is a God of second chances."

Some people didn't want our help, so we let them go. We would help get them sober and out of whatever addictions they had and into appropriate training programs. All these young men were exceedingly polite and relatively easy to work with, because they quickly learned respect. If one of them swore in front of me they would instantly apologize. They became new men with new values.

Rev. Ike freely gave them his books and audios. He helped them rent apartments for a month or until they got work. Additionally, he gave me a budget to pay for their clothing. I would take them shopping to buy clothes like jeans, shirts, and a jacket, because they literally had nothing. With Rev. Ike's financial underwriting of about $200 for each man, we shopped at little mom and pop stores to help the local community businesses, at the reverend's request. He gave each person about a thousand dollars of assistance with no strings attached to re-enter the world safely, confidently, and with a new self-awareness that he encouraged them to have. Rev. Ike helped free their minds and souls, proclaiming them ready to honestly serve for the sake of serving. We freed them out of the prisons in their minds to live as free, honest, ethical, hard-working men.

Another powerful story of redemption about a former prisoner is the story of Petey Greene. For twenty-one of forty-nine years of Petey Greene's life, he was in and out of prison. Lying on his hard, lonely, penitentiary bed one day, he heard Rev. Ike on TV talking about the power of God inside of us, how you can set your mind to anything and achieve it through God in you. The reverend told the story of how Henry Ford had one idea to create an automobile and become a billionaire. Rev. Ike's words captured Petey Greene's heart and spirit. He told himself "*Yes*! I am going to get an idea, get out of here, and be better, do better, and have better."

He was the prison's disc jockey and his fellow inmates loved that he could out-talk anyone and everyone. They nicknamed him "Mr. Loquacious."

Two days after hearing Rev. Ike, a fellow inmate climbed up 350 feet on the prison water tower threatening to commit suicide. "If I don't get to go feed my family," he shouted down from the tower, "I'm going to jump!" The warden asked Petey Greene to talk him down, which Petey did. Two days later, Petey got released from prison for doing that and for exemplifying good behavior.

Once out of prison, he knew to whom he needed to turn to keep his life going in the right direction. He continued to listen intently to Rev. Ike and decided to become a respectable and contributing money-making citizen, always tithing to Reverend Ike with deep gratitude, and encouraging others to do the same. Moving ever forward with the guidance of Rev. Ike, Petey transformed himself into a professional speaker, consultant, and entrepreneur in Washington, D.C. Over time he became a famous TV and radio personality talking about ending poverty, racism, drug usage, and becoming truly free. His work became widely recognized and he won two Emmys for his television show.

His testimonial before Rev. Ike's United Palace audience gave him two standing ovations.

There was a film made on Petey Greene's life story called *Talk to Me* released in 2007. Petey Greene was so popular when he died in 1984 that 10,000 fans came to mourn him.

There were many others who had gotten lost along the way and were guided back by Rev. Ike's shepherdship. We probably will never quite know the true impact of his saving of wayward souls.

REVEREND SAL SABINO

MY STORY WITH REVEREND IKE

t was 1972 and I'd seen the billboards all around Washington Heights of this flashy preacher who drove a Rolls Royce and was dressed to the nines.

My friends and I found it exciting that Ike was rich and famous and word on the street was he could teach you to get what you wanted. My sixteen-year-old curiosity got the best of me, so my friends and I decided to go to this flashy man's church and see what it was all about. We sat in the back rows behind the multitudes of people in the orchestra section of the auditorium.

When Rev. Ike walked into the crowd of churchgoers, an explosion of praise went up. It was the first time I'd laid eyes on the reverend. Truthfully, I thought the entrance was a bit pompous, but everyone seemed to genuinely enjoy the moment. You could feel so much energy as believers broke into joyous cheers. I sat there and listened to him, and I felt his sincerity. Despite my initial reaction, I started to feel something special that touched me inside. I was an active pot user, but by the time the offering buckets were passed I surprised myself, readily putting in the three dollars I was saving for a marijuana bag. My six teenage buddies who were there with me pulled out some of their dollars, eager to join the givers.

Unfortunately, my drug habit didn't get better, but increasingly became more serious as the years passed. I went from a small-time marijuana user to a habitual user and dealer of ever more dangerous illegal drugs. It was an intense life filled with fear, deception, and danger. I became the biggest cocaine salesman in Washington Heights, New York. I was highly visible, known on the streets by the name of "Notorious."

Inside every drug dealer is the constant fear that you'll get caught and the curtain is going to come crashing down. Sure enough, the Feds finally caught up with me. They made certain my career in dealing drugs was over by sending me to prison for nine years. I checked into the penitentiary in 1980 for cocaine use and dealing. During my time in the pen, I often thought about Reverend Ike. I wanted to do better, and as I thought of his effect on me that day long ago, I wanted to go deeper. I wanted to know that feeling again where I could feel God close to me.

I decided that I wanted to clean up my life, surrender completely to God, and work for the Lord. God did just that and I became a minister.

When I came back to New York in 1990, I was a free man, and completely clean of my awful drug habit. It felt good to be out on the streets again, but now I was sober. This time instead of a drug dealer, I was a minister. Out of the slammer, I decided to start a new church in the Bronx. I had made bad choices, and now I wanted to make better choices, like Rev. Ike taught. I wanted to become a more powerful, soul-catching minister. I had already converted several of my drug-selling colleagues into ministers and it meant a lot to me to be able to mentor them.

My church started growing right away and did so for an entire decade. I frequently went back into the United Palace to watch Rev. Ike do his magic. He deeply inspired me, but I wanted to go further and make a bigger difference. I wanted to talk to Rev. Ike, but initially I didn't have the courage.

I was looking for a place to preach in Manhattan, and I'd heard Rev. Ike rented the Palace at certain times when it wasn't being used. It was my dream to preach there on Sunday nights because I loved the building.

I got up my courage and requested to see the reverend. Amazingly, I got an appointment with Rev. Ike.

The meeting took place at his second-floor suite at the United Palace Theatre. When we met, Reverend Ike came out impeccably dressed and ever so gracious. When he greeted me, I felt a warm aura of nobility and class. He was like someone you see from a great Hollywood movie. He told me that he had been praying and believing someone from the neighborhood would rise up to help those in need and use the resource of the Palace to do so. He asked me about my story and I gave him my testimonial.

I told him that I had been a drug dealer, got arrested, came out of prison in 1990, and I was now winning souls as a minister. Rev. Ike told me that he had prayed for a Dominican witness to rise up in this community. "You are the man," he said.

I will never forget that historical and life-defining moment with this amazing man whom I held in such high esteem.

Reverend Ike told me I was welcome to start holding my services at the Palace at 6:00 p.m. on Sunday nights. In early December 1998, as my wife Kenia and I endeavored to launch the Heavenly Vision Church satellite in Upper Manhattan, we started our Sunday evening worship services at the Palace. Within two years, we grew to 500 attendees. My church kept growing, and Rev. Ike grew to trust me. In another year, I was drawing 1,200 attendees.

As Palace attendance started to grow, more things happened. A prophesy from Rev. Ike was fulfilled. He had prophesied we would pack the Palace. He asked me to become the manager of the Palace, and also inspired me start renting out the Palace for events. He asked us to pray before and during the concerts, events, and special conferences and see that those prayers would inspire church attendance. One of Rev. Ike's many unique strategies was to have a group leading a prayer of faith in his Prayer Tower above these secular events. Our group was to pray for transference of multitudes, and it seemed to work almost immediately. Visitors miraculously became parishioners and fans of both the reverend and me.

Our Sunday church services started to grow magically because of these inspired prayers over non-church members. Even as a young man, while I was roaring through the streets of Washington Heights as a victim of drugs, I would hear some of these stories of miracles and about the guy who had chosen to cling to the gift of faith, because he started out as a kid with no money to even buy a sandwich. Meeting this icon and getting so close to him for the last twelve years of his physical life left a mark on me that would stay with me for the rest of my life. I can still hear him say, "Nothing is impossible for God and God is possible for you."

To this very day, his teachings still pour through my mind and spirit, loud and clear: "Trust and obey. You are not people's opinion of you".

> *"Be not conformed to this world, but be ye transformed*
> *by the renewing of your mind…"* (Romans 12:2 KJV)

Rev. Ike took center stage in my life and in the lives of so many others that came to the Palace during his lifetime. Now those same principles he passed to me are repeated in my teachings where they're changing more lives. The influence of his wisdom, personality, and character are branded into my whole person.

Rev. Ike was consistently instructional in all matters of life: ministry, family, business, and health. He was also very loving, but he also had impeccable standards for those he mentored. At the least sign of any weakness or careless mistake, he would attack it like a lion on a hunt. He wasn't afraid to challenge us to be our best. What a giant he was in the faith world.

One of his main teachings for me was "to educate people in prosperity to my church congregation and Latino people in general." He noticed that, even though we got to the point of having a good crowd, offering per capita was relatively low. He knew that failing to make gains with this important ingredient could cause chaos in my ministry. He wanted me to learn and teach the law of sowing and reaping, which I have come to master.

Many lives were turned around through our work together. In 1999, a group of over thirty young gangsters, male and female, came to the Palace from two rival gangs. Miraculously, they made their peace after hearing the gospel first in their chosen places, and then in services at the Palace, where they discovered the love and peace through God in them. Today, a few of the ex-gang leaders are positively influencing others in ministry, as school administrators, and in youth leadership.

The most important thing the reverend ever said to me, that I have repeated endlessly to myself and others is: "Once you discover who you are, it does not matter what you have been." He saw more in me than I saw in myself. He wanted me to succeed, to grow in faith, and to change my self-image. He saw that I was still tied up in my past. I had to let it go and now I am somebody else. I believed that I could be a greater person and a greater minister because of him.

In June 2000, Rev. Ike teamed up with Pastor Rodney Howard Browne, who was born in South Africa, and built a mega-church in Tampa, Florida. Together, Rev. Ike and Pastor Browne sponsored my international traveling ministry.

He said: "You will travel around the world, but you will come to your home, the Palace." To date, I have traveled and preached in many auditoriums, stadiums, and arenas of the United States of America, Latin America, and Europe.

The experience of our meeting was later recorded in my autobiographical book, *Two Ways: A Washington Heights Drug Dealer Turns Around*. I candidly tell my story of how I was a notorious leader in the drug trade business in upper Manhattan, and how I turned my life around, becoming a man of God and an aggressive soul winner, leading my former comrades to Christ.

The reverend was always like a loving and caring spiritual father to me, instructing me, often over the phone. I had frequent invitations to lunch and dinner in his home. He and his wife were always generous, patient, and kind.

"You are at a crossroads," he said to me while having dinner in Tampa Bay one evening. "A man is respected for his convictions. You have a destiny, my Spanish son."

Even his critics admitted the reverend was a wise man, a legend in his own time. Often the very person ready to tear into him was won over seconds after meeting him.

He had what the Bible calls a discerning spirit with words of wisdom. He would have important insight and intuition which came from his deep connection to God.

Rev. Ike was certainly unique, but I have yet to see a more loving, honest, generous, wise gentleman. He would remember people's names, along with details about that individual whom he possibly had a single conversation with. He would remember their visions, dreams, and goals, and get behind them. He was a motivator who celebrated individuals for who they were. He could relate to senior citizens as well as to children with grace and respect as if they were the most important persons on the planet.

Throughout our relationship, I understood the voice of an effective teacher, preacher, and seasoned business leader. I understood Rev. Ike's instructions and welcomed his astute guidance. It was a decisive period of my life, and it was my great gift from God that he was there for me.

I'll forever thank God for this man's vision and presence in my life.

I heard somebody say that a man like Rev. Ike is born every century. After my personal journey with him, I'd say it might be another thousand years before such a man is born. I will honor Rev. Ike and his vision for me and my church forever.

I MEET NO ONE BUT ME

Xavier

Dad delivered thousands of sermons over the course of his lifetime. Fully aware that his ministry was a reflection of him, he embodied his destined obligation to liberate minds by unapologetically teaching the truth as he saw and believed it. He appreciated the concept that the teacher appears when the student is ready, recognizing that, for millions, he was the teacher their consciousnesses had attracted.

One of his most beloved and masterful lessons, "I Meet No One But Me," captures every aspect of his Science of Living philosophy, revealing his mysticism as he brilliantly dissected portions of the Bible from a metaphysical perspective. Those who heard that sermon, as well as the scores of listeners who caught the message via his cassettes or online, experienced my father in his element. Laughing boisterously at his own jokes and poking fun at theologians who missed out by only taking the Bible literally, he delivered a message so rich and complete that a book could be written on its content alone.

Dad knew the subject matter in this lesson might be met with denial or confusion, so he took his time spelling out what he meant by "I Meet No One But Me." Its rich meaning was applicable to every problem he'd ever advised a parishioner about, because he taught that everything anyone had in their life was manifested from their self-image. It all went

243

back to the person. By the end of the message, anyone doubting their power had either slept through it or was not yet ready to take up their authorship in understanding the profound truth he shared. It was a life-changing lesson and one of my father's favorites.

He fundamentally conveyed the same theme time and again: You are the master of your mind and are therefore responsible for your life. Whatever his topic, at the core of the message was the essential truth that everything and everyone in your life reflects your understanding or misunderstanding of your divine nature and birthright. Period. If you want to change the people in your life, change yourself according to God's image of you. You want different circumstances? Become a different person, in alignment with how you were created. While it may sound harsh to some and too simplistic to others, he considered it spiritual law, and he spelled it out masterfully.

Dad cleverly included a subtitle for those who might find the title puzzling or difficult to comprehend: "How to Control People and Conditions in Your Life." While that might have sounded a bit more appealing to some because it implied an ability to change the actions of others you don't like, the talk itself made it clear that it was futile to try to control others. It could be said that he dangled the carrot of control to get people in the door, and once they were there, he made it clear that control of others had nothing to do with creating a good life.

"The people and the conditions in my life are as they are because I am such as I am," Dad explained with that bit of whimsy in his voice because he knew folks were simultaneously intrigued while questioning his logic. "In everyone, I meet some aspect of myself. Some aspect of my subconscious self-image, some aspect of my subconscious self-identity, some aspect of my subconscious self-feeling." He placed himself smack dab in the middle of the lesson, knowing his personal examples helped people embrace what might be difficult to accept.

"I am here to confess that some people have some ways that I don't like. But at the same time, I must realize that everyone is me, though sometimes unrecognized and disliked, because I cannot experience anything or anyone except those which correspond to something within myself."

His whole lesson boiled down to Socrates' admonishment, "Man, know thyself." Dad emphasized this point in most of his sermons because he believed deeply that when man knows his inner self correctly, he will recognize his outer self in all his various disguises. He explained that when you meet someone who rubs you the wrong way or gets on your last nerve, trying to get them to change is futile. Not because change is hard, but because their behavior or whatever else about them resonates with you so pointedly is something within *your* subconscious. "All the people in your world are expressions of something within your subconscious mentality." So the solution is to change yourself, not try to change them. Dad said it was pure mystic science, pure esoteric science, meaning it was impersonal and applicable to everyone. No one was immune to this essential spiritual law, and becoming aware of it was the most liberating thing a person could experience because it placed them in the driver's seat of their life.

My father firmly believed that everyone you meet is as you are, were, or will be. That belief undergirded how respectfully he treated all people. He didn't care whether he was addressing the CEO of a company, or a janitor, he treated them equally with respect. He used that idea to explain the powerful boomerang effect of judgement. "You have to be careful how you judge people. Whenever you judge someone else, you're always judging yourself." He likened this to Jesus saying that one would receive what they meted out. "You're going to be judged with whatever judgment you judge."

This explained why Dad addressed the homeless as "sir" or "ma'am" and spoke to them with dignity and respect. He lived what he preached.

But even he had blind spots. While he generally treated people with respect, he was challenged with respecting those close to him who didn't do what he wanted or fell short of his expectations. He could cut people down without compunction. I only challenged it when I was on the receiving end of the criticism.

He wanted people to understand just how powerful they were when they took control and accepted responsibility for their lives. Living a prosperous life, having money, and experiencing the financial freedom to do what you want, when you want, was guided by this principle as well. "This is what the law of giving is based upon. You give to no one but yourself. This is why I constantly demand, even for the poor, to give. People say that's the one thing many times they can't accept about me and my ministry—that I tell poor people to give."

Dad's critics got all worked up primarily because they believed he instructed the poor to give to fatten his pockets. They did not know and could not understand that he was operating from the mystic secret that says giving is a natural, universal cycle and when we step into it we are entering the flow of abundance, mimicking and participating in a fundamental function of both nature and cosmos, of which we are a part. It's a "never-ending spiral of increase and enjoyment." When you become a giver, you become a receiver. As a receiver, you open to giving more. You give, and you receive. It is an open vibrational resonance, a field one can come to exist within. Within that field, it flows with little thought about it. But until you are there, you need to think yourself into it.

My father took great joy in making scripture understandable by pushing people past the literal interpretation. He saw the Bible as a great source of inspiration and urged people to see themselves in every aspect of it.

Demystifying the Bible was a major component of Dad's work. He felt if people were able to see it as a tool to improve their lives, not just as some historical text to be interpreted by church theologians, they would embrace the true spiritual essence of the Living Word in a way that mattered to the outcome of their lives. Dad knew the Bible provided much more for mankind to learn when one accepts the deep supernatural meanings given and sees beyond the mere words.

According to my father, one of the marks of the master is that he recognizes himself. And when he can recognize himself in others, when he sees the divinity in everyone, every experience can be holy. That was the crux of my father's message at the point in his life when he was far more interested in teaching than preaching.

He wanted people to wake up.[1]

---

[1] You can find Rev. Ike's audio teachings at revikelegacy.com.

DR. DAVID MONTGOMERY

MY STORY WITH REVEREND IKE

As a student at Morehouse University in Atlanta, Georgia, I was out of money and I could not afford to attend school anymore. My friend and fellow student, Kevin Ross, was brilliant at obtaining, booking, managing, and helping us deliver talks. I was enthralled with the idea of taking a year off of school and traveling around speaking everywhere. Kevin manifested paid talks out of thin air. I was overjoyed to earn $8,600, so I could afford to resume my junior undergraduate schooling.

We called ourselves The Sons of Thunder—like Jesus called his disciples James and John, because they were amazingly colorful characters who did not back away from confrontation. We were paid to speak to at-risk youth groups for the Teach for American Company. They paid us thousands to talk at great places like UCLA and gave us fun perks like being picked up in a limousine. It was heady stuff.

While we were on tour in the '90s, Rev. Ike had us present at his church. Afterwards, he invited us to dinner with his family at his home in Rye, New York. It was the first of several such dinners we had together. It was like sitting with a myth, a legend, and an archetype all at once, because the reverend was a master demonstrator. It was a defining moment in my life. I saw I could learn to move from potential into a kinetic space using what Rev. Ike taught me was my God-given birthright. He explained and demonstrated that to us. He told us we are to *be part of the one-mind-of-God and must become as instant as God is.* That took lots of spiritual and mental digesting. Over the years, I have learned the instantaneity of the Divine Mind. It works when I am in alignment with God in me and I listen to my inner desire. It is a still, small voice, it doesn't shout or argue, it's my soul connection.

As a cardiologist working in a large practice, I heard the voice that Rev. Ike taught me to hear. The voice told me, go on your own, build a practice with five other tenant doctors, get a CT scanner, and buy a 22,000 square foot building to see 3,000 patients per year. Many told me it was a bad idea. I was too young and inexperienced; I would never make it. I imagined and felt it so completely. I would sit in the parking lot of the building I desired and felt that I owned it. I would walk through the rooms, and I could see my patients and my colleagues. I could smell the newness of the paint before we moved in. I felt the love of everyone that would be coming to my grand opening. Like my mentor had taught me to do, I owned it before I *owned* it. It all happened as I had imagined and fervently believed.

It was such a great honor when Rev. Ike had me come to Florida to be filmed to be on his telecast. The filming went spectacularly well. The producer nonchalantly told me I should be on TV. I heard it, I felt it, imagined it, and now I have begun a national TV show. I see, feel, and believe that I will become a global TV doctor, as a messenger that matters. Rev. Ike taught me that *you only have what you think you deserve.* My life is the direct result of my thinking and I love how my life, prosperity, and experience is unfolding. I owe so much of that understanding to Reverend Ike. When I graduated with my Doctor of Medicine degree from Northwestern University, I sent a copy of it to Reverend Ike, with this note:

> Dearest Rev. Ike,
>
> I know that this letter, which I write with humility and sincerest regard, will find you peaceful, indulging in health and prosperity. As you know, I have

just graduated with my M.D. from Feinberg School of Medicine at Northwestern University. There are no words that truly capture my gratitude for the influence you've been in my life. In ways that perhaps you don't realize, you have mentored me by your examples, the substance of your words notwithstanding. It is because of these examples that I view the world in a different way, never to return to the old. The word thanks, seems utterly paltry, but is as close as we get in our current manner of speaking. Please know that my use of that word is filled with as much love and respect as any soul can muster. I would like to present you with a copy of my M.D. degree as a small token of thanks. Indeed, I couldn't have accomplished this with pride and with triumph, if it weren't for you.

Respectfully lovingly,
David E. Montgomery, MD, PhD

THE LEGACY CONTINUES
REV. IKE'S SUNSET YEARS

Mark

Rev. Ike's ministry had grown larger and larger, and with that growth, he had taken on more and more responsibility. So much of his work was hands-on because it all sprung from his unique ideas and visions. As his loving wife and the woman who had been by his side through his meteoric rise and phenomenal success, Mrs. Ike began to get concerned. Even though he'd demonstrated superhuman work ethic through the years, she knew he too was human, and he wasn't a young man anymore.

"He was trying to do so much himself," she said. "Trying to make sure he got to the New York church enough, trying to evangelize in different cities, trying to do the television to reach more people, tried to expand his radio reach, keeping up with all the writing that we did. It was all there for him to do 24/7. I could see him starting to hit overload, and then he began to burn out. He was used to giving all of himself, but he got to a point where he started to feel the heaviness of the demands weighing in on him and he kept saying, 'I've got to stop this. I've got to slow down. I've really got to do it.' But a lot of time went by, and he didn't change anything. Then the day came where he finally had to do it, and he just moved away from the daily responsibilities."

Rev. Ike had reached the season in his life that he needed to slow down the pace and intensity of his activities, which had been pretty much a non-stop whirlwind for decades. He had conducted his life with almost an unstoppable devotion to his work, tapping into what seemed to be inexhaustible energy. Now it was time to be there for the sunrises, cherish the sunsets, and contemplate how his work would live on after he had moved on to the next plane.

He had put together a wonderful team of people to help carry the load, so finally he was able to take off and go be by himself. Sometimes it was a cruise, or just time alone at one of the residences. He needed to be in a quiet space where he could read, write, and continue to gain wisdom. More than anything, he wanted to make sure that this body of work continued to be passed forward, that those who had been groomed by his tutelage all those years could take over and continue to run the church and the ministry. He knew he could trust the skills and knowledge this wonderful team of people had learned through the years which would now allow him to opt out of almost everything. The only thing he continued to do was to write.

Since all the properties were offices/residences full of his people working, he had to leave to get away from that to get some rest because those places were a constant hum of work activity with people needing him constantly. He needed a retreat, to rest his overloaded mind and spirit. He'd been going at this for fifty years without a break and it was time.

While it might seem ultra-glamorous to have a lot of homes in different cities, these residences that were purchased by the ministry were utilized first and foremost for that purpose. Each residency had a number of office rooms and staff members who worked there each day. There wasn't one residence that was just his place of home and rest, which explains why Rev. Ike came to *love* cruises, and he often took them alone.

Cruises became his peaceful getaway, and he took many during that time in his life. It was easy for him to depart out of the port in Miami, or sometimes just take off to Europe. He'd get on those ships for sometimes a few days, or sometimes several weeks. He liked that nobody could call him, fax him, or bother him. He could have as much solitude or social interaction as he wanted but 100 percent on his terms. Occasionally, the staff would get faxes while he was gone, but usually it would just be him coming back with a whole bag full of sermon ideas, mailing material, or meditations he'd written while away. "Success Ideas," he liked to call them.

He continued to wind down, focusing on his contemplations and still doing rare appearances, and even a few rare evangelical events. He allowed the system and the ministers he had so carefully put in place take over the services and run the church at United Palace. He discontinued his once-a-month visits to preach at the Beaufort church and turned it over to a younger pastor.

As he wound down even more, he spent most of his time at Bal Harbor in Florida because he loved it there. He allocated many hours a day to writing and organizing his thoughts, ideas, and reflections. A treasure trove of wisdom to be shared with the world even when he had passed from it.

JUDY ADLER

MY STORY WITH REVEREND IKE

n 1980 I was media director for an advertising agency in Richmond, Virginia called Huntsinger and Jeffers. They took on Rev. Ike as a client. For several years, I was his media buyer. I was producing his half hour TV shows for him, and I would buy airtime for the shows on individual stations in markets all over the United States. Usually, it was late night TV that was cheap, with a half hour of nighttime TV costing as little as fifty dollars. After I left the agency, Rev. Ike became unhappy with them, and after some frustrating experiences, he personally called and asked me if I would work for him directly on a freelance basis, which I agreed to do. I had always admired him and had enjoyed working with him before.

For several years, my only function was as a media buyer. Rev. Ike came out with a new half hour show almost every week or so, and I would contact radio and TV stations all over the country to buy time. Usually we were looking for an African American audience, following shows like *Soul Train*, where there was already a built-in audience ahead of us. This worked well for quite a few years. Eventually, he invited me to start overseeing the editing of his shows. I would take several half hour TV show segments and edit them together, along with commercials and promos that he would produce separately. I would then buy the media and place those shows on different television stations. I also was in charge of buying the TV time for the airing his Joy of Living broadcasts which were what he called his church services. I've never been religious, and I'm not a Christian, yet I thought his teachings were full of wonderful truths.

He spoke in a way his audiences could understand. In other words, he spoke to them in their language, taking into consideration their experiences of shortage, fear, and pain, or superstitions. He met people where they were in a way they understood and could feel they had a personal connection with someone who cared about them. It worked beautifully for them and for him to create that bond of trust and understanding so that he could guide them to a much better place in their lives.

He taught them that if they truly believed and had faith, they would succeed and achieve. These words spoken by him, and the premiums offered, were just vehicles to remind them to continually connect to their beliefs. For example, he explained that the prayer cloth itself didn't attract miracles, the prayer cloth was a tangible reminder of the power of faith. That it was their faith that created their miracle, because the power of God is in them. Those TV shows were his outreach to the world. He would promote things like his Good Luck Coin. This was before toll-free calls so the people would write in to get the free Good Luck Coin, or the Cross of Power, or whatever that premium was. His goal with the TV segments was to grow his direct mail list so he could expand his congregation internationally. He had an uncanny knack for knowing his audience and their desire to connect to and support his ministry based on the value they received from him, which was hard to quantify, because many lives were changed for the better dramatically through his teachings. There were many who were just on edge, losing hope and wanting Rev. Ike to pray for their solution. His presence in their lives made a big difference for them.

Rev. Ike walked his talk for two things that mattered to me a lot. First, he was wonderfully generous, and loved to help young people. I had adopted a baby daughter from India whom he met when she was young. I was raising her as a single mother, and he stayed connected to her through her teen years and when she was in college. Periodically, he would just send a check for several thousand dollars every year toward her college education. He helped many, many young people, and was so generous.

Secondly, he taught me that when you pay a bill, pay it with thanks and gratitude, never begrudgingly. Whenever I'd send him an invoice, he would send me back the check with my original invoice and write on it, thank you. He profusely thanked me and others who deserved it, giving so much appreciation.

In September 2001, he was scheduled to be on a big TV interview special. The interviewer planned to criticize and make a satire out of Rev. Ike. He wanted me to be there to help him prepare, plus be there during the interview. The morning of 9/11, I had my ticket, and I was ready to leave the house to go to the airport. My phone rang, and it was Rev. Ike. He said, "Judy, turn on your television." We sat together on the phone, staring unbelievingly at the footage of that first plane that had already crashed into the World Trade Center. Stunned, we stayed on the phone together trying to make sense of it and watched as a second plane hit the second tower. Sharing the few words we could express, we each gazed in disbelief at our respective TVs and watched the buildings collapse. It was surreal. Of course, then all the flights were canceled. I never went to New York and he never had that interview. It was a moment in time I'll never forget.

Eventually, I retired and I kind of lost contact with Rev. Ike for a while. A few years later he called me out-of-the-blue, just to touch base. Later, I got a call from Boston headquarters about the internet. At that time, Reverend Ike's website needed work. There was no promotion of it and nothing interesting going on with it. I was interested in internet marketing and wanted to work with them to build an internet ministry. I gave myself a few months to do a self-taught internet marketing study. I even took some courses and became an internet marketing expert. I considered myself pretty knowledgeable because of my background, and I joined on the ministry again, and became their internet marketing manager, on a freelance basis. That was when I really discovered Reverend Ike's teachings, because in order to write copy, and to promote his products—which were CD recordings at that time—I had to listen to all of them to familiarize myself with what he taught. It was the only way to write effective copy that would be used to launch and market his CDs. I started seriously listening and started enjoying the teachings. I realized that you didn't have to be a Christian or a church person because what he was teaching were universal truths of mind science. I listened to all of them. From everything I learned, I wrote a series of thirty emails to be sent out in sequence. I personally handled the whole online campaign, including writing the long copy and developing a marketing strategy. I developed the website Science of Living online and wrote all the copy for that. Reverend Ike had never been on YouTube before, so I started having short segments from his video teachings edited and uploaded to YouTube. That was before Facebook and a lot of other social media erupted. I would send him emails to let him know that he was going to be on YouTube forever. It was all new to him, but he was excited when I told him that virtually overnight, people would be watching him from his own YouTube channel. To our delight and amazement, they started making these wonderful comments about his videos that I shared online. As the YouTube channel has grown, it's so heartwarming to me to read the comments as people discover that magic of Reverend Ike. "Yes! We love Rev. Ike!" "Reverend Ike has changed my life." "Where was Reverend Ike when I was younger?" "If only I'd had a church like Reverend Ike's that I could go to!"

This is a whole new generation of people, some of the youngest of whom weren't even born when he was alive. Others will say, "Oh, my, mother used to watch Reverend Ike all the time." Or, "My preacher told me such bad things about Reverend Ike. They told me not to listen to him. I'm so sorry that I didn't listen…that I didn't ignore that. Now I thank God, I've discovered him." Comment after comment of people whose lives he's truly impacting.

The bottom line is that Reverend Ike is still changing lives. That is his legacy. To me, it's more powerful than when he was alive because he's reaching a different audience with his life changing mind science teaching. There were still the people of faith that loved Rev. Ike's command of the scriptures and the words of Jesus that taught them the promise of the great things they could do, be, and have. But he also began to attract a big audience that came from an intellectual point of view who understood the philosophy of mind science he taught. He influenced so many people. They loved him and believed in him.

After I retired, Mrs. Ike persuaded me to go with her on many trips to New York together, chatting the whole way. She and I have a special relationship. Often, she would come from Norfolk to Richmond to pick me up. Her cousin and assistant, Pearl Hedgspeth, who is another wonderful lady, would come along. The three of us would go there and spend sometimes almost a week, staying at a hotel and working every day at this big storage facility in New York to preserve Rev. Ike's legacy recordings, tapes, and books. Mrs. Ike is amazing. She is an incredibly strong woman in every way. She is just so dedicated to preserving her husband's legacy.

Rev. Ike was the hardest worker that I have ever known. He never stopped.

As of today, there have been 28,394,000 views on his YouTube channel videos, and most of those are in more recent years. With the internet, we are entering the second phase for Rev. Ike. Neither his life nor his messages are finished. I believe that twenty-eight million is just a drop in the bucket compared to what his legacy will do in the next ten years.

I'll never forget that whenever he called me, he would always say in his wonderful booming voice, "Judy, Judy, Judy," from the famous Cary Grant movie *Only Angels Have Wings* that came out in 1939. At the end of our every conversation, he'd always bless me, and even though I wasn't religious in that sense, it always meant so much to me. I miss him very much. We all do.

ANNETTE EIKERENKOETTER

MY STORY WITH REVEREND IKE

Even though I had been a student of metaphysics from an early age, I did not know of Reverend Ike until I met his son Xavier. It was on our first date, twenty-one years ago on a hike through Corral Canyon, that I would first hear the name Reverend Ike. We stopped to enjoy the view and sat for a while, talking and getting to know each other. Facing away from me in the direction of the canyons Xavier said, "My father is Reverend Ike." I told him that I had not heard of his father, so he began to share some of the stories of his dad's work and a bit of their relationship.

I met Xavier's mother, who graciously welcomed me into the family soon after that first date, but it was not until several years later that I was introduced to his father. I knew by Xavier's tone and posture when he told me about his father that this was not an ordinary father-son relationship, nor was Reverend Ike an ordinary man.

When it came time for me to meet his father, Reverend Ike and Xavier's mom invited us to come to Florida where they were living, and then from there we were to go on a cruise. Although I was excited to meet his dad and spend more time getting to know his mom, I was a bit nervous. However, my nerves were quelled immediately. When I entered their home, Reverend Ike and his wife, who I now call Mom, greeted us with champagne glasses raised in our honor. I was taken aback and quite touched. I felt loved and accepted from the beginning.

My first impression of Reverend Ike was his strong presence coupled with a playful and curious nature. His colorful character certainly spilled over into the furnishings of his home. There was so much to take in, from vibrant rugs, beautiful statues, paintings, and an ornate English silver tea set perched on an ottoman that particularly caught my attention. I learned later that Reverend Ike had an affinity for English and European décor and protocols.

Before we went to Florida, I received one of Reverend Ike's notorious late-night faxes, and in it he wrote, "When you and Xavier come to Florida, I want to take you shopping, and then you can see my more controlling side." I had a good laugh and appreciated his sense of humor and honesty about his controlling nature. Reverend Ike delivered on his generous offer. We had a few days in Florida before boarding the ship. One of those days we went on a shopping excursion. Most of the day we argued about what I would or would not wear, laughing most of the time, of course. I could see how much it meant to him to purchase these beautiful pieces of wardrobe for me, so I stretched a bit of my fashion style to make him happy. There was one particular item that I told him I definitely would not wear so he suggested that I hang it on the wall in a frame. It was just that beautiful and did seem like a work of art, but I opted to leave it in the store.

Every night at dinner on the cruise, Reverend Ike would tell these elaborate stories with his dramatic flair which most of the time ended with his thunderous laugh. He loved to laugh, and I am sure that I would be hard pressed to find one person who wouldn't agree that his laugh was extremely infectious. Another thing I noticed was how his words were like food—salted, peppered, and marinated. It was even more obvious when he described breakfast to us. The way he said the word "pancakes" made me want to skip my morning workout and race to the dining room. We had a wonderful trip all the way around. I was grateful they included me and took the time to get to know me.

After the cruise, Xavier and his parents flew to New York to be at their church, while I flew back to Los Angeles. It was not until a year later that I was introduced to the staff and congregation at the church. That was also the first time I got to witness Reverend Ike in his role as preacher. I do not have a clear memory of the first time I set my eyes on that magnificent building. I think I was a little bit like a deer caught in the headlights. Once again, there was so much to take in. The incredibly ornate architecture of the Palace itself was and is still overwhelmingly beautiful, but I was most struck by the incredible love, appreciation, and loyalty everyone had toward Reverend Ike and his family. There was no doubt that Reverend Ike was in charge and the staff was more than willing to give the attention he commanded. I was so glad that I had an opportunity to see him preach to his congregation. The first thing he did was hold up his study guide, making sure everyone in the church had one in their hands. He was so charismatic and delivered his message of "the God in you" with such conviction and deep reverence along with great humor. He had everyone's undivided attention and it was clear that they were happy to see him.

I was only able to see him preach one other time when he invited Xavier and me to accompany him to a seminar. It was the first time the three of us were alone together. While spending time with them, I was sensitive to an underlying tension in their relationship. It was a bit like walking a tightrope, trying to find the perfect balance between them. There was no doubt they had great love for each other, but there was residual energy left behind from the battle of wills that took place earlier in Xavier's life. Thankfully, I witnessed that tension soften toward the end of Reverend Ike's physical life, allowing for more acceptance between them.

The energy from the crowd at that event was pure excitement and adoration. They were not shy about letting him know how much they loved him. They cheered him on like a rock star. He was inspirational, playful, and his comedic timing was impeccable. I remember feeling proud to be his future daughter-in-law. I can still hear his voice as he introduced me to the participants, "This is my daughter."

I was grateful Reverend Ike had an opportunity to meet my father before he passed. Although my dad was very sick by that time, my brothers and sisters put him in the car and drove him to NY from PA so he could meet Xavier's parents. I am forever grateful to them for doing that for me. I vividly remember the first and only time they met in person. My dad, a talented musician, was playing the beautiful grand piano in their living room. As Reverend Ike walked down the stairs toward my father, he lovingly asked, "And who is this young man?" It warmed my heart to see them embrace each other. Xavier's mom was so gracious, spending a lot of time sitting with my father, knowing he wasn't feeling well. Unfortunately, my mother had already passed away before Xavier and I met so there was no opportunity for all four of them to get acquainted. She would have loved them, and vice versa.

I did not have as many years with him as I would have liked, but the legacy he left continues to inform me of the generosity of spirit that was Reverend Ike. He truly wanted every man and woman to prosper. Through his tireless preaching and teaching of these principles, he gave people the opportunity to know themselves as God knows them, and to play in this world with more dignity and command over their circumstances, not living as victims but as true co-creators with God. I heard one time that an interviewer asked him how many followers he thought he had and he replied, "I hope none." He did not want followers, he wanted to ignite each person's own divine inner guidance. He understood and modeled for everyone as he famously stated, "When you know who you are, there is nothing you cannot be, do, or have." Reverend Ike had an unshakeable faith, not in money or material possessions, but in knowing that God lives in everyone, and it is up to each individual as to how the God in you is expressed. He knew *that* was the true joy of living.

RELEASING THE STRUGGLE—
CELEBRATING THE LOVE

Xavier

After Dad and I went through our most intense differences, I got to a certain point in my life, around my late thirties, when I didn't want to fight anymore. I emotionally put my sword and armor down and focused on the larger picture that I was spending so much psychic energy fighting against. I finally realized that at some level it was a reflection of me. I was allowing the issues to stay alive. It took a lot of deep soul reflection to understand where and how I was perpetuating this battle by keeping feelings of resentment toward him alive. I realized I had to heal this. I knew I had to be the change. When I put all of the blame, all of the vitriol away, I genuinely shifted, and something opened up in our relationship. We stopped fighting and started seeing each other in a different way. More as two men rather than a father and son locked in a dynamic. When that happened, I remember for the first time in my life feeling relaxed around my father. I could enjoy myself and our time together.

My father left us physically on July 28, 2009, two years after he had a major stroke. My wife Annette and I were away in Peru when Mom called to tell us what happened. If he was aware that he had little time left before the stroke, he didn't show it around us.

As you can imagine, saying good-bye to my dad was difficult and painful. His illness and death were unexpected, but it wasn't just that. We felt he had more to give, more teaching to do. The wisdom floating within his seventy-four-year-old mind was poised to express at a whole new level. The magnitude of who he was, what he overcame, what he created, and what he contributed to the world made his illness and decline extremely hard to accept.

In those final days, there was mounting pressure to decide whether to keep him on life support or not. Given that we had reached the end of what medical science could do for him, he was likely to be unresponsive to any kind of radical Hail Mary efforts. His kidneys had already failed, and we had a tracheotomy performed to insert a breathing tube. Dad was unconscious but would open his eyes occasionally and smile at us. There were times I could tell he was aware. The tube was clearly uncomfortable and strange to him. I hated seeing him like that. I wondered what he was thinking. We all felt the energy blanketing the hospital room and pulsing with love for the great Rev. Ike. Frederick Joseph Eikerenkoetter II. Husband, father, son, brother, teacher, preacher, healer, evangelist, revolutionary, philanthropist, mentor, metaphysician, mystic, and so much more.

A woman chaplain performed Last Rites and Dad received the benefaction. In the next day or two, I performed a shamanic ceremony over Dad during his last hours, with only the two of us in the room. I played one of my favorite pieces of music "On Earth as it is in Heaven," by Ennio Morricone from the film *The Mission*. I arrayed various sacred objects around him and in the room on an altar, stones and earth from holy places around the world that held the memory of momentous events throughout the millennia and those who had walked significantly through them; blessed water holding the emotional imprint of the flow of life on our planet; an empty bowl to hold air/wind—the breath of life that would carry Dad's spirit on to his next adventure as an individualized expression of the Infinite; candles dancing with flame whose ascending thermal signature help hold wings aloft during interdimensional travel.

I said blessings over my father and thought to myself that if I were in an indigenous setting, I would take his body out into the landscape and find the place to bury him with my own hands. Or I'd construct a pyre upon which to release his body with fire, or float him down a sacred river on a funerary barge, or leave it on a raised platform in the air as an offering the way ancestors of my various lineages have done—and some still do. All were ways of offering the body back to the Earth and soul back to Heaven.

I sang and chanted, I struck rhythms with my body and drum, and I waved condor feathers over him. The feathers were from the holy land where I had been two years earlier when he had his stroke. To the Quechua, aboriginal people of Peru, the condor is one of the most revered animal spirits, representing higher consciousness and connection to the realm of the Great Spirit. These feathers carried my blessing and that of the host of invisible allies present. I anointed my father with oil.

I had a sense of the readiness of his spirit to depart. His consciousness had already turned its attention away from the physical. When someone dies, it is also a rebirth into the next plane of existence. Energy, consciousness, soul, and spirit are eternal. The physical body is clothing we wear during this Earthly sojourn, a corporeal costume to gain us admittance into this dress-up party called life. It is not who we are, it is a vessel of the spirit we are and a vehicle to move it around while having the terrestrial experience. Understanding this, I shed my last tears, found peace, and knew that those moments and all the time with family and loved ones who had poured out their love and appreciation to him was part of his initiation into the next realm.

The atmosphere teemed with everything he was, everything he did, every person he touched. My grandmother's energy was like a subtle perfume—detectable, yet faint. If she could see him from where she was, perhaps she whispered her approval, and finally, her understanding. The essence of his father was there too. When Dad locked eyes with me, their history and ours intertwined. Unspoken explanations floated between us. Respect and sadness jockeyed for position. Acceptance and permission for both of us to soar into new life assuaged our desire for more time. I thought he was hanging on a bit longer than he might have for me and the rest of the family, but I let him know it was okay to go.

Here was a being who, as a child, had experienced hunger pangs and had shoes stuffed with newspapers to block the holes. He was a man who had demonstrated his faith, and his dreams had come true. And now his life, which had been full of consequence and significance, floated between realms. His magical voice was nearly silent, but its frequency would forever reverberate throughout the multiverse. My father's childhood divinely orchestrated the circumstances for the fulfillment of his purpose. His soul knew its mission and the roles each player would perform to usher him forward. There are no accidents in the universe. None whatsoever. Propelled from within, his path unfolded according to the nudging of his soul. Go this way, turn here, stop, carry on. My father always listened and always marched to that celestial beat whether or not others picked up on its rhythm.

The decision to terminate his life support loomed, and eventually, Mom and I decided it was time. The last moments with him were touching. I reassured him that it was okay to let go of anything he might have been holding on to. I forgave him and let him know he was a good father. Whatever issues we had seemed so miniscule in that space. I told him he provided me with what I needed to be the man I am. Mom spoke to him tenderly and gently, and Annette had her time with him and said her good-bye.

I reminded him that his life had been amazing, that he packed a million years of living into those seven decades, and that he had been an inspiration to countless people, including me. He was a spiritual giant. His legacy would live on forever and his father would be proud of him. "If he could, your dad would say, 'Well done, my beloved son,'" I told him.

Mom, Cousin Pearl, Annette, and I made sure he was as comfortable as possible. Dad was in and out of consciousness while looking at me directly, attempting to communicate. As he navigated this sacred time, surrounded by love and our bittersweet consent for him to transition to his next assignment, a question he asked when the two of us were alone reverberated in my mind as my father, the great Reverend Ike, prepared to leave this realm. "What has my life amounted to?"

With tremendous gratitude in our own way, and the knowing that this wasn't over, we all sang him out of this life and onto the next realm.

> *Swing low, sweet chariot*
> *Coming for to carry me home*
> *Swing low, sweet chariot*
> *Coming for to carry me home…*

There was a private memorial and viewing at Forest Lawn in LA. The services were kept private because my dad had made it clear he did not want his casket to be brought into the church. He just wanted a memorial service, to be cremated, and have his ashes scattered in his favorite bodies of water. We had a ceremony, and we sprinkled his ashes in Rye, New York and in the Bal Harbor area that he just loved so and where he spent a lot of time. That was his favorite place.

We celebrated my father's life at the United Palace in the grand style befitting the great Reverend Ike. The ceremony blessed our family tremendously. During the emotional period of saying good-bye to his physical form, hearing others share their experiences with and thoughts about Dad, comforted us, reminding us of his enormous impact on so many lives.

Congressman Charles Rangel and his wife Alma were dear friends of my parents. At Dad's memorial service, the statesman put my father's contributions into perspective when he said, "I could not help but think, unless Rev. Ike had shattered the image that Black folks had of themselves, unless he shared with so many people the true belief that he, like you and I, were made in God's image, we probably never would have a Barack Obama as president of these United States."

Since his death, my father has visited me many times in my dreams. He does so on a regular basis. I knew right away that he was fine where he was and was enjoying his new experience. For whatever reason, he was done with the Earthly plane. During the years since his death, as my wife and I took on the management and retooling of his ministry, he showed up with encouragement and advice in a way he had never done for me when he was alive.

Years before my father's passing, I had been the presiding bishop of the whole operation, and the only one with the right to succeed my father. The question was, who would become pastor in New York? I had lived in California for twenty-five years, going back and forth at various frequencies, sometimes monthly, sometimes quarterly. I had overseen things for a long time but was not involved day-to-day. My father hadn't pastored there since about 2000. He had placed Reverend Wyns in the main pastoral with others in rotating speaking posts. Reverend Tilley, who had been with him for many years, had stayed on as head administrator. After Dad's transition, I stepped up my overseeing as bishop, increasing my visits to New York. Mom, Annette, and I invited high-powered pastors and speakers to rotate in the pulpit, including Bishop Carlton Pearson, Les Brown, and Susan Taylor. We were getting a feel for the congregation's response in our attempt to find a captain that could take over and build the congregation. Those first years after Dad's transition were a really challenging period for me and my wife, and for my mother. I wanted to make all the right decisions, but we had some disappointing hits and misses when it came to the impossible task of finding the person who could fill my father's shoes.

Then Carlton Pearson called one day and said he had someone special he wanted to introduce us to. He brought Reverend Jack Bomar with him to the Palace. After watching how he moved while assisting Bishop Pearson, having some meals and subsequent conversations together, Mom, Annette, and I thought he might be a good fit. He had a humble spirit of service, a genuine sense of connection to my father's message, and an understanding of what I wanted to accomplish with the church. He even reminded Mom a little of Dad. In 2010 I brought Jack Bomar in as pastor of the United Palace Cathedral. Our instincts were right. The congregation loved him!

Reverend Jack took over the church in New York for a number of years, and then I assigned him to the UCJC church in Beaufort. Later, we turned UCJC over to him and he became a bishop. He's now been with us for twelve years and presides over churches in South Carolina, Georgia, Tennessee, and Hawaii.

My mom has been determined to keep the legacy of my father alive. She is thankful that we found Rev. Jack and very excited about the projects we have in the works that will allow people everywhere to experience the life and teachings of my father. Pastor Jack is a young, energetic, loving young man who loves the work, and is so committed to what he's doing.

The Eikerenkoetter family, Bishop Jack Bomar, and the congregation of United Church in Beaufort, South Carolina, are in the process of erecting a building in Rev. Ike's honor called the Rev. Ike Resource Center/Library-Museum on the church property. Bishop Jack is spearheading this project. It will contain Rev. Ike legacy artifacts, his wonderful writings, lessons, and books.

BISHOP JACK BOMAR

MY STORY WITH REVEREND IKE

As a youngster, I remember my mother listening every night at midnight to Reverend Ike. She was an avid supporter of his, with prayer cloths and literature decorating our home. I would hear his captivating voice booming through the radio, so I met him in spirit early in my childhood, and though I never met him while he was alive, I never forgot his teachings and preaching. Little did I know at the time that my life and his would eventually be deeply intertwined.

One of Reverend Ike's most successful pastors and a friend of mine, Bishop Bernard Jordan, recommended that I listen to Rev. Ike's sermons daily for a year and miracles would happen in my life, and in the life of my church, and they did. My life has been miracle after miracle.

A few years later, I was pursuing my theology doctorate at McCormick Theological Seminary in Chicago, Illinois, when I had a dream that I needed to meet Mrs. Eikerenkoetter at United Palace. I knew my colleague and friend, Bishop Carlton Pearson, had been pastoring there once a month since Rev. Ike's passing in 2009. Bishop Carlton knew that I had pastored at churches in Chicago, Georgia, Tennessee, and California, so I called and asked if he wanted a volunteer assistant.

Bishop Pearson entreated me in June 2010 to join him in New York at the Palace. I did and was lovingly received. After the service, over dinner with the Eikerenkoetters, they invited me to come and preach at the church. It went well and I ultimately agreed by September 2010 to a one-year contract to provide leadership to regrow the United Palace church in Washington Heights, New York, and help rebuild the church which had dwindled since Rev. Ike's passing. I started The Blessing Hands Outreach specifically to the Dominican Republic neighborhood. The political and social leaders loved all that we were doing with and for them. As we grew, I even went by invitation to the Dominican Republic and Haiti.

When I was invited to the United Palace to be the pastor, I had my first dream of Rev. Ike. He was standing in front of me full of joy and broke into song, singing "He Walks with Me and He Talks to Me and Tells Me That I Am His Own." So, I happily joined him in song, as we sang a compelling duet. What a dream!

I now believe that he was spiritually overseeing from the other side what my interaction with his son, Bishop Xavier Eikerenkoetter, the leader of the Palace, would be. I had to make countless tough decisions at United Palace, which was totally different from what I was accustomed to doing. Politicians, entertainers, drifters, and everyone else seems to show up, and each had a different agenda that they wanted to promote. I would go into meditation and prayer, and God would provide me with answers. I felt that Rev. Ike was always blessing me from on high to help me make important decisions about who had honorable intentions to the church or me personally. I was able to make a profound difference in rebuilding there.

In 2013, Bishop Xavier asked me to make a lateral move to pastor the mother church in Beaufort, South Carolina. Things went so well there that I became the full-time pastor of United Church in Beaufort, which is the first church that Rev. Ike founded near his birth home in Ridgeland. I had to prove myself to the church and the community. We won the souls, hearts, and minds of the community as everyone started to prosper, gaining their health back, and raising their consciousness. We became, as Rev. Ike says, "a point of contact that inspires people to be all they can be, do all they can do, and have all they can have."

Around 2015, while still at the Beaufort church, I received a telephone call from the leaders of the church in Hawaii where I had previously preached. The church was going through difficult times, so I left Beaufort after fulfilling my obligation to be there for a year, having given them one and a half years.

I started teaching Rev. Ike's principles in Hawaii. The results were astounding. "Oh! It's a miracle," the congregants in the Hawaiian Unity Church would say as they began to notice significant differences. The Hawaiian church had been in over $200,000 of debt forever, the roof was caving in, and termites were eating their building until I arrived and began to preach and teach the principles of Rev. Ike. Voilà! The money began to flow in.

For example, in the beginning, after doing three Sunday church services in Hawaii at 8:00, 9:30, and 11:00 a.m., I was ready to head off to our church town hall fundraising meeting. Before I left home, a voice in my head said, "The money is in the house." I thought it meant to get my own money to start the tithing. I went to the town hall, and while walking in, a White lady pulled me aside and said, "Bishop, Black folk are accustomed to giving, not White folk." I answered her by saying, "Consciousness does not know or recognize color."

With only 10 percent of our struggling congregation of 400 attending our vision quest fundraising meeting, I took a deep breath to upgrade my courage and be in alignment with Spirit. The forty attendees liked my opening statement. After I presented the complete vision, an older White congregant innocently asked, "Okay, so where's the money?" I answered that the Spirit just told me, "It is in your pocket." It was amazing. Before we left the town hall, we had $100,000 to fix up the church. We only needed $80,000. Everyone was profoundly inspired, becoming true believers again. It was a miracle, and everyone kept affirming that it was. The God in you Rev. Ike taught really worked!

After helping the Hawaiian church rebuild its membership and viability for a year and a half, I returned to the Beaufort church again as its pastor. Now we are preparing to open the spectacular Rev. Ike Museum here on the church grounds on his birthday in June 2023.

I lift the consciousness that the people had inside of themselves all the time but didn't recognize or use. I teach them that the one thing that is everything is consciousness. I have been so blessed to take over the special church which launched Rev. Ike's ministry and to carry on his work with this wonderful community, right where it began.

A NEW ERA OF REVEREND IKE

Mark

For all the uncertainty, struggles, and doubt the family experienced in trying to take Rev. Ike's work forward with their best efforts, they needn't have worried. Rev. Ike's promise to have his work continue beyond his lifetime was true, but it was impossible at the time to see how his plan for his legacy gift to the world would be delivered. Today, there have been more than twenty-eight million views of Rev. Ike's messages, far greater than the numbers he reached while he was physically present on this Earth. We know he's still nearby, and that he's still directing the show from on high. Our collective plan is to take the story and the beautiful work of this extraordinary man and bring it to a 100 million people in this decade.

In each of us he touched, he left an indelible mark. He sculpted our souls with a thundering truth—delivered with the velvet gloves of his deep love for humanity. Through all of us who are committed to sharing his legacy, Reverend Ike will be forever pouring his love into every single soul he can touch.

From seven years of age when his grandmother told him to sit down in front of his Bible and preach to his cousins, Rev. Ike studied each and every day to prepare himself to speak God's truth, to inspire, and to heal. He communed ceaselessly with God and gave himself absolutely to the calling God put inside of him. He kept his own fire of spiritual connection to the Divine burning and did like the Apostle Paul admonished:

Rejoice always, pray without ceasing, give thanks in all circumstances; for this will of God for (and in) you in Christ Jesus (Thessalonians 5:15–18 ESV).

As the years went by, he wanted his legacy to be awakening others to do the same or more. He comprehensively emphasized that healing, health, prosperity, abundance, and love are now.

People touched by Rev. Ike's work weren't just taught a new way of doing things, they were given the formula to create a whole new paradigm for themselves, recognizing the God that lives inside of them, and with that knowledge, that everything is possible. Millions of people manifested more wealth, health, and a bigger purpose than they had ever previously wished for. Through his inspired teachings, they changed everything in their lives and the lives around them. In a documentary made after Rev. Ike's passing, Reverend Al Sharpton beautifully credited his work with the following tribute: "Some broke the shackles on our arms; you helped break them on our minds." While the majority of Rev. Ike's followers came from the Black community, people of all colors and backgrounds today are seeking the mental, emotional, and spiritual freedom that he taught. The teachings seem to have been made as much for these times as any. There is a spiritual awakening across the planet that is calling people everywhere to look within to find the answers.

When I interviewed Gary Richards, the reverend's personal assistant and chauffeur, he told me that Rev. Ike had at least two books in the back of his cars at all times. The *Rev. Ike Study Guides* and the newest copy of one of my *Chicken Soup for the Soul* books. I am honored and touched that he cherished my books, but more than that, I think he always realized he played a pivotal role in my meteoric rise to success as arguably the world's best-selling non-fiction author. As he saw fifty-nine of my books reach that *New York Times* number one spot and hundreds of millions of lives changed through the readings of those books, he knew, as I did, that our journeys became intertwined for a reason and a better world was created because of it.

Those seeds of spiritual truth, success, and financial freedom he sowed in me from my early days with him reaped a wildfire of goodness for me and for the planet, as my books are translated into fifty-four languages around the world.

Now that you've had the opportunity to read the story and hear the illumined teachings of Rev. Ike, I hope you'll contemplate what it means for you. I hope you'll highlight the stories that speak to your heart and go back to them to explore them more deeply, pondering what specific purpose they might serve your life, and opening up to where your new understandings might take you.

BIGGER IN DEATH THAN IN LIFE

Xavier

Some people have such a significant impact on their respective societies that it reverberates for generations, and perhaps indefinitely. These souls come into the Earthly plane with a certain destiny and a work to do that if accomplished, creates positive movement for the world at large. The destiny contains within it the means (courage, talent, strength, and unseen assistance) to achieve its ends.

In death, Dad's influence still has an impact. Even the more traditional denominations are subtly including his concepts while loosening rigid religious dogma. His lingering mystique is that his teachings are still influencing and shaping popular culture and new religious icons. Some say they see several prominent ministers carrying the essence of his mind power message as well as his charismatic personality and prosperity philosophy, and many more who have the mark of his influence.

I can't help smiling because I know Dad's stuff when I hear it. My father is considered a legend as an international pastor to millions. Many spiritual leaders celebrate Dad in their sermons and generously credit his teachings for impacting their lives and ministries. Among them are Rev. Michael Bernard Beckwith, founder and senior minister of Agape International in Los Angeles; Rev. Gaylon McDowell, senior associate minister at Christ Universal Temple in Chicago; Rev. Kevin Kitrell Ross, senior minister at Unity of Sacramento; Pastor Greg Stamper, cofounder of Celebration Spiritual Center in Brooklyn; and many others.

277

My father's influence was vast, reaching people from all walks of life, including celebrities like John Lennon, who I've heard watched my dad on television at night and wrote the song "Whatever Gets You Through the Night" after hearing him say the phrase. Billy Joel wrote a song called "So Long, Reverend Ike." I've heard stories of the rock band KISS rubbing the prayer cloth before they went on stage for concerts, and Michael Jackson reportedly loved my father's clothes. Other people my father inspired include R&B singer Jeffrey Osborne, and Susan L. Taylor, former editor of *Essence* magazine.

My father was a student of success. If you were successful, he wanted to be around you and find out what you had done to become successful. And he was very interested in helping you maximize your success. Yet successful or not, he would never look down on anyone because he saw the divinity in everyone. If there was a homeless man on the street, Dad saw the man, not his condition, and approached him as such. He would sometimes slip the homeless man some money, but he would always greet them with, "Hello, sir," in that voice that was trying to get the man in them to stand up and feel their self-worth. It has been said that some would straighten up and kick their trash out of the way when they saw him coming. He treated them with respect and that inspired them to want to appear more respectful, and I'm sure that deep down, they wanted to respect themselves. That is the effect he had on many people.

Even though my family transitioned out of the church organization and are no longer associated with the United Palace, my father's message continues growing stronger among new generations seeking the spiritual understanding and divine empowerment that traditional religion fails to provide. Thankfully, technology affords easy access to Dad's riveting sermons, and his timeless Science of Living spiritual psychology is reaching millions. His YouTube channel has over a 150,000 subscribers and is growing by the day. People are quite grateful to be able to view Dad in action and are pleased they get to immerse themselves in his message, which feels as fresh and meaningful today as it did almost fifty years ago.

Ultimately, my dad's legacy is love. He loved himself, he loved his family, and he loved being able to bring a smile to someone's face when they were sad. He loved all people, but he realized the divine plan behind his being born Black and stepped fully into his purpose to help his people know the truth about themselves. Even though he facetiously proclaimed himself green (the color of money), Dad did not deny his racial heritage and proved his deep, abiding love for Black people in giving the best of himself to them. That love for humanity and his desire for Blacks to awaken to their inner divinity permeated everything he did. His thought-provoking challenges to traditional religion still resonate with those questioning its role in their lives—maybe more than ever before. He dared us to go higher, broader, and deeper in our understanding of God and Self and to be transformed by it.

Reverend Ike's legacy lives on.

ACKNOWLEDGMENTS

I t would take a separate volume to truly acknowledge the individuals who contributed to the Reverend Ike legacy through the years.

The Eikerenkoetter family and Mark Victor Hansen want to let these wonderful individuals know that we understand each of their special contribution to his life, to his work, and to this story.

From the family:

Rev. Katy Posey
Rev. Pearl Hedgspcth

From United Church in Beaufort, SC:

Bishop Jack Bomar
Mother Cleo Stokes
Rev. Herbert Kemp
Deacon Joseph Holmes
Mother Mary Ward

From Christ United Church in New York:

Rev. Alfred and Jessie Miller
Bishop Robert Jiggetts
Rev. James Wyns, Jettie Wyns, and Rev. Yolanda Wyns
Rev. Barbara Tilley

Rev. Lilly Braxton
Evan Inlaw
Rev. Kevin Ross, Sacramento, CA
Bishop Bernard Jordan, New York
Lucille Willard and Stan Hoffman
Cheryl and Jessica Tittle, for keeping Rev. Ike Legacy, LLC going
Joan Clancy
Judy Adler
Eugene Farber
Dave Corbett
Bob Proctor

Xavier Eikerenkoetter gives special thanks to:

"Crystal Dwyer Hansen for tireless efforts as unseen co-co-author, and manager of all things."

"Eula Eikerenkoetter for being my mom and laying open her life and life partner for this story."

"Annette Eikerenkoetter, my gift-from-God wife, for handling so much around this project and beyond, especially me!"

"Great personal thanks to my co-author, Mark Victor Hansen, for stepping in to help me finish this work when I was at an impasse."

Mark Victor Hansen gives special thanks to:

"Mrs. Eula Eikerenkoetter and Xavier Eikerenkoetter. I have deep and humble gratitude to both of you for entrusting me with this special project that is so dear to all of our hearts."

"My wife Crystal Dwyer Hansen, who acted as the other half of my heart and my mind in this most important project. I couldn't have done it without you."

"Annette Eikerenkoetter who was always there with a smile, to direct me to the exact materials I needed no matter how many times I asked."

We're thankful for our publisher Anthony Ziccardi for recognizing this treasure of a man and wanting to tell his story.

If we've forgotten anybody, please know it wasn't intentional. We appreciate each of you who played any part big or small.

The Grand Foyer to the United Palace.

The ornately gilded and decorated theater—one of the Loew's Wonder Theatres was purchased by Rev. Ike in 1969 for his congregation.

Frederick Eikerenkoetter (Rev. Ike) at eighteen years of age attending a youth conference at the Church of Our Lord Jesus Christ in New York City with Bishop R. C. Lawson. He had received a monetary gift from "Lady T" to attend.

Mrs. Ike (Eula Dent Eikerenkoetter) holding Xavier, their son. Late 1965 or early 1966.

**Frederick Joseph Eikerenkoetter II (Rev. Ike)
at three or four months old, 1935.**

Frederick Eikerenkoetter (Rev. Ike) at around five years of age.

Rema Matthews Eikerenkoetter (Rev. Ike's mother).

**Frederick Eikerenkoetter (Rev. Ike) at twenty years of age
(in bible college between South Carolina and New York).**

Joseph Frederick Eikerenkoetter I (Rev. Ike's father).

Frederick Eikerenkoetter (Rev. Ike), early twenties.
(Possibly military chaplain service photo.)

TO A WORLD OF CONFUSION, SIN AND SICKNESS WE JOYFULLY DECLARE

IT IS NO SECRET WHAT GOD CAN DO

PRAYER AND GOSPEL CRUSADE

Conducted by

Rev. FREDERICK J. EIKERENKOETTER II

YOUNG EVANGELIST SINCE AGE 14

Preaching the Gospel with Power and Praying the Prayer of Faith for You. Come with Your Burdens, Leave with a Song!

Bibleway Church of Christ

RIDGELAND   SOUTH CAROLINA

SUNDAY, MAY 10th TO SUNDAY MAY 24th

—1959—

—8:00 P. M. NIGHTLY—

All the Gospel for All the People of All Faiths

SEE NEWSPAPER FOR BROADCASTING SCHEDULE

Flyer advertising Rev. Ike's early meetings, 1959.

Rev. and Mrs. Ike on their honeymoon in
New York City, February 19, 1964.

Eula Mae Dent (sitting at the piano on extreme left
with hand on face) meets Rev. Ike for the first time at
Mount Calvary Church in Boston, MA in 1962.

Rev. Ike's first trip to Egypt.

Headshot of Rev. Ike.

Rev. Ike and his son, Xavier, in office at the United Palace, circa 1973.

Rev. Ike at one of his Evangelistic Meetings, late 1970s.

Rev. Ike interfacing with children.

Rev. Ike with Rolls Royce, mid-1970s.

Rev. Ike and his son Xavier, 1995.

Rev. Ike interview with TV host Tom Snyder.

Testimony of Gary Richardson, healing from hole in his heart, given by his nana, 1973.

The famous Robert Morton pipe organ, which was
used in vaudeville performances, was also used to
open up Rev. Ike's services at the United Palace.

Rev. Ike on the Evangelistic Circuit, late 1980s.

Rev. Ike in church service at United
Palace in New York, early 1980s.

Rev. Ike and his 98 children (!)

from the Carrie Steele-Pitts Home in Atlanta, Georgia.

Rev. Ike's Atlanta Report starts on page 6.

(Atlanta) All these young people came to be with Rev. Ike at The Omni in Atlanta on Sunday, April 27, to tell Rev. Ike how his teachings have helped them develop self-control, self-respect and peace within. They also voted to adopt Rev. Ike as their Godfather. Rev. Ike says, "They give me so much love that they make me feel like I'm the richest man in the universe. — Because *love* makes you *rich!*"

"Rev. Ike, we've adopted you as our Godfather!"

"Rev. Ike and his 98 children," late 1970s.

Rev. Ike preaching at Madison Square Garden, 1975.

Rev. Ike preaching at the United Palace, 1975.

Rev. and Mrs. Ike, attending a wedding
in Dallas, TX, circa 1987.

Rev. Ike, Xavier, Annette (Xavier's wife),
and Mrs. Ike on a family cruise.

Credit: Winston J. Vargas

Rev. Ike at the piano. Credit: Winston J. Vargas

Left to right: Rev. Run, Rev. Ike, Rev. Al Sharpton, Bishop Bernard Jordan. Next generation ministers mentored or inspired by Rev. Ike, outside the exclusive Plaza Hotel in New York after an awards ceremony. Rev. Ike was presented the "Lifetime Achievement Award in Mentoring" by Rev. Sharpton. Credit: Cedric Thompson